I'VE GOT A COOK IN
KALAMAZOO!
KALAMAZOO!
KALAMAZOO!
KALAMAZOO!
KALAMAZOO!
KALAMAZOO!
KALAMAZOO!
KALAMAZOO!

A very special thanks to Richard H. Jones of Paper Point of Kalamazoo for invaluable help in the preparation of the cookbook, 1978.

We extend our gratitude to DeLano Services, Inc., of Allegan for the type-setting and reprinting of this cookbook, November 2007.

The reprinting of this cookbook was made possible through the generous grant of the Santreece Foundation, whom we thank for their continuous sup-port of the mission of the Junior League of Kalamazoo, November 2007.

I'VE GOT A COOK IN KALAMAZOO!

COVER DESIGN AND ILLUSTRATIONS BY PAMELA OLHEISER POHLONSKI

**JUNIOR LEAGUE OF
KALAMAZOO**

Women building better communities

2007

**JUNIOR LEAGUE OF
KALAMAZOO**
Women building better communities

Copyright © 1978
Junior League of Kalamazoo
(Formerly Service Club of Kalamazoo, Inc.)
Kalamazoo, Michigan

All proceeds from the sale of I'VE GOT A COOK IN KALAMAZOO will benefit the programs, projects and grants of the Junior League of Kalamazoo.

For additional copies, cookbooks may be ordered at www.jlkalamazoo.org; by using the order blanks in the back of this book; or by writing directly to:

I'VE GOT A COOK IN KALAMAZOO
Junior League of Kalamazoo
2121 Hudson Street, Suite 101
Kalamazoo, Michigan 49008

Checks should be made payable to the Junior League of Kalamazoo for the amount of $25.00 plus $5.00 postage and handling per book. Michigan residents add $1.50 sales tax per book.

Please contact us with additional questions at (269) 342-5562.

First printing: 8,850 copies, November, 1978

Second printing: 10,000 copies, November, 1979

Third printing: 10,000 copies, September, 1981

Fourth printing: 10,000 copies, September, 1984

Fifth printing: 1,000 copies, November, 2007

ISBN 0-9606506-0-1

COOKBOOK COMMITTEE

Cochairwomen	Sharon Garside
	Geri Fuzy Penniman
Cover and Illustrations	Pamela Olheiser
Editor	Mary Ellen Godfrey
Testing Cochairwomen	Greeta Douglass
	Amanda Clark Morrill
Sectional Chairwomen	
Appetizers and Beverages	Sandra Wotta
Breads	Ann Paulson
Desserts	Barbara Brandt
	Mary Maynard
Game	Sharon Garside
Meats and Seafood	Sally Shipman Early
Microwave	Irene Shippy
On the Lighter Side	Irene Shippy
Poultry	Patricia Ellwood
Salads and Dressings	Leatha Linders
Soups	Doris Statler
Vegetables	Susan Brown
Wine Selections	Barbara Brandt
	Bacchus Wines & Spirits
Typing Chairwoman	Shirley McCarty
Recipe Solicitation	Jan Shugars
	Mel Van Peenan
Proofreading Chairwoman	Mary Ellen Godfrey
Layout	Ann Paulson
	Patricia Ellwood
	Geri Fuzy Penniman
Captions	Christine Oosterbaan
Index	Ann Paulson
Marketing and Publicity Cochairwomen	Norma Stancati
	Shirley Weiss
Testers	Members of Service Club

COOKBOOK COMMITTEE, 2007

Chair

Lindsay Oosterbaan

Co-Chair

Nancy Tinklenberg

Committee

Heather Reece

Cathy Todd

Anne Drummond

Nicole Colosky

Grace Gatmaitan

Karen Garceau

Nicole Keorkunian

Jackie Lincoln

TABLE OF CONTENTS

Trade names of products used only when necessary.

INTRODUCTION

"I've Got a Gal in Kalamazoo" has been danced to and sung for over 35 years, since its creation by songwriters Mack Gordon and Harry Warren for the Glenn Miller band in the movie "Orchestra Wives."

The real-life "Gal in Kalamazoo" was chosen in September, 1942, by the male students of Kalamazoo College, Kalamazoo, Michigan. Sara Woolley, later to become Mrs. Donald Knight, was selected on the basis of beauty, popularity, cheerfulness, and pep as the girl who would best fit the song.

Servicemen around the world wrote for her picture and some even traveled to Kalamazoo to prove such a city existed. As the song increased in popularity so did the requests for the "Gal" to appear in connection with America's war effort. Sara made many appearances around the country for defense bond drives and USO programs.

After college, the real "Gal in Kalamazoo" stayed in Kalamazoo to raise a family and participate in volunteer community work. Service Club was an organization which Sara Knight joined. Over the years, this organization has consistently worked to benefit children in the community.

Service Club began in February, 1928, with 40 members and a $600 budget. Among its first projects were driving for well-child clinics and raising funds for Pretty Lake Vacation Camp. Throughout the years, the club has expanded its role in the community, its membership, and its budget. This year, as it celebrates 50 years of community involvement, it currently numbers 110 active members and over 200 honorary members—a group which includes Mrs. Knight. Service Club sponsors Pretty Lake Vacation Camp, Volunteer Services, Children's Services, Child Abuse and Protection Council, and Senior Citizen and Teen programs by offering innumerable hours of service plus financial assistance.

Service Club hopes that *I'VE GOT A COOK IN KALAMAZOO* will become as popular as the song and will offer many hours of enjoyment creating unique and taste-pleasing recipes. We have gathered our recipes from the entire community, tested them thoroughly, and selected what we felt were the most original and attractive for your enjoyment. We have included a selection of ingredients to reflect all tastes; a balance between quickly prepared and lengthy dishes to accommodate all life-styles; and a variety of cooking procedures to reflect today's use of microwaves, woks, food processors, etc. All recipes have been written in similar form and ingredients listed in the order in which they are added to the recipe to reduce confusion. All amounts have been standardized throughout all recipes and, when possible, preparation time has been noted.

Service Club of Kalamazoo sincerely offers *I'VE GOT A COOK IN KALAMAZOO* to you as a pleasurable alternative to singing and dancing "our tune."

The Cookbook Committee
Service Club of Kalamazoo, Inc.
November, 1978

On June 19, 1980, we affiliated with the Association of Junior Leagues, Inc., and are now the Junior League of Kalamazoo.

INTRODUCTION, 2007

The Junior League of Kalamazoo is proud to bring to you the 30th Anniversary Commemorative Edition of the *I'VE GOT A COOK IN KALAMAZOO!* cookbook. Originally printed in 1978 by the Service Club of Kalamazoo, the cookbook's success is legendary. We know that you'll enjoy these classic time-tested recipes.

By purchasing this cookbook, you are supporting the Junior League of Kalamazoo and its mission to promote voluntarism, develop the potential of women, and improve the community through the effective action and leadership of trained volunteers. The Junior League of Kalamazoo proudly embraces its rich history of positively impacting thousands of individuals in the Kalamazoo area. Focusing its efforts on the health, education and well-being of women and children, the Junior League of Kalamazoo provides volunteer service and financial assistance to myriad community organizations.

Because of the efforts of the Junior League of Kalamazoo and its predecessor, the Service Club of Kalamazoo:

• Children attend a residential camp experience free-of-charge.
• Children of all abilities can play together at a barrier-free playground.
• People with loved ones in the hospital receive free lodging and emotional support.
• Children are taught healthy nutritional choices.
• Children are engaged in literacy programs that encourage family involvement.
• Community leaders are developed who are lifelong volunteers.

Thank you for your support of the Junior League of Kalamazoo and bon appetit!

Fondly,

Katie Williams
President, Junior League of Kalamazoo
November, 2007

I'VE GOT A COOK IN KALAMAZOO!

In 1976, my provisional year in Service Club, I signed up for the cookbook development committee. I loved to cook and bake but never dreamed this project would bring me lasting friendships and plant the idea for starting a business of my own.

Our chair person, Sharon Garside, knew a cookbook would be a good fundraiser if it had thoroughly tested recipes, used terms consistently and appealed to cooks of all abilities. Sharon had her own retail business in Richland. She sold community cookbooks and knew the good ones sold well.

We requested recipes, developed a rating system, recruited typists and testers. No names appeared on the recipes that were handed out. Each recipe was tested three times; only those receiving the highest ratings were considered for the book.

Testing was sometimes stressful but mostly it was an adventure. Our families were our guinea pigs. You couldn't beat kids for honest appraisals; they had no trouble saying exactly what they thought about a dish. When she presented yet another chicken recipe for dinner, Pat Dolan's children said, "Mom, if we have to test one more chicken recipe, we will start to grow feathers."

As we prepared the book for publication, it became evident that our committee was blessed with experts, among them Irene Shippy, who was our microwave guru; Barbara Brandt, who owned Bacchus and selected the wines; Chris Oosterbaan, our poet laureate, who wrote catchy subtitles for the recipes; Pam Olheiser Pohlonski, who created the graphics and drawings; and Mary Ellen Godfrey, who was our editor and proofreader.

At the time there were no home computers, cell phones or fax machines. The Service Club newsletter was typed on stencils on an electric typewriter and run off on a mimeograph. In the cooking department, microwaves and food processors were just finding their way into our kitchens.

I was the first cookbook chair after the book was published. At one meeting, Susan Brown told the committee about a wonderful cookbook seminar a friend of hers had attended. It was put on by Ellen Rolfes and Helen Hays, members of the Memphis Junior League who started a business teaching women how to market community cookbooks. Chris Garrett and I were sent to Memphis for training. We came home brimming with ideas for marketing *I'VE GOT A COOK IN KALAMAZOO.*

We were shameless promoters. Mary Maynard sent a book to cookbook author and bread making expert Bernard Clayton, Jr. He sent back a warm endorsement which we used in our sales brochure. We did cooking demonstrations in local stores and on television. We learned that free samples of our recipes were great sales tools.

In 1980, thanks to Debbie Hudgins' efforts, our cookbook was selected for a feature article in the *Ladies Home Journal*. Assistant LHJ food editor, Jan Turner Hazard, selected the recipes she wanted made and set a mid-October date for the visit.

On the appointed day, Jan, copy editor Lys Margold and photographer Nick Samardge arrived. For the next three days the cookbook committee worked nonstop. We scouted locations; they chose the Delano Homestead at the Nature Center and Susan Brown's backyard. We presented the requested recipes for the photo shoot. Nick took hundreds of pictures; only two were used in the magazine.

On the last night of the visit, the cookbook committee hosted an elegant sit-down dinner for Jan, Lys, and Nick at Gerri Penniman's home. The menu featured star recipes from *I'VE GOT A COOK IN KALAMAZOO*. It would be another year before the article appeared in print.

After working on the cookbook committee, serving as newsletter editor and public relations chair, I decided that someone might be willing to pay me to do the things I loved and had been doing as a volunteer. With a small loan from my husband and my trusty electric typewriter, I started Pandemonium, The Copy Company, which later became Paulson Communications. My first paying client was Bacchus; my second client was Hays Rolfes & Associates in Memphis, TN. Twenty-seven years later I am still in business and I still love what I do.

Ann Paulson
November, 2007

MELTING POT

As a member of the cookbook marketing committee in 1979, I wrote a letter to Sue B. Huffman, food editor of the *Ladies Home Journal,* requesting that *I'VE GOT A COOK IN KALAMAZOO* be considered for one of their monthly cookbook features. With the letter, I sent my own copy of the cookbook.

In her response, Ms. Huffman wrote that our cookbook was chosen because of the quality and accuracy of our recipes and for the well-defined profile of our diverse "melting pot" community.

I'VE GOT A COOK IN KALAMAZOO gave Service Club of Kalamazoo a project that would raise funds on an on-going basis and allow us to respond to the ever growing needs in our community. It also gave us the opportunity to develop and run a small business, learn about marketing and sales, and spread the word about the good work of Service Club.

The cookbook arrived at a particularly opportune time for many Service Club members. In the late 70s and early 80s women were returning to work for a variety of reasons: some to establish careers before marriage and children and some to new ventures which included starting their own businesses. As we returned to the workplace, many of us used the skills we had honed working on the cookbook project.

I was inspired to take my passion for cooking and develop it into a thriving catering business. One day, after I finished doing a cooking demonstration at Hudson's, the store manager offered to hire me to do cooking demonstrations for them. That was 22 years ago! A Cook's Palette owes its success in part to the work I did on various cookbook committees.

The Junior League of Kalamazoo and members of Service Club of Kalamazoo applaud the success of *I'VE GOT A COOK IN KALAMAZOO* and welcome its return in this special reprinting.

Deborah Brooks Hudgins
November, 2007

Please note: Microwave directions in this book are for use with units having 600-700 watts (and above). If unit with lower wattage is used, baking times will need to be lengthened.

Common microwave wattage in 2007 is 1200 watts.

RAMOS GIN FIZZ

1½ ozs. gin
1 egg white
Juice of ½ lemon
2 tsps. sugar
3 drops orange flower water
½ oz. curaçao
3 ozs. half-and-half
Nutmeg, grated

Place ingredients in blender with small amount of shaved ice. Strain into chimney glass. Dust with nutmeg and serve.

Preparation time: 5 minutes

Serves: 1
Easily increased

Greeta Douglass

HOT BUTTERED RUM

BATTER:
1 lb. brown sugar
½ cup butter
½ tsp. cinnamon
½ tsp. nutmeg
¼ tsp. ground cloves

Rum
Cinnamon sticks

Mix together batter ingredients.

To make drink: Use 1 to 2 teaspoonfuls batter to 6 ounces hot water and 1 shot (1 ounce or to taste) rum. Garnish with cinnamon stick.

Suggestion: Could also use batter in coffee.

Note: Batter stores well in refrigerator.

Preparation time: 10 minutes

Easy
Can make ahead

Serves: 10-12

Norma Stancati

MULLED WINE
Hits the spot on a cold winter's night

1 gal. red Italian wine
1 orange studded with 50
  cloves
1 T. whole allspice
4 sticks cinnamon
¾ cup brown sugar, packed
1 small orange, sliced
  (slices cut in half)
Brandy or rum (optional)

Two hours before serving: Mix all ingredients in a pan and bring to a boil. Turn off heat; let sit for 2 hours. Warm to serve. If desired, brandy or rum may be added.

Preparation time: 15 minutes

Easy
Must make ahead

Yield: 1 gallon

Jana Hletko

FROZEN KAHLUA EGGNOG
Unique ice cream taste-use as a light dessert

3 eggs, separated
1 cup sugar (divided)
1 cup whipping cream
3 T. rum
Nutmeg, freshly grated
Whipped cream (for
  garnish)
Kahlúa

Beat egg yolks until thick and lemon colored; add ½ cup sugar and beat until creamy. Beat egg whites until stiff; add ½ cup sugar and continue beating. Whip cream until stiff enough to fold. Combine mixtures and add rum. Freeze. Serve in glasses; top with whipped cream flavored with Kahlúa. Sprinkle with nutmeg. Coffee may be substituted for Kahlúa.

Preparation time: 15 minutes

Easy
Must make ahead

Serves: 4-6
Can increase

Shirley Weiss

BRANDY SLUSH
Delicious afternoon refresher

1 can (6 oz.) frozen
concentrated orange
juice, thawed
1 can (6 oz.) frozen
concentrated lemonade,
thawed
2 tea bags steeped in 1 cup
hot water (1 minute)
1 cup sugar dissolved in
3½ cups water
1 cup brandy (½ pint)
7 Up

Mix together first 5 ingredients and freeze overnight. When ready to serve, put 1 or 2 scoops slush in glass and fill with 7 Up.

Preparation time: 3 minutes

Easy
Must make ahead

Serves: 6-8

Chris Harrison

TEA-BASED RUM PUNCH

1 qt. boiling water
16 tea bags
2 cups sugar
Juice of 12 lemons
2 cans (6 oz. each) frozen
concentrated orange
juice, thawed
2 cans (46 oz. each) apricot
nectar
1 can (46 oz.) pineapple
juice
3 fifths rum (2 light and
1 dark may be used)
8 dashes of Angostura
bitters
Maraschino cherries
Orange slices

Four hours ahead: Pour water over tea bags and allow to sit at room temperature until strong. Mix with remaining ingredients. Serve in a punch bowl with ice mold. Garnish with maraschino cherries and orange slices.

Preparation time: 5 minutes

Easy
Must make ahead

Serves: 24
Can increase

Cathy VanderSalm

18

SANGRIA

1 gal. dry red wine
2 cups orange juice, freshly
  squeezed
½ cup lime juice, freshly
  squeezed
½ cup lemon juice, freshly
  squeezed
¼ cup sugar
2 cups sparkling water or
  soda, chilled
Orange slices

Combine first 6 ingredients. To serve, add ice; garnish with orange slices.

Preparation time: 15 minutes   Easy   Yield: 1¼ gallons
                                    Serve immediately

Amanda Clark Morrill

BEER PARTY PUNCH
Tastes like a whiskey sour

1 can (12 oz.) frozen
  concentrated lemonade
12 ozs. bourbon
2 cans or bottles (12 oz.
  each) beer (any brand)

In a punch bowl, combine lemonade and bourbon. Stir in beer. Add lots of ice. Serve in punch cups.

Preparation time: 3 minutes   Easy   Yield: 12 servings
                                    Serve immediately   (4 oz. each)
                                                         Can increase

RUM DUM
Yummy hot weather drink

1 can (6 oz.) orange juice
1 can (6 oz.) pineapple juice
Rum

Mix and serve in a glass with ice.

Preparation time: 1 minute   Easy   Serves: 1
                                                         Can increase

Jan Beisel

MOTHER'S EGGNOGG
A treat for the entire family

2 eggs, well beaten
1 cup condensed milk
  (Eagle Brand preferred)
1 tsp. vanilla
¼ tsp. salt
1 qt. milk
½ pt. whipping cream,
  whipped
Nutmeg
Whiskey or rum (optional)

Mix eggs, condensed milk, vanilla, salt, and milk. Fold in whipped cream. Dust with nutmeg.

Optional: Whiskey or rum may be added.

Preparation time: 5 minutes

Easy
Can make ahead

Serves: 4-6

CLAMDIGGER
Unique, tangy taste

1 can (8 oz.) Bull Shot or
  beef broth
1 qt. Clamato juice
4 T. dill sauce
4 dashes of Tabasco sauce
4 dashes of lemon pepper
8 drops of Worcestershire
  sauce (according to taste)
4 shots (1 oz. or to taste)
  vodka
Dill pickle or celery stick

Mix first 6 ingredients. Adjust seasonings to taste. When ready to serve, add vodka and garnish with dill pickle or celery stick.

Preparation time: 5 minutes

Easy
Can make ahead

Serves: 4
Can increase

John Garside

20

CHAMPAGNE PUNCH
Lovely, light, and potent

1 qt. ginger ale
1 qt. club soda
1 fifth sauterne
1 fifth white rum
1 fifth domestic champagne

Before combining, refrigerate all ingredients until well chilled. After combining, the punch is champagne color; it may be colored to suit table colors.

An ice ring may be used for added decoration and to keep punch chilled. Make ice ring with distilled water (to keep it clear).

Preparation time: 3 minutes

Easy
Serve immediately

Yield: 38 punch glasses (4 oz.)

Mary Jo Garling

SIR JOHN'S BRANDY ICE
Excellent as light dessert or after-dinner drink

1 scoop toffee ice cream
1 oz. brandy
1 oz. creme de cacao
Crushed ice (2 cubes)

Mix all ingredients in a blender. Serve in a small goblet.

Preparation time: 3 minutes

Easy
Serve immediately

Serves: 1
Can increase

John Garside

YOGURT WHIP
Refreshing—a child pleaser

1 container (8 oz.)
  strawberry or raspberry
  yogurt
2 containers apple juice
  (use yogurt container for
  measuring)

Whip in blender and serve over ice.

Preparation time: 2 minutes

Easy
Serve immediately

Serves: 4

Bernadine Simpson

ASPARAGUS ROLL-UPS

Unique—excellent flavor!

24 slices sandwich bread
1 pkg. (8 oz.) cream cheese
3–5 ozs. blue cheese
¾–1 cup butter
24 spears fresh asparagus,
  parboiled

Remove crusts from bread slices. Flatten bread with a rolling pin. Soften cheeses and mix with softened butter. Spread mixture on bread slices. Place a spear of asparagus on each bread slice. Roll up and dip in melted butter. Cut each roll into fourths and freeze. Bake at 400° for 15 minutes.

Microwave: Microwave on high cheeses and butter for 15 to 30 seconds. Continue with above directions.

Preparation time: 40 minutes
Baking time: 15 minutes

Easy
Must make ahead

Yield: 96 pieces
Can freeze

Anne Rapp

MARINATED CHICKEN WINGS

2 lbs. chicken wings
1 cup soy sauce
1 cup brown sugar, packed
1 T. prepared mustard

Mix together all ingredients. Let stand overnight, turning wings occasionally. Bake at 350° for 45 minutes, basting several times. Serve warm.

Microwave: Microwave on high for 15 to 16 minutes, turning after 8 minutes.

Preparation time: 5 minutes
Baking time: 45 minutes
Microwave: 15-16 minutes

Easy
Must make ahead

Easily doubled

Sandra Wotta

CHEESE-BACON SPREAD

½ lb. Monterey Jack cheese
8 strips bacon, cooked,
  drained, finely chopped
1 T. onion, chopped
1 tsp. dry mustard
Mayonnaise
  (enough to spread)

Mix ingredients and spread on crackers. Place under broiler until bubbly.

Microwave: Arrange 10 to 12 crackers in a circle on a glass plate or wax paper. Microwave on high for 45 seconds to 1 minute, rotating dish ¼ turn halfway through cooking time.

Preparation time: 15 minutes

Easy

Serves: 8-10
Easily doubled

Jean Locklin

FLAMING CHEESE
An elegant and impressive hors d'oeuvres

1 lb. Monterey Jack cheese
½ lemon
¼ cup brandy, warmed

Slice cheese ½ inch thick and put on a sizzle platter or steak plate. Put this in the oven for a few minutes to soften the cheese but not melt it. Squeeze lemon over cheese. Pour warm brandy over all; flame. Serve with crackers. Keep warm at table by using a hot tray (hostess tray).

Preparation time: 15 minutes

Easy   Serves: 12
Serve immediately

Judith Betten

CAPERED CHEESE BITES

6 English muffins, split
1 cup mayonnaise
  (Hellmann's preferred)
1½ cups (6 oz.) sharp
  cheddar cheese, grated
2 T. capers, chopped
5-6 whole green onions,
  chopped

Place split muffins on baking sheet. Mix remaining ingredients in small bowl. Spread on muffins. Cut each slice into 8 triangles. Bake at 350° for 25 to 30 minutes. Serve warm.

To freeze: Bake only 10 minutes—to set cheese. Cool; place in plastic bag and freeze. Finish baking time just before serving.

Preparation time: 25 minutes
Baking time: 25-30 minutes

Can make ahead   Yield: 96 pieces
                                    Can freeze

Jeannie Coulter

SAUSAGE RYES

1 lb. hot sausage
  (Bob Evans preferred)
1 lb. ground chuck
1 lb. Velveeta cheese
½ tsp. garlic salt
1 T. Worcestershire sauce
1 can (8 oz.) mushrooms
1 loaf party rye

Brown the meats. Add cheese and cook until it melts. Add seasonings and mushrooms; mix well. Spread on slices of party rye. Place on baking sheets and freeze. After frozen, store in plastic bag. To serve, heat under broiler until hot and bubbly.

Hint: Could be used for a light supper or lunch. Cheese may be sprinkled on top.

Preparation time: 20 minutes
Baking time: 5-10 minutes

Easy   Serves: 20
Can make ahead   Can freeze

Fran Garvey

23

SWEET-AND-SOUR MEATBALLS
A tempting tanginess you'll enjoy

2 lbs. hamburger
¼ tsp. instant garlic
½ tsp. salt
¼ tsp. pepper
2 eggs, beaten
½ cup bread crumbs,
  seasoned (Progresso
  preferred)
1 onion, grated

Mix together first 7 ingredients and roll into small meatballs.

SAUCE:
1 bottle (12 oz.) chili sauce
6 ozs. grape jelly
Juice of 1 lemon
  or 1 T. lemon juice

Mix sauce ingredients in pan and simmer for 5 minutes. Add meatballs; cover. Simmer for 1 hour. Stir gently and not too often.

Preparation time: 25 minutes
Cooking time: 1 hour

Easy
Can make ahead

Serves: 24
Easily doubled

Marilyn Belenky

PIGS IN THE BLANKET
Tangy sauce, too!

1 pkg. smokey link
  sausages
2 cans (8 oz. each)
  refrigerated crescent rolls

Unroll crescent rolls; leave in squares. Put smokey links on long side of squares and roll up. Cut each roll in thirds and bake according to directions on roll package. Serve hot with dip.

DIP:
1 cup sour cream
1 tsp. horseradish
2 tsps. mustard
1 tsp. garlic powder

Dip: Mix together dip ingredients; refrigerate. Best if made a few hours ahead.

Preparation time: 10 minutes

Very easy
Can make ahead

Yield: 24 pieces
Easily doubled

Sandra Wotta

FILO CHEESE TRIANGLES
Well worth the effort

3 cups small curd cottage cheese

1½ cups Monterey Jack cheese, grated

3 eggs

6 T. parsley, minced

1 T. onion, minced

¾ tsp. pepper

1 lb. filo pastry sheets (about 30)

1½ cups butter, melted

Combine cheeses, eggs, parsley, onion, and pepper. Separate 3 sheets of filo pastry; spread butter between layers and restack. Cut into 6 crosswise strips. Spoon 1 tablespoonful filling onto 1 pastry strip to within 1½ inches from the end. Fold pastry over filling. For second fold, bring folded edge to left side of strip to form a triangle. Continue folding until pastry strip is completely folded like a triangle. Fill and fold remaining 5 strips in the same way. Repeat 9 times with remaining 27 pastry sheets-making a total of 60 triangles. Cover filled triangles and remaining pastry sheets with a damp towel to prevent drying. Place filled triangles on a baking sheet. Bake at 350° for 15 minutes, or until light golden brown. These may be frozen before or after baking. Bake frozen unbaked triangles at 350° for 20 minutes. To reheat frozen baked triangles, bake at 300° for 5 minutes.

Preparation time: 1 hour
Baking time: 15 minutes

Can make ahead

Yield: 5 dozen
Can freeze

Judy Brown

BROOK LODGE WATER CHESTNUTS
A favorite with men

1 can (8 oz.) water chestnuts, quartered

1 lb. bacon, slices cut in half

SAUCE:

½ cup catsup

⅓ cup sugar

1 tsp. soy sauce

Wrap bacon around chestnuts and secure with toothpicks. Bake on foil-lined baking sheet at 350° for 30 minutes. Pour off grease. May be frozen at this point. Blend sauce ingredients in blender or food processor. At serving time, dip chestnuts in sauce, put on baking sheet, and reheat at 350° for 20 minutes.

Variation: Sauce may be doubled and used with chicken wings or shrimp. Shrimp may or may not be wrapped in bacon.

Preparation time: 10 minutes
Baking time: 30 minutes

Easy
Can make ahead

Can freeze
Doubles easily

TOASTED MUSHROOM ROLLS

½ lb. mushrooms, cleaned,
  finely chopped
¼ cup butter
3 T. flour
¾ tsp. salt
¼ tsp. monosodium
  glutamate (MSG)
1 cup half-and-half
2 tsps. chives
1 tsp. lemon juice
1 loaf white bread
  (family size)

Preheat oven to 400°. Sauté mushrooms for 5 minutes in butter. Blend in flour, salt, and MSG. Stir in cream; cook until thick (spreading consistency). Add chives and lemon juice; cool.

Remove crusts from bread and roll slices thin. Spread bread with mixture and roll up. Cut each roll in half and toast on all sides for 10 minutes in a 400° oven.

Variation: Lobster or crab meat may be added as pleasant variations.

Microwave: Prepare mushrooms. Microwave on high for 2 minutes in butter. Blend in flour, salt and MSG. Stir in cream and microwave on high for 2 to 3 minutes. Continue with above directions.

Preparation time: 20 minutes
Baking time: 10 minutes

Easy
Freezes well

Yield: 3½ dozen

Arlene Foster

PIZZA APPETIZERS
Tiny tantalizing pizzas

1 can (2¼ oz.) ripe olives,
  chopped
½ cup canned tomatoes,
  well drained, chopped
  (Del Monte stewed
  tomatoes preferred)
1 cup sharp cheese, grated
1 tsp. Parmesan cheese,
  grated
1 tsp. onion, grated
⅛ tsp. oregano
⅛ tsp. garlic salt
7 slices toast, buttered
  (Pepperidge Farm
  preferred)

Mix together all ingredients except toast. Spread mixture on toast. Cut each slice into six pieces. Bake at 400° for 10 minutes.

Variations: Could be used for a light supper or lunch. Very good on English muffins.

Preparation time: 15 minutes
Baking time: 10 minutes

Easy
Can make ahead

Yield: 42 pieces
Can freeze

Jane Todd

26

HOT SPINACH BALLS

4 eggs
2 cups herb-seasoned
  stuffing
1 medium onion, minced
½ cup Parmesan cheese
½ tsp. thyme
1 tsp. salt
½ tsp. pepper
½ tsp. garlic powder
2 pkgs. (10 oz. each) frozen
  chopped spinach, cooked,
  drained
¾ cup butter, melted

Beat eggs well. Combine stuffing, onion, cheese, and seasonings. Mix together eggs, spinach, and stuffing mixture. Pour melted butter over it; mix well. Chill thoroughly. Roll into 1-inch balls. Bake at 350° for 15 minutes.

Preparation time: 15 minutes
Baking time: 15 minutes

Easy
Can make ahead

Yield: 40-50 balls
Easily doubled

Cheryl Simpson

SPINACH-HAM DIP

2 T. butter
1 medium onion, chopped
1 can (4 oz.) mushrooms,
  chopped
1 pkg. (10 oz.) frozen
  chopped spinach
1 cup ham, cooked, finely
  ground (or deviled ham)
2 pkgs. (3 oz. each) cream
  cheese
1 tsp. dijon mustard
¼ tsp. sweet basil
¼ tsp. dill
Salt and pepper to taste

Sauté onion in butter; add mushrooms. Add spinach, ham, and mustard. Heat while blending in the cream cheese. Add herbs and salt and pepper to taste. Heat in double boiler and serve warm. This could be served as a vegetable over toast points.

Microwave: Heat onions and mushrooms in butter on high for 2 to 4 minutes, until tender. Add drained spinach, ham, and mustard. Blend in cream cheese and spices. Microwave on high until hot.

Preparation time: 20 minutes
Cooking time: 10 minutes

Easy
Can make ahead

Sally Ward Hume

CRAB SUPREME

12 ozs. cream cheese,
  softened
2 T. Worcestershire sauce
1 T. lemon juice
2 T. mayonnaise
1 small onion, finely grated
Dash of garlic salt
4 ozs. chili sauce (Heinz
  preferred)
1 can (6½–7 oz.) crab meat,
  drained, minced
Dried parsley, chopped
  (for garnish)

Blend first 6 ingredients well; spread on a shallow platter. Spread chili sauce thinly over cheese mixture. Spread crab meat over chili sauce. Sprinkle top with chopped dried parsley. Serve with crackers.

Preparation time: 15 minutes

Easy
Can make ahead

Serves: 10

Mary Bower

CRAB MEAT ÉLÉGANTE
A connoisseur's selection

1 pkg. (8 oz.) cream cheese
1 T. milk
1 can (6½ oz.) crab meat,
  flaked, drained
2 T. onion, finely chopped
½ tsp. cream-style
  horseradish
¼ tsp. salt
Dash of pepper
1 can (4 oz.) mushrooms,
  drained, chopped
1 T. chili sauce
Dash of Tabasco sauce
⅓ cup almonds, sliced,
  toasted
Paprika

Mix together all ingredients except almonds and paprika. Put into ovenproof dish. Sprinkle with paprika and almonds. Bake at 375° for 15 minutes, or until piping hot. Serve with crackers.

Preparation time: 10 minutes
Baking time: 15 minutes

Easy
Can make ahead

Yield: 1½ pints

Chris Garrett

CRAB À LA FLORENTINE

1 can (6 ½–7 oz.) Alaskan
  king crab meat or
  equivalent amount of
  frozen crab meat
1 pkg. (10 oz.) frozen
  spinach
2 T. onion, minced
¼ cup butter (divided)
1 tsp. salt (divided)
½ tsp. dried dill weed
Dash of pepper
1 cup milk
2 T. flour
White pepper to taste
1 egg yolk
1 tsp. lemon juice
¼ cup dried bread crumbs
1 T. Parmesan cheese,
  grated

Drain crab (thaw and drain, if frozen). Cook spinach according to package directions; drain. Sauté onion in 1 tablespoonful butter; add to spinach with ½ teaspoonful salt, dill weed, and pepper. Melt 2 tablespoonfuls butter; blend in flour and white pepper. Gradually add milk. Cook and stir until boiling and thick. Slightly beat egg yolk; add small amount of hot mixture to yolk to blend. Return egg to hot mixture on low heat for 1 minute. Add lemon juice and crab meat (reserve a little crab for garnish, if desired). Spoon enough spinach mixture into ovenproof shells to cover bottoms. Top with crab mixture. Garnish with reserved crab. Top with mixture of 1 tablespoonful melted butter, bread crumbs, and cheese. Bake at 350° for 10 to 15 minutes. Serve hot.

Preparation time: 45 minutes
Baking time: 10 minutes

Serves: 8

Neoma Kilway

CRAB CANAPÉS

10 slices white bread
  (Pepperidge Farm
  preferred)
1 cup mayonnaise
  (Hellmann's preferred)
1 tsp. curry powder
1 can (6½ oz.) crab meat,
  drained
Salt and pepper to taste
1 cup (4 oz.) Swiss cheese,
  grated

Cut bread into rounds with cookie cutter or rim of drinking glass. Toast rounds under broiler on 1 side only. Combine mayonnaise and curry powder; blend thoroughly. Spread the mayonnaise mixture on the untoasted side of bread rounds. Place crab meat on top of each round; add salt and pepper to taste. Sprinkle cheese over all and toast under broiler until cheese melts.

Preparation time: 15 minutes   Easy   Yield: 30 appetizers

Helen Handelsman

PINEAPPLE CHEESE BALL
Very refreshing

2 pkgs. (8 oz. each) cream cheese
1 can (8½ oz.) crushed pineapple, drained
1 tsp. salt
¼ cup green pepper, chopped
2 T. onion, chopped
1½ cups pecans, chopped

In medium bowl, beat cream cheese. Combine rest of ingredients except pecans; mix well. Shape into ball and refrigerate for several hours. Roll ball in pecans. Serve with assorted crackers.

Preparation time: 15 minutes

Easy
Must make ahead

Serves: 18-20

Ann Kneas
Sandy Reece
Marianne Struckmeyer

TANGY CHEESE POT

1 jar (5 oz.) Old English cheese spread
1 jar (5 oz.) Roka Cheese spread
1 pkg. (3 oz.) cream cheese
¼ cup dry white wine
1 small onion, finely chopped
Garlic salt to taste
Parsley or chives (for garnish)

Mix together ingredients and put into a crock. Sprinkle with parsley or chives. Refrigerate several hours or overnight to allow flavors to mingle. Keep indefinitely in refrigerator.

Preparation time: 10 minutes

Easy
Must make ahead

Sandra Wotta

CH-EASY SPREAD

2 lbs. Velveeta cheese
1½ bottles (8¼ oz. each)
  cream-style horseradish
1 cup plus 2 T. mayonnaise
10 drops Tabasco sauce
5 ozs. beer

Melt together all ingredients in double boiler until smooth. Fold in beer. Put in bowl or crock and refrigerate. Serve with crackers.

Microwave: Cut up cheese chunks and put in 2-quart glass casserole. Microwave on high for 4 minutes. Stir occasionally. Add remaining ingredients and micro-wave on high for 1 to 2 minutes. Stir to blend all ingredients. Pour into crock.

Preparation time: 15 minutes
Microwave: 6 minutes

Easy
Can make ahead

Yield: 1 quart

Joan deMink
Isabel Stout

CHEESE-ONION SOUFFLÉ
A soufflé always adds a glamorous touch

1 cup onion, thinly sliced
½ cup ripe olives, sliced
1 cup cheddar or Swiss
  cheese, grated
1 cup mayonnaise
  (Hellmann's preferred)

Mix together all ingredients. Put in pie plate or flat baking dish. Bake at 350° for 20 to 30 minutes. Serve hot with party pumpernickel slices or favorite crackers.

Variation: To change flavor, bacon or crab may be added.

Preparation time: 20 minutes
Baking time: 20-30 minutes

Easy

Serves: 12

Polly Peters

CHINESE CHEESE

1 pkg. (8 oz.) cream cheese
Soy sauce
Worcestershire sauce
Sesame seeds

Put cream cheese in a shallow dish. Mix equal amounts of soy sauce and Worces-tershire sauce and pour over cream cheese until it comes halfway up the cheese. Spread sesame seeds in single layer on baking sheet. Bake at 350° for about 10 minutes, or until toasted. Sprinkle seeds over cheese. Serve with crisp crackers.

Preparation time: 10 minutes

Easy

Serves: 10

Julie Crockett

MEXICAN MIX
Tasty south-of-the-border flavor

2 large tomatoes, peeled,
chopped
3–4 green onions, chopped
1 can (4 oz.) green chilies,
chopped
3 T. olive oil
1½ T. vinegar
1 tsp. garlic salt

Mix ingredients and chill for several hours. Drain off most of liquid before serving. Serve with plain Doritos.

Preparation time: 10 minutes

Easy
Can make ahead

Serves: 8

Gretchen Ishler

GUACAMOLE
Something snappy to liven up a party

1 large or 2 small avocados,
peeled, chopped
½ small onion, chopped
1 T. lemon juice
½ tsp. salt
1 can (4 oz.) roasted peeled
green chilies

Put ingredients in blender or food processor and blend to desired consistency. Refrigerate. Serve with Doritos.

Variation: Add 1 medium tomato, peeled and chopped; several sprigs of coriander, chopped; and a pinch of sugar. This can be used as a topping for tacos, nachos, and salads.

Preparation time: 10 minutes

Easy
Can make ahead

Serves: 4-6

George Ann Castel

SAVORY VEGETABLE DIP

½ cup mayonnaise
½ cup sour cream
1 tsp. dried dill
1 tsp. Beau Monde spice
1 tsp. instant onion
Pinch of garlic salt

Mix together all ingredients and refrigerate for several hours before serving.

Preparation time: 10 minutes

Easy
Must make ahead

Serves: 8

Mary Oudsema

SHRIMP MOUSSE
Really elegant when done in a special mold

1 env. unflavored gelatin
¼ cup cold water
1 can (10¾ oz.) tomato soup
1 pkg. (8 oz.) cream cheese
½ cup green pepper,
  chopped
½ cup onion, chopped
½ cup celery, chopped
1 cup mayonnaise
  (Hellmann's preferred)
2 cans (6½ oz. each) small
  shrimp, drained

Dissolve gelatin in ¼ cup cold water; set aside. Combine soup (undiluted) and cream cheese; warm over low heat until melted. Add gelatin mixture. Set aside and cool. Mix green pepper, onion, celery, mayonnaise, and shrimp into the soup-gelatin mixture. Refrigerate for 2 days. Serve with plain crackers.

Preparation time: 30 minutes   Must make ahead   Serves: 8

Peg La Pine

SERVICHE
Straight from San Salvador

2 lbs. white fish fillets
2 cups lime juice
1 large onion, minced
20 pitted green olives,
  sliced
3 ripe tomatoes, peeled,
  minced
1 cup tomato juice
½ cup water
½ cup catsup
½ cup olive oil
2 tsps. salt
1 tsp. oregano
1 tsp. Tabasco sauce
Green hot chilies
  (optional garnish)
Avocado (optional garnish)

Fish may or may not be poached. If poached, marinate in lime juice to cover for 15 to 20 minutes; drain and rinse. If unpoached, marinate in lime juice to cover for at least 5 hours-preferably overnight. Drain; rinse in cold water. Cut fillets into 1-inch cubes.

Add remaining ingredients. Can be prepared the day before. Serve chilled with bread and crackers. Optional garnishes: green hot chilies and avocado.

Preparation time: 30 minutes   Must make ahead   Serves: 8-12

Jean Kavanaugh

MARINATED VEGETABLES

2 cups mayonnaise
(Hellmann's preferred)
1 cup sour cream substitute
1 cup (or less) horseradish
1 T. lemon juice, freshly
squeezed
1 tsp. salt
1 tsp. Accent
1 pkg. (10 oz.) frozen
artichoke hearts
1 pkg. (10 oz.) frozen
Brussels sprouts
1 pkg. (10 oz.) frozen long
baby carrots
Fresh mushrooms
1 can (8 oz.) water
chestnuts
Fresh zucchini, sliced
Fresh cauliflower

Mix together the first 6 ingredients. Slightly cook and then cool frozen vegetables so that they are crisp. Add all the vegetables to the mayonnaise mixture. Marinate overnight. Serve in bowl with toothpicks.

Preparation time: 15 minutes

Easy
Can make ahead

Serves: 24

Betsy Morren

TUNA-MUSHROOM SPREAD

1 can (10 oz.) tuna fish,
water packed
1 pkg. (8 oz.) cream cheese
(or low-calorie substitute)
1 can (2½ oz.) mushrooms,
chopped
Paprika or parsley
(for garnish)

Drain tuna and mushrooms; mix thoroughly with cream cheese (mixer can be used). Sprinkle with paprika or parsley for color. Serve with crackers.

Preparation time: 5 minutes

Easy
Can make ahead

Serves: 6–8

Jean Paulson

CHILLED ARTICHOKE HORS D'OEUVRE
A grand opening for a fine repast

1 artichoke, whole
1 T. vegetable oil
1 T. lemon juice
1 cup mayonnaise
2 tsps. dry mustard
1 tsp. Worcestershire
sauce
3 eggs, hard cooked

Trim ends from artichoke leaves. Cook whole artichoke in boiling water to which the vegetable oil and lemon juice have been added. Cook for 45 minutes to 1 hour, or until fork tender. Drain. Pull off leaves and chill. Mix and chill mayonnaise, mustard, and Worcestershire sauce. To serve: Arrange leaves in circles on plate. Put a dab of mayonnaise mixture on each leaf and decorate with a sliver of egg.

Microwave: Prepare artichoke. Wrap in wax paper or place in covered dish. Microwave on high for 4 to 4½ minutes, or until base is fork tender.

Preparation time: 20 minutes
Cooking time: 45 minutes
Microwave: 4–4½ minutes

Easy
Can make ahead

Serves: 4–6

Sharon Garside

MUSHROOMS VINAIGRETTE

1 lb. mushrooms
3 T. olive oil
4 T. vinegar
½ tsp. salt
½ tsp. oregano, crushed
Dash of pepper
1 T. parsley
1 clove garlic, minced

Wash and drain mushrooms. If large, cut in half and trim. Place in medium saucepan with small amount of water and bring to boil. Cover and simmer for 5 to 10 minutes. Drain. Mix together remaining ingredients and pour over drained mushrooms. Chill for several hours. Pour off some of liquid before serving.

Variation: This would also be good with shrimp, artichoke hearts, or peeled cherry tomatoes.

Microwave: Prepare mushrooms as above. Place in 1½-quart casserole; add 4 tablespoonfuls water. Cover and microwave on high for 5 to 6 minutes, stirring after 3 minutes. Do not overcook. Continue with above directions.

Preparation time: 10 minutes
Cooking time: 10 minutes

Easy
Can make ahead

Serves: 8–10

Mary Maynard

BEER-CHEESE PUFFS

1 cup beer
¼ cup margarine
1 cup flour
1 tsp. Worcestershire sauce
½ tsp. salt
⅛ tsp. cayenne
1½ cups cheddar cheese,
  shredded
4 eggs
Paprika

FILLING:
1 can (15½ oz.) salmon,
  drained, flaked
3 T. salad dressing
2 T. stuffed olives, diced
2 T. onion, diced
1 T. parsley, chopped
⅛ tsp. garlic salt
Dash of chili powder

Mix together beer and margarine in medium saucepan. Bring to a boil. Reduce heat to low; add flour and stir vigorously until mixture forms a ball-about 1 minute. Remove from heat. Add seasonings and cheese. Beat vigorously for 2 minutes to blend mixture and cool it slightly. Add eggs, 1 at a time, beating until smooth after each addition. Drop by teaspoonfuls on ungreased baking sheets. Sprinkle tops with paprika. Bake at 400° for 15 minutes, or until browned. Cool on wire racks. Puffs may be made several days ahead and kept in airtight container.

To serve: Cut off tops of puffs. Scoop out centers and fill with 1 teaspoonful filling. Replace tops and serve.

Filling: Combine all ingredients and mix well. Best to make ahead to let flavors mingle.

Preparation time: 30 minutes
Baking time: 15 minutes

Can make ahead

Yield: 10 dozen

Mardee Mott

SCRAMBLED EGG DIP

3 eggs
1 T. butter
3 T. vinegar
3 T. sugar
1 pkg. (8 oz.) cream cheese,
  softened
Green onions, chopped
Green olives, sliced

In skillet, *softly* scramble eggs in butter, vinegar, and sugar. Mix in cream cheese. Add onions and olives to taste. Refrigerate in serving dish. Serve on party rye or Triscuits.

Preparation time: 15 minutes

Easy
Can make ahead

Yield: 2 pints

Kay Hutchinson

36

CHICKEN LIVER PÂTÉ

¼ cup chicken fat (or butter)
1 small onion, chopped
1 lb. chicken livers, drained
1 jar (4 oz.) mushrooms,
  sliced, drained
⅓ cup dry white wine
⅓ cup butter, cold
1 T. brandy
1 tsp. salt
1 large dash of Parisienne
  spice (or equal dashes
  of white pepper, cloves,
  ginger, allspice)

Melt chicken fat; add onion and cook for a few minutes. Add livers and cook until they have lost their redness. Add mushrooms and wine. Cover and simmer for about 5 to 10 minutes, until livers are cooked but not hard and dry. Cool. Put mixture in blender or food processor and blend until smooth. Add remaining ingredients. Blend well. Check seasonings and store in pint container. Refrigerate at least 1 day. To serve, bring near room temperature. Accompany with toast, crackers, or French bread. Keeps for about 1 week.

Microwave: Microwave butter on high for 15 to 30 seconds. Add onion and microwave for 2 minutes. Chop chicken livers. Add to butter and onion and microwave, covered, 3 to 4 minutes. Continue with above directions.

Preparation time: 30 minutes   Must make ahead   Serves: 8
                                                        Can freeze

George Ann Castel

MOCK BOURSIN AU POIVRE

1 pkg. (8 oz.) cream cheese
1 clove garlic, crushed
1 tsp. caraway seed
1 tsp. basil
1 tsp. dill
1 tsp. chives, chopped
Lemon pepper

Blend together all ingredients but lemon pepper; shape into ball. Roll in lemon pepper until covered. Refrigerate a day or more to blend flavors. Serve with crackers (Bremner wafers preferred).

Preparation time: 10 minutes   Easy   Serves: 8–10
                                   Must make ahead

Ann Pryser

The following dips may be served with assorted fresh vegetables:

AUNT ALICE'S DIP

1 can (4¾ oz.) deviled ham
1 pkg. (8 oz.) cream cheese
¼ cup chutney (Major
   Grey's preferred)
Dash of Worcestershire
   sauce

Mix ham and cream cheese. Chop chutney into small bits. Add pieces and liquid of chutney to bowl with cream cheese and ham. Add Worcestershire sauce and mix well. Refrigerate.

Hint: If there is any left over, this makes an excellent sandwich spread.

Preparation time: 10 minutes

Easy
Can make ahead

Serves: 6–8

Brenda Murphy

CRUDITÉS AND CURRIED DIP

3 ozs. blue cheese
1 cup mayonnaise
½ cup chili sauce
Dash of Worcestershire
   sauce
Curry powder to taste

Rub cheese through a sieve. Mix together mayonnaise, chili sauce, Worcestershire sauce, and cheese in a medium-size bowl. Add more curry powder than seems to be needed, then add more to taste. Refrigerate. Serve with vegetables.

Preparation time: 10 minutes

Easy
Can make ahead

Serves: 8-10

Gail Kasdorf

MITCHELL'S FRESH-FROZEN JUMBO SHRIMP

Place *frozen* shrimp in large pot; barely cover with any kind of beer. Sprinkle with a little garlic salt, parsley flakes, salt, and a few peppercorns. When beer comes to a boil, let it boil about 2 to 3 minutes.

Mitchell's Tavern
Paw Paw

Welcome to the wonderful world of soup. Here you may let your creative instincts bubble. The recipes that follow will all stand on their own merits, but each of them may be altered to suit your fancy. In so doing, you will be able to use up all kinds of odds and ends from your refrigerator! For instance—use tired, but still valuable, lettuce leaves by cooking them briefly in chicken stock with some thinly sliced unpeeled potatoes. Blend and add to cucumber soup. Delicious!

Remember to freeze those tasty bones from roasts and chops for later use in soup.

You may easily make your own equivalent of canned cream soup. Just make a cup of medium white sauce and add the appropriate vegetables and seasoning. For mushroom soup, sauté ½ cup chopped fresh mushrooms with 2 tablespoonfuls minced onion in a little butter. Season with garlic and freshly ground white pepper. Chopped fresh parsley also adds a nice touch. Just read the labels on the soup cans and you'll see they are easily duplicated, at little cost and with much less salt.

Very little equipment is *necessary* for making soup. You do need a good sharp knife, and although a blender or food processor is handy, you may use a simple food mill for all blended soup. A garlic press is nice. Many a soup has been given a lift by the discreet addition of garlic. It adds a full flavor that is hard to duplicate.

Those French canning jars with the wired glass tops that come in ½-gallon and gallon sizes are wonderful for storing quantities of soup in the refrigerator.

Do consider investing in an extra pepper mill for white pepper if you don't have one.

There is one more very important thing that will make all soups better. Whenever possible, use fresh ingredients-especially herbs. Consider starting an herb garden in pots. You can set them out in the ground in the summer and bring them back inside in the winter.

HAPPY STIRRING!

MINESTRONE
"Stew-like"

¼ lb. lean salt pork, diced
1 qt. rich beef stock
1 cup potatoes, cut in large
   cubes
1 cup carrots, cut in large
   pieces
1 cup turnips, cut in large
   pieces
¾ cup rice, uncooked
1 cup onion, sliced
½ cup green peas
½ cup lima beans
¼ small head cabbage,
   shredded
¼ lb. fresh spinach,
   shredded
1 leek (white part only),
   shredded
½ cup celery, sliced in large
   pieces
4 medium tomatoes,
   diced, or 3 cups canned
   tomatoes
2 T. tomato paste
2 T. parsley, chopped
½ tsp. sage
½ tsp. ground black pepper
Salt to taste
Parmesan cheese, grated
   (for garnish)

Cook pork in water to cover in a large covered kettle for 30 minutes. Add stock; bring to a boil. Add potatoes, carrots, turnips, and rice. Cover and cool for 10 minutes. Add all remaining ingredients except Parmesan cheese. Slowly bring to a boil and cook until soup is *very* thick and vegetables are tender. Serve as a main dish, sprinkled with Parmesan cheese.

Note: Soup may be thinned with chicken broth.

Preparation time: 30 minutes
Cooking time: 1–2 hours

Yield: Twelve
8-oz. servings

Betty Upjohn

41

HEARTY HAM SOUP

1½–2 lbs. meaty ham bone
  or smoked ham hocks
  plus some extra ham
8–10 cups water
8–10 whole black
  peppercorns
5 whole cloves
1 tsp. salt (omit if using
  ham hocks)
1–2 cloves garlic
½ head cabbage, coarsely
  chopped
2 large potatoes, pared,
  thinly sliced
2 carrots, thinly sliced
1 medium onion, chopped
Salt and pepper to taste
6–8 thick slices rye bread
Parmesan cheese, grated
Swiss cheese, cut in strips
Parsley, minced
  (for garnish)

In 4½-quart Dutch oven, combine ham bone, ham, water, peppercorns, cloves, salt, and garlic. Bring to a boil. Reduce heat. Cover and simmer for 2½ hours. Remove ham bone and cut meat off bone. Strain broth. Return broth and meat to Dutch oven. Add cabbage, potatoes, carrots, and onion. Cover and simmer for 40 minutes, or until vegetables are tender. Season with salt and pepper. Ladle hot soup into heatproof bowls. Top with a slice of rye bread which has been liberally covered with Parmesan cheese. Top Parmesan with strips of Swiss cheese. Place under broiler for about 2 minutes, or until Swiss cheese melts. Garnish with parsley.

Preparation time: 20 minutes
Cooking time: 3–3½ hours

Yield: Twelve
8-oz. servings

Diane Basso

BROCCOLI SOUP

4 T. butter
2 T. flour
3 cups milk
⅔ cup broccoli, cooked
1 bouillon cube
2 T. sherry
½ cup half-and-half
Salt and pepper to taste

In a blender or food processor, blend butter, flour, milk, broccoli, bouillon cube, and sherry. Put in double boiler and cook for 30 minutes, or until thick. Add half-and-half.

Preparation time: 10 minutes
Cooking time: 30 minutes

Yield: Eight
4-oz. servings

Susan Brown

GAZPACHO

¼ cup almonds, ground
2 shallots, peeled, chopped
1 tsp. salt
1 tsp. white pepper
1 cup salad oil
½ cup cider vinegar
2 eggs
1 can (16 oz.) Italian
  tomatoes
2 medium cucumbers,
  peeled, seeded, chopped
1 tsp. ground cloves
1 tsp. ground cumin
Cayenne pepper to taste
3 slices stale white bread
  (remove crusts)
4 cups chicken stock
1 cup whipping cream,
  unwhipped
Seedless grapes, peeled

Put almonds, shallots, salt, white pepper, oil, and vinegar in blender; blend until smooth. Set aside in bowl. Blend remaining ingredients except grapes in blender until smooth. Add to first mixture. Chill. At serving time, put 5 or 6 grapes in bottom of each cup before adding soup.

Preparation time: 30 minutes   Must make ahead   Yield: Ten 8-oz.
                                                            servings

Laurie DeHaven

CHILLED CREAM OF TOMATO SOUP
No-cook soup!

1 can (10¾ oz.) condensed
  tomato soup
1 ⅓ cups milk
⅔ cup mayonnaise
1 tsp. lemon juice
Several dashes of Tabasco
  sauce
½ cup cottage cheese
¼ cup green onions, thinly
  sliced

Mix together tomato soup and milk and slowly add to mayonnaise. Add remaining ingredients. Chill.

Preparation time: 10 minutes   Easy   Yield: Six 6-oz.
                                 Must make ahead   servings

Dorrie Kelly

43

GAZPACHO SOUP

1 clove garlic, crushed
6 T. lemon juice
3 cups fresh tomatoes,
  peeled, chopped
½ cup green pepper,
  chopped
½ cup onion, chopped
¼ cup parsley, chopped
2 cups cucumber, chopped
2–3 tsps. salt
Tabasco sauce to taste
⅓ cup olive oil
2 cups tomato juice
½–1 lb. shrimp, cooked
  (optional)

Mix together all ingredients. Vegetables can be coarsely chopped by hand or finely chopped in food processor. Chill thoroughly. If desired, soup may be served with shrimp (added at serving time).

Preparation time: 30 minutes
Chilling time: Several hours

Must make ahead
Can freeze

Yield: Eight
8-oz. servings

Sandra Wotta

LOBSTER-SHRIMP CHOWDER

¼ cup celery, chopped
2 T. onion, finely chopped
2 T. butter
1 can (10¾ oz.) condensed
  cream of shrimp soup
  (Campbell's preferred)
1 can (10¾ oz.) condensed
  cream of mushroom soup
1 soup can (10¾ oz.) milk
1 cup half-and-half
1 can (5 oz.) lobster meat
  (or an equivalent amount
  frozen)
¼ cup dry sherry
1 T. parsley, chopped

Cook celery and onion in butter until tender. Add shrimp and mushroom soups, milk, and half-and-half; heat through (may be made a few hours ahead to this point). Add lobster, sherry, and parsley just before serving. Heat through.

Preparation time: 10 minutes
Cooking time: 10 minutes

Easy
Base can be made
ahead

Yield: Six
8-oz. servings

Lynn Deis

44

MY LENTIL SOUP

Delicious as a main course with tossed salad and bread

1 lb. lentils
2–4 lb. ham bone (fresh or smoked) with meat
½–1 lb. spicy sausage
1 can (6 oz.) tomato paste
1 large onion, chopped
1 clove garlic, chopped
2½ tsps. salt
1 tsp. dried oregano
¼ tsp. ground sage
Dash of cayenne pepper
4 tomatoes, chopped
2 carrots, sliced
2 stalks celery, chopped
Parmesan cheese, grated

Cover lentils with water; soak overnight. Simmer ham bone with sausage in 10 cups water for 3 hours. Remove meat from bone; thinly slice sausage. At this point, stock may be chilled and unwanted fat removed. Strain stock and return to clean pot, adding lentil water and additional water to make 10 cups. To liquid, add meat, tomato paste, onion, garlic, salt, oregano, sage, cayenne, and lentils. Cover and simmer for 30 minutes, stirring occasionally. Add tomatoes, carrots, and celery. Cover and simmer for 30 to 40 minutes longer. Serve in large bowls with a spoonful of Parmesan cheese on top.

Note: By using fresh ham and freshly made sausage, you avoid nitrates and/or nitrites.

Preparation time: 2 days
Cooking time: 4 hours

Can make ahead
Can freeze

Yield: Sixteen
8-oz. servings

Susan Balz

GEORGIA PEANUT SOUP

¼ cup margarine
¼ cup onion, finely chopped
¼ cup celery, finely chopped
1 cup creamy peanut butter
1 T. flour
4 cups beef bouillon
2 tsps. lemon juice
Whipping cream, whipped, unsweetened (for garnish)
½ cup cocktail peanuts, chopped

In a large heavy saucepan, melt margarine. Add onion and celery; sauté until tender. Stir in peanut butter and flour; blend well. Gradually stir in beef bouillon and lemon juice until smooth. Cook over medium heat for 20 minutes, stirring occasionally. To serve, garnish with whipped cream and peanuts.

Note: For variation, use curry powder to taste instead of lemon juice. Substitute chicken broth for beef bouillon. Garnish with parsley.

Preparation time: 30 minutes
Cooking time: 20 minutes

Easy
Can make ahead

Yield: Eight
6-oz. servings

GREEN PEA AND CHICKEN SOUP
Garden fresh

5 cups fresh peas
6 T. butter
1 onion, finely minced
1 small head leaf lettuce,
　cut in fine strips
15 leaves fresh spinach
1 sprig parsley
A few sprigs chervil
　(if available)
2 tsps. sugar
½ tsp. salt
1¾ cups water
3 cups chicken stock
½ cup chicken breast,
　cooked, cut in fine strips
3 egg yolks
1½ cups half-and-half

In a large pan, put 4 cups peas, butter, onion, lettuce, spinach, parsley, chervil, sugar, salt, and water. Cover. Bring to boil and cook until peas are tender. Put mixture through a vegetable mill or blend in a food processor. Return to pan. Add chicken stock; simmer for 15 minutes. Cook 1 cup peas in separate pan and add to pot along with chicken. Mix egg yolks with half-and-half; gradually add to soup, stirring constantly. Cook soup until it thickens; *do not let boil.*

Preparation time: 30 minutes
Cooking time: 1 hour

Can make ahead

Yield: Twelve
8-oz. servings

Sharon Garside

DIETER'S CHILLED CREAM SOUP

2 cups any low calorie
　vegetable (spinach,
　green beans, asparagus,
　broccoli, cauliflower,
　celery, etc.)
⅔ cup cottage cheese
Salt and pepper to taste
Onion juice or curry powder
　to taste
Buttermilk (if needed)
Parsley (for garnish)
Croutons

In blender, puree vegetables and cottage cheese. Add seasonings to taste. If necessary add buttermilk to thin. Chill. Garnish with parsley. Serve with croutons.

Preparation time: 10 minutes

Easy

Yield: Four
6-oz. servings

Woodena Stainton

POTATO SOUP
Superb in its simplicity

3 cups potatoes, diced
½ cup celery, diced
½ cup onion, diced
1½ cups water
2 chicken bouillon cubes
¼ tsp. salt
2 cups milk
8 ozs. sour cream dip with
  chives*
1 T. flour
Parsley, chopped (for
  garnish)

*If unavailable, substitute
may be made by combining
8 ozs. sour cream; 1 T. fresh
chives, chopped; ½ tsp.
onion salt; ½ tsp. salt; and
¼ tsp. white pepper, freshly
ground.

In a large saucepan, combine potatoes, celery, onion, water, bouillon cubes, and salt. Cover and cook for about 20 minutes, or until vegetables are tender. Add 1 cup milk; heat through. In medium bowl, blend sour cream dip and flour; gradually stir in remaining 1 cup milk. Pour about ⅓ hot potato mixture into sour cream mixture; return to saucepan. Cook and stir until thickened. Garnish with parsley.

Preparation time: 15 minutes
Cooking time: 3 minutes

Easy
Can make ahead

Yield: Eight
8-oz. servings

SEAFOOD-SAFFRON SOUP

1½ cups onions, sliced
1½ cups potatoes, cubed
½ cup milk
1½ cups strong chicken
  stock
1½ lbs. halibut or sole
2½ cups whipping cream,
  unwhipped
½ tsp. saffron
½ tsp. turmeric (optional)
Black pepper, ground,
  to taste

Combine onions and potatoes with milk and chicken stock. Cook until tender. Blend in blender or food processor and strain through sieve. Poach fish in chicken stock to cover until tender (do not overcook). Drain. Remove bones from fish. Place potato mixture over low heat; add cream, saffron, turmeric, and pepper. Bring to a boil; simmer for 5 minutes. Add fish, correct seasoning, and heat through.

Note: Coho is an excellent substitute for halibut.

Preparation time: 15 minutes
Cooking time: 1 hour

Can make ahead

Yield: Eight
8-oz. servings

Sally Shipman Early

47

SHRIMP-ARTICHOKE SOUP

1 can (10¾ oz.) condensed
cream of mushroom soup,
undiluted
1 can (10¾ oz.) condensed
cream of celery soup,
undiluted
1 can (14 oz.) artichoke
hearts, cut in quarters
1 can (4½ oz.) or 1 bag
(8 oz.) small cocktail
shrimp, cooked, cleaned
1 can (8 oz.) water
chestnuts, sliced
Salt and pepper to taste
Curry powder (optional)
Chicken broth to thin,
if desired

Combine all ingredients and heat through.

Preparation time: 10 minutes
Cooking time: 10 minutes

Easy
Can make ahead

Yield: Four
8-oz. servings

Jan Cornell

FRESH CUCUMBER SOUP

2 cucumbers, peeled,
seeded, coarsely chopped
1 cup chicken broth
¼ cup celery leaves
1 cup half-and-half
3 sprigs parsley
2 T. butter, melted
2 T. flour
Fresh dill, chopped
(for garnish)
Fresh chives, chopped
(for garnish)

In a blender or food processor, blend cucumbers, chicken broth, celery leaves, half-and-half, parsley, butter, and flour. Heat, stirring constantly, until smooth and thick. Sprinkle with dill and chives and serve.

Preparation time: 10 minutes
Cooking time: 15 minutes

Easy
Can make ahead

Yield: Eight
4-oz. servings

Susan Brown

ZUCCHINI SOUP

1 lb. sweet or hot Italian
sausage, cut in pieces
2 cups celery, chopped
2 lbs. zucchini, cut in
¼-inch pieces
1 cup onions, chopped
2 cans (28 oz. each)
tomatoes
2 tsps. salt
1 tsp. Italian seasoning
1 tsp. oregano
1 tsp. sugar
½ tsp. basil
¼ tsp. garlic powder
2 green peppers, cut in
½-inch pieces
2 cups water

Brown sausage in large deep pan. Drain off fat. Add celery; cook for 10 minutes. Add all ingredients except green peppers; cook over low heat for 20 minutes. Add peppers; cook, covered, for 10 minutes longer.

Preparation time: 30 minutes
Cooking time: 1 hour

Yield: Twelve
8-oz. servings

Bonnie Eldridge

CREAM OF TOMATO SOUP
Great way to use garden vegetables

1 peck (1/4 bushel) ripe
tomatoes, skinned
1 bunch celery (trim off
large leaves)
7 medium onions
3 green peppers
14 sprigs parsley, chopped
14 bay leaves
14 whole cloves
1½ cups flour
1 cup butter
10 tsps. salt
Milk to taste

Grind vegetables in food processor or blender. Tie bay leaves and cloves in cheesecloth bag; heat with vegetables. In a separate saucepan, blend together flour, butter, and salt; simmer but don't brown. Add to vegetable mixture and simmer for ½ hour.

Freeze mixture for indefinite length of time or can, using appropriate process for tomatoes. If using glass jars, have jars and tops warm. At serving time, heat with as much as an equal part milk, according to taste.

Preparation time: 1 hour
Cooking time: 30 minutes

Can make ahead
Can freeze

Yield: 5 quarts

Ellie Bailey

CRAB BISQUE

½ cup butter
1 medium onion, diced
½ cup flour
1 tsp. garlic salt
1 tsp. Aćcent
1 tsp. liquid Maggi
 (optional)
1 drop Tabasco sauce
1 tsp. dry mustard
1 T. paprika
1 T. instant chicken bouillon
White pepper to taste
5 cups milk or half-and-half
1 cup dry white wine
 (vermouth is good)
2 cups crab meat
Splash of dry sherry
¼ cup parsley, chopped

Melt butter in heavy pan. Add onion and sauté until transparent. Stir in flour and let it bubble. Add seasonings to milk and stir into flour mixture. Bring to a boil, stirring constantly. Add wine and let boil again. Reduce heat and simmer for 20 to 30 minutes. Add crab meat and sherry. Heat but do not let boil. Add parsley just before serving.

Preparation time: 15 minutes   Easy   Yield: Eight
Cooking time: 45 minutes   8-oz. servings

Valaire Addison

CANADIAN CHEESE SOUP

1 medium carrot, grated
½ medium onion, minced
1 stalk celery, diced
1 qt. chicken stock, well
 seasoned
4 T. butter
⅓ cup flour
16 ozs. sharp cheddar
 cheese, grated
3–4 cups milk
Salt to taste
White pepper to taste

Cook vegetables in chicken stock until tender. Melt butter and add flour to make roux; stir constantly so that roux does not brown. Add roux to chicken stock; cook until it thickens. Add cheese; stir until completely melted. Do not let soup boil after cheese is added. Thin with milk to creamy consistency. Season with a pinch of salt and white pepper. Serve piping hot.

Preparation time: 30 minutes   Yield: 2 quarts
Cooking time: 30 minutes

Michael W. Lampos

NEW ENGLAND CLAM CHOWDER
Has Down Easter seal of approval

3 slices bacon, sliced
1 small onion, diced
3 stalks celery, diced
3–4 small potatoes, cubed
2 cans (7–8 oz. each)
  minced clams (reserve
  juice)
1 cup water
2 cups milk
½ pt. half-and-half
1 can (10¾ oz.) condensed
  cream of celery soup (or
  cream of potato soup)
2 T. flour mixed with ½ cup
  water
1 T. lemon juice
2 T. butter
⅛ tsp. pepper

Fry bacon until crisp; remove from pan. Saute onion and celery in bacon fat until tender. Drain off bacon fat. Combine onion, celery, potatoes, clam juice, and water in pot; simmer for 15 minutes. Add bacon, milk, half-and-half, canned soup, flour mixture, lemon juice, butter, pepper, and clams. Simmer for ½ hour.

Note: 1 to 1½ cups cubed cooked white-fish and 1¼ cups sherry may be added as a variation.

Preparation time: 15 minutes   Easy   Yield: Eight
Cooking time: 45 minutes   8-oz. servings

Jan Cornell

POTAGE PRINTAINER
Springtime soup

2 T. butter
2 leeks, chopped
1 small onion, chopped
1½ qts. hot water
2 potatoes, pared,
  quartered, thinly sliced
1 carrot, thinly sliced
2 tsps. salt
¼ cup white rice, uncooked
8 stalks fresh asparagus,
  chopped
½ lbs. fresh spinach,
  washed, chopped
1 cup half-and-half

Melt butter in a 3 to 4-quart kettle. Add leeks and onion; cook, covered, over low heat for about 5 minutes. Add hot water, potatoes, carrot, and salt; bring to a boil. Reduce heat. Cover and simmer for 15 minutes. Add rice and asparagus; simmer, covered, for 25 minutes. Add spinach and simmer for 10 minutes longer. Stir in half-and-half; bring just to a boil.

Preparation time: 30 minutes   Yield: Ten
Cooking time: 1 hour   8-oz. servings

51

BONEN BEAN SOUP

1 cup Great Northern beans,
    culled
3 cups water
1 tsp. salt
6 cups cold water
1 ham bone
¼ cup onion, chopped
¼ cup celery, chopped
Salt to taste
1 lb. kielbasa, sliced
2–3 T. bacon grease
3 T. flour
Paprika
Parsley, chopped

To prepare beans: Rinse beans in cold water. Bring 3 cups water to a boil; add salt and beans. Bring to a second boil, uncovered, and boil for exactly 2 minutes. Remove from heat, set the cover loosely on the pan, and let set for 1 hour. Drain.

To make soup: in a large (3 to 4-quart) kettle, put 6 cups cold water, beans, ham bone, onion, and celery. Slowly simmer until completely tender—2 to 3 hours. Salt to taste. When beans are tender, remove ham bone and add kielbasa to soup. In a small skillet, put bacon grease. Melt; stir in flour. Brown flour until golden, stirring constantly. When brown, add a little bean liquid to thin; stir into soup. Garnish individual servings with paprika and parsley.

Preparation time: 1+ hours
Cooking time: 3 hours

Yield: Eight
8-oz. servings

Louisa Paulson

WILD DUCK SOUP
Hunters (and nonhunters!) love it

¼ cup butter
1 tsp. dry mustard
1 large onion, chopped
Meat from 1 wild duck,
    cooked, chopped
¾ cup red wine (optional)
1 qt. water
1 pkg. (6 oz.) long grain and
    wild rice with seasoning
    (Uncle Ben's)
Salt and pepper to taste

Melt butter and mix in mustard. Place onion, meat, wine, and water in 5-quart pan. Simmer, covered, for 1 hour. Add rice and cook until done, adding more water if too thick. Season with salt and pepper to taste.

Note for nonhunters: Substitute white wine for red and chicken or shrimp for duck.

Preparation time: 1 hour
Cooking time: 1½ hours

Easy

Yield: Eight
6-oz. servings

Mardee Mott

TOSTADA SOUP
Olé!

1 small fryer
2 medium tomatoes, chopped
1 medium onion, chopped
2 cloves garlic, chopped, or ¼ tsp. garlic powder
¼ cup of margarine
½ can (10 oz.) tomatoes and green chilies
4–6 ozs. Monterey Jack or American cheese, thinly sliced or grated
6–8 tostadas,* cut in fifths

*May be found in Mexican food section of grocery.

Boil fryer in 6 cups water until tender. Remove from broth, cool and cut into bite-sized pieces. Sauté tomatoes, onion, and garlic in margarine. Add to chicken broth along with tomatoes and green chilies. Add about 1½ cups chicken and heat. Just before serving, add cheese and then tostadas. Do not let soup boil after adding tostadas because they will disintegrate (they will break up a little anyway). Serve immediately.

Preparation time: 1 hour
Cooking time: 1 hour

Base may be made ahead

Yield: Eight 8-oz. servings

Patricia Ellwood

CHICKEN GUMBO SOUP

6–8 chicken breasts
1 green pepper, chopped
1 medium onion, chopped
Butter (for sautéing)
1 can (28 oz.) tomatoes
1 can (6 oz.) okra, or 1 pkg. (10 oz.) frozen okra, or 2 cups fresh okra
2–3 handfuls rice, uncooked
Salt and pepper to taste
1 T. gumbo filé powder (optional)

Cook chicken in 2 quarts water. Remove chicken from broth, reserving broth. Refrigerate chicken. Sauté green pepper and onion in butter. Add to broth along with tomatoes, okra, and rice. Simmer for 1 to 1½ hours. Cut chicken into pieces and add to pot. Simmer for ½ hour longer. Season with salt and pepper.

Note: Gumbo filé powder may be added. Stir in carefully so it does not lump. Do not let boil after adding filé.

Preparation time: 15 minutes
Cooking time: 2 hours

Can freeze

Yield: Eight 8-oz. servings

Marianna Zeman

53

CHICKEN SOUP
A real "health food"

1 (1 lb.) chicken
6 cups water
½ cup onion, diced
1 cup celery, diced
2 T. butter
1 cup carrots, diced
1 cup turnips, diced
1 large tomato, peeled,
  seeded, chopped
¼ cup parsley, chopped
¼ tsp. white pepper, freshly
  ground
1–2 tsps. salt

Cook chicken in water until tender; remove from broth and cut meat into bite-sizes pieces. Sauté onion and celery in butter in heavy pan. Add carrots, turnips, tomato, parsley, pepper, salt, and chicken broth. Simmer for 1 hour, or until vegetables are tender. Add chicken and dill; let simmer at least 1 hour.

Note: Good with dumplings.

Preparation time: 1 hour
Cooking time: 1–2 hours

Can make ahead

Yield: Ten 8-oz.
servings

Doris Statler

DANISH DUMPLINGS

4 T. butter
½ cup water
⅔ cup flour
1 tsp. salt
1 tsp. sugar
½ tsp. nutmeg
2 eggs

Bring butter and water to a boil and add flour all at once, stirring constantly. Cook until mixture leaves sides of pan. When cool, add seasonings and eggs, 1 at a time; beat well after each addition. Drop by teaspoonfuls into hot liquid or broth. Dip spoon into hot liquid after dropping each dumpling so that mixture will not stick to spoon. Cook, uncovered, for 4 or 5 minutes. At this point, dumplings are ready to be used in soup.

Note: For a different taste, use garlic, onion, salt, freshly ground pepper, and a little chopped parsley instead of sugar, salt, and nutmeg.

Preparation time: 20 minutes
Cooking time: 5 minutes

Easy
Serve immediately

Yield: 24
dumplings

CREAM OF BROCCOLI SOUP

1½–2 lbs. fresh broccoli
8 cups chicken stock
Bouquet garni*
2 T. butter
2 T. flour
Nutmeg, freshly grated
2 egg yolks
1 cup whipping cream,
   unwhipped
Croutons or lemon slices
   (for garnish)

*Combine 2 sprigs parsley,
1 sprig thyme, and 1 large
bay leaf in a cheesecloth
bag tied with string.

Combine broccoli, chicken stock, and bouquet garni; cook, covered, for 35 to 40 minutes, or until broccoli is very tender. Drain off liquid and reserve. Puree broccoli in blender. In a saucepan, melt butter and then stir in flour. Gradually stir in liquid; bring to a boil, stirring constantly. Add broccoli puree. Season with nutmeg. In a bowl, mix egg yolks and whipping cream. Stir 2 tablespoonfuls hot soup into eggs and cream. Gradually pour mixture Into soup, stirring constantly. Reheat soup *without boiling*. Top with crisp buttered croutons or thin lemon slices.

Preparation time: 30 minutes
Cooking time: 50 minutes

Yield: Twelve
8-oz. servings

Dori Lawrence

ONION SOUP AU GRATIN
With American flair

4 T. butter
2 T. vegetable oil
6 medium onions, sliced
1 tsp. flour
½ tsp. dry mustard
½ cup dry white wine
   (vermouth is good)
2½ cups beef stock
Salt and pepper to taste
French bread, thickly sliced
4 T. sharp cheddar cheese,
   grated
4 T. Parmesan or mozzarella
   cheese, grated

Melt butter into hot oil in casserole. Add sliced onions. Sauté slowly until onions are dark brown—20 to 30 minutes. Add flour and mustard; stir until smooth. Continue stirring and add wine and stock. Simmer for 15 minutes. Season with salt and pepper. Toast French bread. Put into a medium-size or individual casseroles. Add soup. Sprinkle each top with 1 tablespoonful cheddar cheese; brown fully under broiler. Sprinkle with oil. Add Parmesan cheese; return to broiler until brown.

Preparation time: 15 minutes
Cooking time: 45 minutes

Easy

Yield: Four
8-oz. servings

Kay McAndrew

SPANISH BEAN SOUP
Main-dish soup

1 lb. dried garbanzos or
navy beans
3 qts. water
3–4 T. oil
1 small frying chicken
1½ lbs. good soup beef
1 large onion, chopped
3 cloves garlic, crushed or
minced
2 leeks, sliced
¼ lb. slab bacon, finely
diced
½ lb. smoked ham, cubed
¼ lb. chorizo (Spanish
sausage) or pepperoni,
sliced
2 cups carrots, sliced
Salt to taste
Cayenne pepper to taste
5 medium potatoes, peeled,
cut in julienne strips

Soak garbanzos in cold water to cover overnight. Drain, rinse lightly, and simmer in 3 quarts water for 30 minutes. (A 20-ounce can of cooked chick-peas may be substituted for garbanzos. Add them for the last 30 minutes of cooking.) In a large heavy kettle or Dutch oven, heat oil and sauté chicken and beef with onion, garlic, and leeks. Add garbanzos with their cooking liquid and simmer for 30 minutes longer. Remove chicken and beef, discard skin and bones, cut into bite-sized pieces, and return to soup. Sauté bacon until half-cooked and add to the soup along with ham and sausage. Simmer, with lid ajar, for about 1 hour. Add carrots and cook for 30 minutes longer. Add salt to taste, stir in potatoes, and let bubble for another 30 minutes. Season to taste with cayenne pepper.

Preparation time: 1 or 2 days,
depending on type of bean used
Cooking time: 2 hours

Yield: Twenty
8-oz. servings

Barbara Beardsley

CHILLED CUCUMBER SOUP
Soupendipity

1 fairly large cucumber,
peeled, seeded, coarsely
chopped
1 cup French onion sour
cream dip
⅓ whole lemon, chopped
⅓ medium onion, chopped
Salt to taste
Lemon pepper to taste

In blender or food processor, blend all ingredients; chill.

Note: Thickened with blended cottage cheese, this makes a delicious vegetable dip.

Preparation time: 15 minutes

Must make ahead
Easily doubled

Yield: Four
4-oz. servings

Anne Rapp

56

HINTS

1. Unless specified, flour is measured unsifted.
2. One package or 1 scant tablespoonful of active dry yeast is equivalent to one 0.6-ounce package of cake yeast.
3. A candy thermometer allows accurate measurement of liquid temperatures; thus the one major pitfall of yeast baking—"dead" yeast—is avoided. The proper temperature for recipes in which the yeast is dissolved before being added to other ingredients is 105°–115°; for Rapidmix, it is 120°–130°.
4. Always add flour gradually; humidity and temperature affect the amount of flour required.
5. To determine if dough has doubled in bulk, press the tips of 2 fingers lightly and quickly into it. If the dent remains, dough is doubled.
6. Always preheat the oven.
7. When using glass or Corning Ware pans, LOWER the oven temperature 25°.
8. Start testing for doneness about 10 minutes before end of baking time.
9. Bread is done if it sounds hollow when tapped on the bottom.

OVEN PANCAKES

¼ cup butter
2 eggs
½ cup flour
½ cup milk
½ tsp. nutmeg, grated

Melt butter in a 9-inch round baking dish or an iron skillet. Beat eggs; add flour, milk, and nutmeg. Mix until blended but not smooth. Pour into baking dish. Bake at 425° for 15 to 20 minutes. Pancake will puff and brown. Sprinkle powdered sugar on top. Cut into pieces. Serve with syrup, marmalade, or jelly. Recipe can be doubled or tripled; use larger pan. Resembles a popover-soufflé combination.

Preparation time: 5 minutes
Baking time: 15–20 minutes

Easily doubled

Serves: 2–3

Geri Penniman
Ginny Scott

Hint: For a baked apple pancake, add 1 teaspoonful sugar and a pinch of salt to oven pancake batter. Pour batter in a hot skillet; spread with 1 apple, peeled and sliced, that has been sprinkled with ½ tablespoonful lemon juice. Bake as for oven pancake. To serve, sprinkle with cinnamon sugar.

Sally Shipman Early
Dorrie Kelly

SUPER PANCAKES
Beauties to behold

2 cups flour, sifted
2 tsps. sugar
1 tsp. salt
1½ tsps. baking powder
1 tsp. baking soda
3 eggs, beaten
1 cup buttermilk
1 cup sour cream
2 T. butter, melted

Blend dry ingredients in a bowl. Beat together eggs, buttermilk, sour cream, and butter. Add to dry ingredients and mix gently by hand; do not beat too hard. Cook on a hot griddle.

If batter is too thick, add a little more buttermilk. Blueberries may be added to batter. Serve hot with syrup and butter.

Preparation time: 15 minutes
Cooking time: 15 minutes

Easy
Serve immediately

Serves: 6–8

Jan Orwin

FUNNEL CAKES

2 cups vegetable oil
2 eggs, beaten
1½ cups milk
2 cups flour, sifted
1 tsp. baking powder
½ tsp. salt

Pour oil in electric skillet and heat to 375°. Combine beaten eggs and milk in mixing bowl. Sift flour, baking powder, and salt; add to egg mixture. Beat until smooth. Batter should be medium weight, resembling pancake batter. Hold a finger over the hole, and pour ¼ cup batter into a small-holed (⅜ to ½-inch) funnel. Starting at the center of the skillet, draw a spiral with the batter so that each ring just touches the next one. Fry 2 minutes; turn over and fry 2 minutes. Drain on paper town. Sprinkle with powdered sugar. Serve with syrup, jelly, or a mixture of melted butter and lemon juice.

Preparation time: 10 minutes
Cooking time: About 4
  minutes per cake

Serve immediately

Serves: 5–6

Mary Hilton

APPLE FRITTERS

Vegetable oil (for frying)
2 T. sugar
1 cup flour
½ tsp. salt
1½ tsps. baking powder
⅓ cup milk
1 egg, slightly beaten
1 cup apples, chopped
1 T. butter, melted

TOPPING:
¼ cup sugar
2 tsps. cinnamon

Heat oil (about 1 inch deep) to 375°. Meanwhile, in medium bowl, mix together sugar, flour, salt, and baking powder. Combine milk and egg; add to dry ingredients. Stir until well mixed. Add apples and butter, stirring until well blended. Drop teaspoonfuls of dough into hot oil; fry about 30 seconds on each side, until golden brown. Drain on paper towel. While fritters are warm, toss them in mixture of sugar and cinnamon.

Hint: Drop dough into center of fryer; fritters will drift to the side and turn over when starting to turn golden. Do not puncture them while in fryer. Use slotted spoon to remove fritters.

Preparation time: 10 minutes
Cooking time: 20 minutes

Easy
Serve immediately

Yield: 30–36

Sandra Wotta

MEL'S CRISP HERB TOAST

½ lb. butter, softened
¼ cup sesame seeds
½ tsp. marjoram
2 T. chives, chopped
½ tsp. basil
½ tsp. rosemary
1 loaf Pepperidge Farm Very
   Thin Bread*

*If Pepperidge Farm bread
is unavailable, a loaf
of unsliced bread may
be sliced very thin and
substituted.

Blend butter and herbs. Spread slices with herb butter. Cut slices in half, diagonally. Place on ungreased baking sheet. Bake at 350° for 15 to 20 minutes. Serve warm. Can be made ahead and reheated before serving. Store in tightly closed container.

Preparation time: 10 minutes
Baking time: 15–20 minutes

Very easy
Can make ahead

Serves: 10
Easily doubled

Mel VanPeenan

HERB BUTTER

½ cup butter or margarine,
   softened
1 tsp. parsley flakes
¼ tsp. oregano
¼ tsp. dried dill weed
1 clove garlic, minced
Parmesan cheese, freshly
   grated

Blend butter, herbs, and garlic. Slice one 14-inch loaf Italian or French bread into 1-inch slices. Spread slices with herb butter, and reassemble loaf on a piece of foil. Shape foil around loaf, twisting ends and leaving top open. Sprinkle top with freshly grated Parmesan cheese. Heat at 400° for 10 to 15 minutes. Can be made ahead and reheated.

For hard rolls: Split rolls and spread with herb butter; sprinkle with Parmesan cheese. Place rolls under broiler until butter bubbles up and cheese turns golden. May be made in food processor.

Preparation time: 10 minutes
Baking time: 10–15 minutes
Broiler time: 3–5 minutes

Very easy
Can make ahead

Serves: 4–6
Can be frozen
Easily doubled

Ann Paulson
Jan Wright

LEMON BUTTER

½ lemon, juice and rind
1 T. butter, softened
1 cup sugar
1½ tsps. flour
1 cup water
2 eggs, separated

Grate rind of ½ lemon; squeeze juice. Mix together lemon rind, juice, butter, sugar, flour, water, and egg yolks. Beat egg whites until stiff and fold into first mixture. Cook in a heavy saucepan over medium heat until it is the consistency of heavy cream or mayonnaise. Spread on toast.

Preparation time: 15 minutes
Cooking time: 15 minutes

Easily doubled
Serve warm

Yield: 2 cups

Jeannette T. Bonsor

BANANA-BRAN BREAD

1½ cups flour, sifted
½ tsp. baking soda
½ tsp. salt
2 tsps. baking powder
½ cup margarine
⅓–½ cup sugar
2 eggs
2 T. water or milk
1 tsp. vanilla
1½ cups bananas, mashed
⅔ cup bran (Miller's Bran)
⅔ cup raisins, plumped
½ cup nuts, chopped

Sift together flour, baking soda, salt, and baking powder. Set aside. Cream margarine and sugar; beat in eggs one at a time, beating well after each addition. Beat in water (milk), vanilla, and mashed bananas. Using a wooden spoon, stir in flour mixture, bran, raisins, and nuts. Pour into 1 greased 9 × 5 × 3-inch loaf pan or 2 greased 7 × 3½ × 2-inch pans. Cover pan with another pan of the same size. Bake at 350° for 20 minutes; remove covering pan and continue baking for 30 to 40 minutes. Bread is done when toothpick inserted in the center comes out clean. Small loaves usually take 50 minutes. Remove pan from oven; let cool 5 minutes; remove bread from pan; cool on wire rack.

Hint: To plump raisins, cover with very hot water, allow to stand for 5 minutes, then drain.

Miller's Bran can be found in the health food section of your grocery store or in a health food store.

Preparation time: 20 minutes
Baking time: 50–60 minutes

Easy
Can make ahead

Yield: 1 large loaf or
2 small loaves
Can be frozen

Ann Paulson

62

BANANA BREAD

½ cup butter
1 cup sugar
2 eggs
½ cup buttermilk
1 cup bananas, mashed
2 cups flour
1 tsp. baking soda
1 cup dates, chopped
½ cup nuts, chopped

Cream butter and sugar. Beat in eggs, one at a time, beating well after each addition. Combine buttermilk and mashed bananas. Stir together flour and baking soda; add alternately with banana mixture to creamed mixture. Stir in nuts and dates. Pour into 2 greased 8½ x 4½ x 2½ inch loaf pans. Bake at 350° for 45 to 55 minutes.

Preparation time: 25 minutes
Baking time: 45–55 minutes

Easy
Can make ahead

Yield: 2 loaves
Can be frozen

Geri Penniman

BISCOTTI
Great to dunk in coffee

2 cups plus ½ cup flour
2 tsps. baking powder, heaping
4 eggs, large size*
1 cup sugar
½ cup vegetable oil (Mazola preferred)
2 T. anise extract or aniseed

*If extra-large eggs are used, it will be necessary to add more flour.

Sift 2 cups flour and baking powder and set aside. Beat eggs on highest speed of mixer for 2 minutes, or until they are thick and lemon colored. With beater running on high, gradually beat in sugar and then oil. Add aniseed. Stir in sifted flour mixture and enough flour (about ½ cup) to make a soft dough. Flour hands well. Quickly cut dough into 2 or 3 portions and place on greased baking sheets. Dough spreads quite a bit; put no more than 2 on a sheet. Bake at 350° for 20 minutes, until light brown. Remove loaves from oven, and cut into ½-inch slices. Place slices, flat side down, on an ungreased baking sheet. Toast at 400° for a few minutes, until light brown. Watch carefully; do not allow slices to get too brown. Store in tightly closed container.

Preparation time: 15 minutes
Baking time:
   Approximately 20 minutes

Can be made ahead

Yield: 2–3 loaves

Vi Anderson

DATE-NUT BREAD

1 cup dates, chopped
½ cup sugar
½ cup margarine
1 cup boiling water
2 eggs, beaten
2 cups whole wheat flour
1 tsp. baking soda
½ tsp. salt
1 cup pecans or walnuts,
  chopped

Put chopped dates, sugar, and margarine in a bowl. Pour boiling water over mix, and let cool a little. In another bowl, beat eggs and then add flour, baking soda, and salt, which have been stirred together. Add mixture from first bowl; quickly mix the 2 parts together. Stir in chopped nuts. Pour into greased 9 × 5 × 3-inch loaf pan. Bake at 350° for 45 to 50 minutes. Remove from pan and allow to cool completely.

Preparation time: 25 minutes
Baking time: 45–50 minutes

Easy
Can make ahead

Yield: 1 large loaf
Can be frozen

Jessie B. Quinn

ZUCCHINI-WHEAT GERM BREAD

3 eggs
1 cup vegetable oil
1 cup sugar
1 cup brown sugar, packed
3 tsps. maple flavoring
2 cups zucchini, unpeeled,
  coarsely shredded (about
  4 medium)*
2½ cups flour
½ cup wheat germ
2 tsps. baking soda
2 tsps. salt
½ tsp. baking powder
1 cup walnuts, finely
  chopped
⅓ cup sesame seeds

Beat eggs at high speed; with mixer running, slowly add oil, sugars, and maple flavoring; continue beating until thick and foamy. Stir in zucchini. Combine flour, wheat germ, baking soda, salt, baking powder, and walnuts. Stir gently into zucchini mixture. Divide batter equally between 2 greased and floured 9 × 5 × 3-inch or 3 greased and floured 7 × 3½ × 2-inch loaf pans. Sprinkle sesame seeds evenly over tops. Bake at 350° for 1 hour for larger loaves or 40 to 50 minutes for smaller loaves, or until a toothpick inserted in center of the loaf comes out clean. Cool in pan for 10 minutes, turn out on wire racks, and cool completely.

*This is easily done in a food processor.

Preparation time: 15 minutes
Baking time: 40–50 minutes

Easy

Yield: 2–3 loaves
Can be frozen

Jane Gilman Miller

GLAZED LEMON-NUT BREAD

¼ cup butter, softened
¾ cup sugar
2 eggs
2 tsps. lemon peel, grated
2 cups flour, sifted
2½ tsps. baking powder
1 tsp. salt
¾ cup milk
½ cup walnuts, chopped

TOPPING:
¼ cup sugar
2 T. lemon juice

Cream butter and sugar until light and fluffy. Add eggs and lemon peel; beat well. Sift flour, baking powder, and salt. Add to creamed mixture alternately with milk, beginning and ending with flour. Stir in chopped nuts. Pour into 8½ × 4½ × 2½-inch greased loaf pan or two 7 × 3½ × 2-inch greased loaf pans. Bake at 350° for 50 to 55 minutes for large loar or 35 to 40 minutes for small loaves. Let cool in pan 10 minutes, then spoon over the lemon juice and sugar which have been mixed together. Remove from pan and cool.

Preparation time: 20 minutes
Baking time:
   50–55 minutes (large)
   35–40 minutes (small)

Easy
Can make ahead

Yield: 1 large loaf or
   2 small loaves
Can be frozen

Lenore Lofstrum
Woodena Stainton

Hint: To increase the amount of juice extracted from lemons, microwave each lemon 30 to 45 seconds before slicing.

BROWN BREAD

1½ cups raisins and/or nuts
1½ cups water
1 T. butter
1 egg
½ tsp. salt
¾ cup sugar
2 tsps. baking soda
2¾ cups flour

Simmer raisins and nuts in water for 10 minutes. Half nuts and half raisins, or any combination of the two, may be used. Stir in butter. Cool. Beat egg. Sift together salt, sugar, baking soda, and flour. When raisins and nuts are cool, stir in egg and flour mixture. Pour into greased 9 × 5 × 3-inch loaf pan. Bake at 350° for 1 hour.

Preparation time: 20 minutes
Baking time: 1 hour

Easy
Can make ahead

Yield: 1 large loaf
Can be frozen

Betty Moler

PECAN BREAKFAST RING

ROLLS:
2 cans (8 oz. each)
 refrigerated crescent rolls
2 T. butter, softened
½ cup sugar
1–2 tsps. cinnamon
¼ cup pecans, chopped

TOPPING:
2 T. honey
2 T. butter
¼ cup powdered sugar
1 tsp. vanilla
¼ cup pecan halves

Separate rolls into triangles. Spread each with butter. Combine sugar, cinnamon, and pecans. Sprinkle over triangles. Roll up each triangle starting from wide end. Place rolls, point side down, in a greased ring mold, making 2 layers of 8 rolls each. Bake at 375° for 40 to 45 minutes, or until rolls are a deep golden brown. Remove from pan at once and drizzle with topping.

Topping: In a saucepan, combine honey, butter, and sugar. Bring to a boil, stirring constantly. Remove from heat; stir in vanilla and pecans. Cool slightly.

Preparation time: 15 minutes
Baking time: 40–45 minutes

Very easy
Serve immediately

Serves: 6–8

Rose Losenski

CHERRY-NUT COFFEE CAKE
Marvelous aroma

2 cups sugar
1 cup butter
2 eggs
1 tsp. almond extract
1 tsp. vanilla
2 cups plus 2 T. flour
2 tsps. baking powder
½ tsp. salt
1 can (13 oz.) evaporated
 milk
1 cup nuts, chopped
1 jar (6 oz.) maraschino
 cherries, chopped

Cream butter and sugar; beat in eggs and extracts. Sift flour (reserve 1 tablespoonful), baking powder, and salt, and add alternately with evaporated milk to the creamed mixture, beginning and ending with dry ingredients. Sprinkle reserved flour on chopped cherries. Stir cherries and nuts into batter. Pour into well-greased and floured 10-inch tube pan (with removable bottom) or a springform pan. Bake at 350° for 70 to 80 minutes. Remove from pan.

Hint: Food processor can be used to chop cherries.

Preparation time: 20 minutes
Baking time: 70–80 minutes

Easy
Can make ahead

Serves: 16–20
Can be frozen

Jan Shugars

SOUR CREAM COFFEE CAKE
They'll never know it came from a box

1 pkg. (18½ oz.) yellow cake mix
1 pkg. (3 oz.) instant vanilla pudding
4 eggs
8 ozs. sour cream
½ cup vegetable oil

TOPPING:
2–3 T. flour
2 tsps. cinnamon
½ cup sugar
⅓ cup nuts, chopped

Combine all cake ingredients in a mixing bowl. Beat 10 minutes at medium speed. Make topping by combining all ingredients and mixing well. Pour ½ the batter into a greased 10-inch tube pan; sprinkle with ½ the topping. Add remaining batter, and sprinkle with rest of topping. Cut through batter with a knife to marbleize. Bake at 350° for 50 to 55 minutes.

Microwave: Grease and sugar the tube pan. Pour in ½ the batter; sprinkle with ½ the topping. Repeat. Microwave 10 to 11 minutes on high, rotating dish a quarter-turn once. Frost if desired.

Preparation time: 15 minutes
Baking time: 50–55 minutes
Microwave: 10–11 minutes

Very easy
Can make ahead

Serves: 16–20
Can be frozen

Bernadine Simpson

Hint: For a quick, make-ahead hors d'oeuvre, thinly slice an entire loaf of day-old Vienna bread. Butter each slice, and sprinkle with celery salt or sparingly with celery seed. Heat at 250° for 20 minutes on ungreased baking sheets. Store in a tightly closed container. Reheat before serving.

Jessie B. Quinn

DUTCH KOEK
Just plain delicious

½ cup butter
  (no substitutions)
1 cup sugar
1 egg
½ cup almond paste
1 cup flour

Cream butter and sugar. Beat in egg. Mix in almond paste, then stir in flour. Spread in a buttered 9-inch pie pan. Bake at 325° for 50 minutes. Cut in wedges. Serve warm. May be garnished with sliced almonds if desired.

Preparation time: 10 minutes
Baking time: 50 minutes

Easy
Can make ahead
and reheat

Serves: 8–12
Can be frozen

Amanda Clark Morrill

67

CHRISTMAS MARMALADE
Looks like Christmas

3 oranges
1 lemon
1 can (20 oz.) crushed
  pineapple
3 lbs. sugar
½ cup water
1 bottle (6 oz.) green
  maraschino cherries,
  halved
1 bottle (6 oz.) red
  maraschino cherries,
  halved
Paraffin

Put oranges and lemon, rind included, through a food grinder. Put ground oranges and lemon, crushed pineapple, sugar, and water in a 3 to 4-quart saucepan. Boil hard for 30 minutes. Remove from heat; stir in cherries. Pour into sterilized jelly jars. Seal with paraffin. Nice for gifts!

Preparation time: 20 minutes
Cooking time: 30 minutes

Very easy

Yield: 7 half-pints

Gayl Werme

CHEESE-ONION BISCUITS

2½ cups flour
1 T. baking powder
½ tsp. salt
½ cup shortening
  (Crisco preferred)
4 ozs. cheddar cheese,
  shredded
¼ cup onions, minced
1 egg
1 cup milk

Sift flour, baking powder, and salt. Cut in shortening. Stir in cheese and onions. In a separate bowl, beat together egg and milk; stir into flour mixture. Drop by tablespoonfuls on well-greased baking sheets. Bake at 425° for 15 to 20 minutes.

Preparation time: 15 minutes
Baking time: 15–20 minutes

Easy
Serve immediately

Yield: 25–30
biscuits

Mary Kelley

68

YEAST ROLLS

1¼ cups milk, scalded
½ cup shortening (Crisco preferred)
⅓ cup sugar
1 tsp. salt
1 pkg. active dry yeast
¼ cup water (105°–115°)
2 eggs, well beaten
5 cups flour
Melted butter

Combine scalded milk, shortening, sugar, and salt; cool to lukewarm. Dissolve yeast in warm water and add to milk mixture. Stir in beaten eggs; beat thoroughly. Add flour and mix to a soft dough. Cover and let stand 10 minutes. Knead on a lightly floured board for 5 to 8 minutes, until dough is smooth and elastic. Place in a greased bowl, turn once, cover, and let rise until doubled. Punch down. Let rise again. Punch down. Divide dough into 2 or 3 portions. Roll 1 portion into a circle ½ inch thick. Cut into rounds with a 1½ or 2-inch biscuit cutter. Brush surface of each round with melted butter. Fold rolls in half, buttered sides together; stretch slightly to elongate. The tops should overlap the bottoms. Pour melted butter into baking pans to a depth of about ⅛ inch; place rolls in pans so that they just touch each other. When pan is full, brush tops of rolls with melted butter, cover, and let rise until doubled—about 2 hours. Bake at 400° for 15 minutes. An 8 × 8-inch pan will hold about 16 rolls; a 14 × 10-inch pan will hold 36 rolls. Cool rolls either in the pan or on a rack. Wrap in foil for freezing.

Note: To make easy sweet rolls, spread warm rolls with Thin Butter Icing (see page 89) and sprinkle with chopped nuts. Dough may also be used to make other sweet rolls.

Preparation time: 30 minutes   Easy   Yield: About 5 dozen
Baking time: 15 minutes   Can be frozen

Louisa S. Paulson

69

REFRIGERATOR ROLLS
No knead

1 cup milk, scalded
1 cup water, boiling
4 T. sugar
2 tsps. salt
¼ cup butter, softened
¼ cup shortening
2 eggs
2 pkgs. active dry yeast
5 ½ cups flour

Combine milk, water, sugar, salt, butter, and shortening. Cool to lukewarm. Add eggs and beat well. Mix yeast with 2 cups flour, then add to liquid mixture. Gradually stir in remaining flour. Cover bowl. Allow dough to rise for 30 minutes; stir down and cover again.

Refrigerate overnight. Punch down and turn onto floured surface. Knead for 1 to 2 minutes. Shape into rolls. Place on greased baking sheets. Cover and let rise until doubled. Bake at 325° for 15 minutes.

Hint: For brown 'n serve rolls, bake at 275° for 25 to 30 minutes, or until rolls just begin to change color. Cool; wrap in foil and freeze until ready to use. Thaw in freezer bag for 30 minutes. Bake at 425° for 10 to 12 minutes.

Preparation time: 20 minutes   Easy   Yield: 4–5 dozen
Baking time: 15 minutes   Can be frozen

Pat Dolan

CRUSTY WHITE ROLLS
A versatile dough

2 pkgs. active dry yeast
6 cups flour,
  unbleached
  (approximately)
2 cups water (105°–115°)
¼ cup vegetable oil
2 T. sugar
1 T. salt

Combine yeast and 2 cups flour in large mixing bowl. Add water, oil, sugar, and salt. Beat at low speed on electric mixer for 30 seconds, scraping sides of bowl constantly. Beat 3 minutes at high speed. By hand, stir in enough of the remaining flour to make a stiff dough. Turn onto lightly floured surface and knead until smooth and elastic—8 to 10 minutes. Place in greased bowl, turn once, cover and let rise until doubled—about 1½ hours. Punch down. Divide dough in half; roll each half into a long rope; divide each rope in 6 to 12 pieces. Pieces may be shaped into round or oblong rolls. Place on greased baking sheets which have been sprinkled with a little cornmeal. Cover and let rise until almost doubled—about 40 minutes. Bake at 375° for 20 to 30 minutes, or until rolls are golden brown.

For a harder crust, rolls should be sprayed with water just before they are put in the oven and every 5 minutes for the first 10 minutes. Large rolls are ideal for submarine sandwiches.

(continued)

CRUSTY WHITE ROLLS (continued)

Hint: This dough may be used for pizza crust. Allow dough to rise once. Spread it on 4 well-greased 12-inch pizza pans, top, and bake immediately at 425° to 450° for 20 minutes. Dough may also be used for French or braided breads (2 loaves); increase baking temperature to 400° and baking time to 30 minutes.

Preparation time: 15 minutes   Easy   Yield: 12–24 rolls
Baking time: 20–30 minutes   Easily doubled   Can be frozen

Bonnie Eldridge
Irene Shippy

BUTTERFLAKE ROLLS

2 cakes (0.6 oz. each) yeast
   or 2 pkgs. active dry yeast
¾ cup water (105°–115°)*
1 T. sugar
1 cup flour, sifted
½ cup butter
¼ cup sugar
1 tsp. salt
4 egg yolks
3 cups flour, sifted
Softened butter

*If cake yeast is used, water temperature should be 85°.

Dissolve yeast in water; add sugar and stir until dissolved. Blend in 1 cup flour. Cover and let rise in a warm place until light and bubbly—about 20 to 30 minutes. Cream butter. Gradually add sugar, salt, and egg yolks, creaming well. Add to yeast mixture. Beat in 3 cups flour, 1 cup at a time. Knead on floured board 1 to 2 minutes. Place in a greased bowl, turn once, cover, and let rise until almost doubled—about 1½ hours. Punch down. Divide dough in half. Roll each half of dough on a lightly floured surface to an 18×6-inch rectangle. Spread center third of rectangle with softened butter. Fold 1 side of dough to overlap center. Spread this fold with butter. Fold opposite side to overlap. Reroll into an 18 × 6-inch rectangle. Cut into 1 × 6-inch strips. Coil each strip into a loose "snail" on a well-greased baking sheet. Cover and let rise until doubled—about 30 to 45 minutes. Bake at 375° for 12 to 15 minutes.

Preparation time: 1½ hours   Best served warm   Yield: 3 dozen
Baking time: Can be frozen
   12–15 minutes per batch

Kay Davison

FAT A BALLEN
A real Dutch treat

1 qt. milk
1 pkg. active dry yeast
½ cup sugar
1 egg, beaten
1 tsp. salt
1¼ cups raisins
5¾–6¼ cups flour
Vegetable oil (for frying)
Sugar

Heat milk to lukewarm. Pour into large bowl, add yeast, and stir to dissolve. Add sugar, salt, and beaten egg. Gradually beat in flour until the dough is elastic. Stir in raisins. Cover bowl and let rise until doubled.

Preheat oil to 375° in heavy pan or deep-fat fryer. Drop dough by tablespoonfuls into hot fat and fry for 5 minutes. Drain on paper towel. Cool on wire rack until warm. Shake in bag with sugar. Best served warm. These may be reheated in brown paper bag in the oven.

Preparation time: 20 minutes
Cooking time:
  5 minutes per batch

Easy
Can make ahead
and reheat

Yield: 4–6 dozen
Can be frozen

Joan deMink

SEMMEL
Say "zemmel"

1 pkg. active dry yeast
¼ cup water (105°–115°)
5 cups flour
2 tsps. salt
½ cup shortening
2½ cups milk

Dissolve yeast in water; set aside. Place flour and salt in a 4-quart mixing bowl; add shortening, yeast, and 2 cups milk. Stir vigorously to make a sticky moist dough, adding approximately ½ cup more milk. Cover bowl with plastic wrap and let rise overnight. In the morning, stir dough down, and drop by rounded spoonfuls about 1 inch apart on greased baking sheets. If the spoon is dipped in warm water, dough will not stick to it. Bake at 425° for 12 to 15 minutes, or until lightly browned.

Preparation time: 25 minutes
Baking time: 12–15 minutes

Easy
Best served warm

Yield: About 24 rolls
Can be frozen

Don Epp

72

CINNAMON ROLLS

1 pkg. active dry yeast
4½ cups flour, sifted
1 T. sugar
1 cup milk, scalded
7 T. sugar
7 T. lard or shortening
1 tsp. salt
3 eggs, beaten
Melted butter
Brown sugar (optional)

FILLING:
½ cup butter or margarine, softened
1 cup dark brown sugar, packed
2 T. cinnamon
1 T. milk
4 ozs. pecan pieces (optional)

Combine yeast, 1½ cups flour, and 1 T. sugar in a large mixing bowl; stir to blend. Add lard and remaining sugar to the scalded milk; cool to lukewarm. Add liquid mixture and salt to flour mixture and mix briefly with mixer, scraping bottom and sides. Add eggs and beat for 3 minutes at high speed. By hand, mix in remaining flour. Turn dough out on a floured surface and knead 3 to 5 minutes until dough is smooth and elastic. Place in a greased bowl, turn once, cover, and let rise until doubled. Punch down; let rest 10 minutes. Divide dough in half and roll into 12 × 20-inch rectangles. Brush dough with melted butter. Spread each rectangle with half the filling; sprinkle with nuts. Starting on the 20-inch side, roll up, jelly-roll fashion, and cut into ½-inch slices. Butter a 3-quart and a 1½-quart ring mold. Pour melted butter in the bottoms of the molds; sprinkle brown sugar on the bottoms, if desired. Put 3 layers of rolls in each pan. Cover and let rise until doubled. Bake at 350° for 30 to 40 minutes, or until top layers are brown. Remove from oven; let rest about 10 minutes. Run knife along edges and invert on platter, or foil if they will be frozen. To serve, pull apart.

To make filling: Cream together butter and brown sugar; stir in cinnamon and milk.

Note: This recipe will also make three 9 × 5 × 3-inch loaves of cinnamon bread. To make loaves, proceed as for rolls. Divide dough into 3 equal parts; roll dough into 8 × 20-inch rectangles; roll up, starting at the narrow side. Pour melted butter in the bottoms of three 9 × 5 × 3-inch loaf pans. Sprinkle melted butter with additional brown sugar, cinnamon, and ground pecans. Place shaped loaves in pans; cover and let rise until doubled. Bake at 350° for 25 to 30 minutes, or until tops are brown. Remove from oven; let rest 10 minutes, then invert.

Preparation time: 45 minutes   Can be frozen   Yield: One 3-quart and
Baking time: 30–40 minutes   one 1½-quart mold or
                                                    three 9 × 5 × 3-inch loaves

Carole Hawk

CRANBERRY COFFEE CAKE

½ cup margarine
1 cup sugar
2 eggs
2 cups flour
1 tsp. baking powder
1 tsp. baking soda
½ tsp. salt
1 cup sour cream
1 T. orange juice (fresh
  squeezed preferred)
1½ tsps. orange rind, grated

FILLING AND TOPPING:
1 can (16 oz.) whole
  cranberry sauce
½ cup pecans, chopped

Cream margarine and sugar; beat in eggs one at a time. Sift together flour, baking powder, baking soda, and salt and add to creamed mixture. Stir in sour cream which has been mixed with orange juice and orange rind. Crush whole cranberries. Pour half the batter into a greased and floured bundt pan. Add half the cranberries; repeat with batter and cranberries. Sprinkle top with pecans. Bake at 350° for 50 to 60 minutes. Remove from pan. Drizzle with powdered sugar icing (see page 89) while still warm.

Variation: Chop 1 pound raw cranberries in food processor. Grease and flour a 9-inch springform pan, fitted with a tube. Pour in half the batter; sprinkle with 2 cups chopped cranberries. Top with remaining batter. To remaining cranberries, add 2 tablespoonfuls of sugar and 1½ teaspoonfuls orange rind. Mix well. Sprinkle cranberries on top of batter; sprinkle with chopped nuts. Bake at 350° for 45 to 55 minutes. Remove from pan and frost. Frosting looks pretty if drizzled on with a fork.

Preparation time: 30 minutes
Baking time:
    50–60 minutes (bundt)
    45–55 minutes (springform)

Can make ahead

Serves: 16–20
Can be frozen

Ann Paulson
Kathy Shurtz

Hint: For a taste treat with pancakes or French toast, drain 1 small can mandarin oranges, reserving half the liquid. In a small saucepan, heat oranges with reserved liquid, 1 cup maple-flavored syrup, and 3 tablespoonfuls butter. When the syrup is hot, pour it over pancakes or French toast. Blueberries, cherries, or other canned fruits may be substituted for the oranges. This may also be refrigerated and then rewarmed.

Jana Hletko

SUPERIOR YEAST COFFEE CAKE
Start the night before

1 pkg. active dry yeast
4 cups flour
1 cup milk
½ cup butter
½ cup sugar
1 tsp. salt
2 eggs
1 tsp. vanilla
Melted butter

In a large bowl, combine yeast and 2 cups flour. In a saucepan, heat milk, butter, sugar, and salt, stirring until butter almost melts. Pour liquid mixture into flour and yeast. Add eggs and vanilla and beat at low speed for 3 minutes. Gradually stir in remaining 2 cups flour.

Transfer dough to greased bowl, cover with plastic wrap, and refrigerate overnight.

Divide dough in half. Roll 1 piece into a 10 × 15-inch rectangle; brush with melted butter. Spread with desired filling, leaving a 1-inch border on 1 long and 2 short sides. Roll like a jelly roll, starting on the long side which has filling to the edge. Pinch edges to seal, and tuck under the ends of the roll. Brush with melted butter. Place on a greased 11 × 17 × 1-inch pan. Repeat with remaining dough. Cover with a cloth and let rise until doubled. Bake at 350° for 30 to 40 minutes. Drizzle with Thin Butter Icing (see page 89) while still warm.

Hint: Dough may be rolled out more easily if rolled on a pastry cloth.

CREAM CHEESE FILLING:
8 ozs. cream cheese,
  softened
½ cup sugar
1 egg
1 tsp. vanilla

Beat cream cheese until fluffy. Gradually beat in sugar. Add egg and vanilla and beat well. This is enough for 2 coffee cakes.

NUT FILLING:
1½ cups walnuts or pecans,
  chopped
  medium fine
1 egg
Approximately 3 T. cream
  or half-and-half
½ tsp. vanilla
1 cup powdered sugar,
  sieved

Mix all ingredients together in a bowl. If the mixture is too soft, add more nuts; if it is too firm, add more cream. This is enough filling for 1 coffee cake. To make Poteca (Yugoslavian Christmas spiral), coil prepared roll snail fashion on a baking sheet.

Preparation time:
  15 minutes initially;
  1 hour next day
Baking time: 30–40 minutes

Must be started
the night before

Yield: 2 coffee cakes
Can be frozen

Dorrie Kelly

75

POPPY SEED COFFEE CAKE

1 cup sugar
2 cups flour
2 tsps. baking powder
1 cup vegetable oil
1 cup evaporated milk
2 eggs, beaten
1 tsp. vanilla
1 T. poppy seeds

Place first 8 ingredients in bowl and mix well. Pour into a greased 10-inch tube pan. Mix brown sugar and nuts and sprinkle on top. Bake at 350° for 35 to 45 minutes.

TOPPING:
½ cup brown sugar, packed
½ cup nuts, coarsely
    chopped

Preparation time: 15 minutes
Baking time: 35–45 minutes

Easy
Can make ahead

Serves: 16–20
Can be frozen

Jo Andrews
Leatha Linders

BANKET
Dutch letters

PASTRY:
2 cups flour
⅛ tsp. salt
⅛ tsp. baking powder
1¼ cups butter, very cold
½ cup ice water

FILLING:
½ lb. almond paste
1 cup sugar
1½ eggs,* beaten
1 egg white, unbeaten

*To get ½ egg: beat 1 egg, pour into measuring cup, and remove half. Two small eggs may be substituted, if desired.

Measure unsifted flour into bowl of food processor fitted with steel blade. Add salt and baking powder. Turn on and off once to mix. Cut butter into ½-inch pieces, drop into processor, and turn on and off rapidly 3 to 4 times until mixture resembles coarse meal. Add the ice water and turn machine on for 2 to 3 seconds, or until dough begins to leave the sides of the bowl. Turn dough onto a lightly floured surface. With the heel of your hand, rapidly smear the dough, a small portion at a time, 6 to 8 inches out in front of you. This insures complete blending of the butter into the dough. Form dough into a round or a ball. Wrap tightly in plastic wrap and refrigerate overnight.

The next day, make the almond filling in the food processor fitted with steel blade. Break the almond paste into small pieces and put into the

(continued)

BANKET (continued)

bowl. Turn machine on and off 3 to 4 times. Add sugar and turn machine on for about 5 seconds. Add beaten eggs and process until well blended— 5 to 10 seconds. Divide dough into 5 equal parts. Roll each piece into a 4 × 12-inch rectangle. Drop filling by teaspoonfuls onto the middle of the dough lengthwise, leaving ½ inch at each end. Fold 1 long side of dough over the filling; fold other side over and seal edges with a little ice water. Place rolls, seam side down, on ungreased baking sheets. Three rolls will fit on an 11 × 17 × 2-inch pan. Prick tops with a folk at ½-inch intervals. Brush tops with unbeaten egg white. Bake at 375° for 30 to 40 minutes, or until light golden brown. Cool on wire racks.

This is a Dutch pastry, traditionally served at Christmas. With practice, it can be made in the shape of letters. The pastry and filling may be made by using conventional methods. Make pastry like piecrust. Use an electric mixer for making filling.

Preparation time:	Must start	Yield: Five
30–40 minutes	night before	12-inch rolls
Baking time: 30–40 minutes	Best served warm	

Mita Mitchell

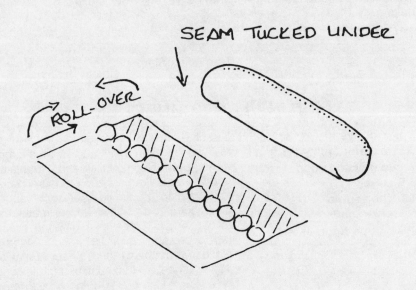

SEAM TUCKED UNDER

ROLL-OVER

ARABIC BREAD
Fun to make

6 cups flour, all white, or 3 cups whole wheat and 3 cups white
2 tsps. sugar
1 T. salt
1 pkg. active dry yeast
2¼ cups water (105°–115°)

Mix together flour, sugar, and salt in a large bowl. Dissolve yeast in ¼ cup warm water. Add yeast mixture and 2 cups warm water to flour. Knead well, adding more flour if necessary. Place in a greased bowl, turn once, cover, and let rise until doubled. Punch down. Divide dough into 10 to 12 balls. Place balls on a board or leave on countertop, cover, and let rise for 1 hour. On a floured surface, roll each ball into a circle 6 inches in diameter, starting at the center and rolling toward edge.

Baking Directions: Turn oven to broil, or highest temperature. **For gas stove:** Put 2 circles of bread on a firm baking sheet; place in oven. Let them rise and separate for 2 to 3 minutes. Take them out of oven and put under broiler to brown top. The bottom may also be browned (10 to 20 seconds per side). Remove bread from oven, and cover with a cloth. Flatten with a rolling pin when cool. **For electric stove:** Place baking sheet 6 inches below broiler. Close oven door. After 60 seconds, turn over each "loaf." Return to oven; keep door open a few inches while bread separates. When top is brown, turn over bread and brown bottom. Remove bread from oven and cover with a cloth. Flatten when cool.

Hint: Great with Greek-Style Sandwiches (see page 133)!

Preparation time: 20 minutes
Baking time:
   2–4 minutes per batch

Can be frozen

Yield: 10–12 "loaves"

Bernadine Simpson

EIN TELLER SCHNECKEN

1 pkg. active dry yeast
¼ cup water (105°–115°)
¾ cup milk, scalded
2 T. sugar
4 T. shortening
1½ tsps. salt
2½–3 cups flour, sifted

Dissolve yeast in warm water. Combine the milk, sugar, shortening, and salt in a large mixing bowl. Cool to lukewarm. Gradually add 2½ cups flour. Knead on floured surface, adding remaining flour, until dough is smooth and satiny—approximately 3 to 5 minutes. Place in a greased bowl, turn once, and cover. Let rise in a warm place until doubled (about 1 hour). Place a 15-inch sheet of aluminum foil, dull side up, on a baking sheet (or a 12-inch pizza pan).

(continued)

EIN TELLER SCHNECKEN (continued)

TOPPING:
¼ cup butter, melted
¾ cup sugar
¼ cup brown sugar, packed
2 tsps. cinnamon
½–¾ cup nuts, finely chopped

Grease foil and turn up edges to form a 12-inch circle. Punch down dough; divide into 2 equal pieces. Roll each piece into a "rope." Cut each rope into 10 to 12 equal pieces. Melt butter. Mix together sugars, cinnamon, and nuts. Roll each piece of dough into a 6-inch rope, ½ inch thick. Dip rope in melted butter, then in cinnamon-sugar topping. Wind into flat coil in the center of the pan. Continue making coils, placing them so that they just touch. Sprinkle remaining topping mixture over rolls. Cover and let rise until doubled. Bake at 375° for 20 to 25 minutes. Remove from oven and drizzle with Powdered Sugar Frosting (see page 89) if desired.

Preparation time: 60 minutes
Baking time: 20–25 minutes

Can make ahead and reheat

Yield: 20–24 rolls
Can be frozen

Billie Hayward

SWEDISH CARDAMOM BRAID

2 pkgs. active dry yeast
½ cup water (105°–115°)
½ cup milk
½ cup sugar
1 tsp. salt
¼ cup butter, softened
5½ cups flour, sifted
2 eggs, beaten
1½ tsps. cardamom, ground
½ cup light raisins

GLAZE:
1 egg white, slightly beaten
2 T. sugar (approximately)

Soften yeast in warm water. Scald milk. Stir in sugar, salt, and butter; cool to lukewarm and add to yeast. Stir in 2 cups flour; beat well. Add beaten eggs, cardamom, raisins, and enough flour to make a stiff dough. Knead on floured surface 5 to 8 minutes. Place in a greased bowl, turn once, cover, and let rise until doubled. Punch down. Divide in half; divide each half into 3 equal parts. Roll each piece into a rope about 14 inches long. Loosely braid the 3 strands. Tuck under ends. Place on a greased baking sheet. Repeat with remaining dough. Let rise 45 minutes or until almost doubled. Brush loaves with beaten egg white; sprinkle with sugar. Bake at 350° for about 35 minutes.

Preparation time: 30 minutes
Baking time: 35 minutes

Make ahead
Can be frozen

Yield: 2 loaves

TWISTED MAPLE-BUTTER RINGS

1 pkg. active dry yeast
¼ cup water (105°–115°)
¼ cup butter
3 T. sugar
1½ tsps. salt
½ cup milk, scalded
2 eggs
3¼–3½ cups flour

FILLING:
¼ cup butter, softened
½ cup brown sugar, packed
⅓ cup sugar
¼ cup maple syrup
    (or pancake syrup)
2 tsps. flour
1 T. cinnamon
½ tsp. maple flavoring
½ cup walnuts, chopped

Dissolve yeast in warm water. Let stand about 10 minutes. Combine butter, sugar, salt, and milk in a large bowl. Stir in unbeaten eggs and softened yeast. Gradually add flour to form a stiff dough. Cover bowl with plastic wrap and let dough rise in a warm place for 1 to 1½ hours.

To make filling, cream soft butter, add sugars, and beat well. Stir in maple syrup, flour, cinnamon, maple flavoring, and nuts.

Punch dough down; toss on well-floured surface to coat with flour. Divide in half. Roll ½ into a 14 × 8-inch rectangle. Spread with ½ of the filling. Starting with the 14-inch side, roll up dough. Cut roll in half lengthwise almost to end. Twist strips together, cut side up. Repeat with remaining dough. Grease two 8 or 9-inch round cake pans. Shape twists into rings and place in pans. Cover and let rise about 45 minutes. Bake at 350° for 20 to 30 minutes. Frost with Maple-Flavored or Plain Powdered Sugar Icing (see page 89).

Preparation time: 60 minutes
Baking time: 20–30 minutes

Can make ahead
Best served warm
Can be frozen

Yield: Two
8 or 9-inch
coffee cakes

Jan Cornell

DATE COFFEE CAKE

2 pkgs. active dry yeast
¼ cup water (105°–115°)
1 cup milk, scalded
3–3¼ cups flour
½ cup margarine
4 T. sugar
1 egg, well beaten

Dissolve yeast in warm water and let stand 10 minutes. Cool scalded milk. Add cooled milk and 1 cup flour to yeast. Cream margarine, sugar, and egg and add to first mixture. Add 2 to 2¼ cups more flour and mix until elastic. Cover and let rise in bowl until doubled. Punch down dough; roll into a rectangle ¼ inch thick. Spread margarine on dough; sprinkle on brown sugar mixed

(continued)

DATE COFFEE CAKE (continued)

FILLING:
⅓ cup margarine, softened
⅓ cup brown sugar, packed
1½ tsps. cinnamon
1 can (12 oz.) date filling (Solo brand preferred)

with cinnamon. Spread on date filling. Roll up like a jelly roll. Cut into 1½-inch slices. Arrange ½ inch apart on greased baking sheets. Cover and let rise until doubled. Bake at 375° for 15 to 20 minutes.

If canned date filling is unavailable, the following recipe may be substituted: In a heavy saucepan, combine 8 ounces chopped dates, 1 cup chopped pecans, ¼ cup packed brown sugar, ⅔ cup water, and 1 tablespoonful lemon juice. Cook, stirring constantly, until of spreading consistency (3 to 5 minutes).

Preparation time: 60 minutes
Baking time: 15–20 minutes

Can make ahead
Best served warm

Serves: 10
Can be frozen

Sandy Shauman

SWEDISH RYE BREAD

1 cake (0.6 oz) yeast*
4 T. butter, melted
2 cups milk, lukewarm
½ cup brown sugar, packed
1 T. salt
½ tsp. caraway seeds, crushed
½ tsp. anise seed, crushed
2 cups rye flour
4 cups white flour

*To make recipe with active dry yeast, mix 1 pkg. yeast with rye flour, beat in liquid, and gradually add white flour.

Crumble yeast into a bowl. Melt butter in a saucepan. Add milk and heat until lukewarm. Add sugar, salt, and caraway seeds and then add to yeast in bowl. Stir in rye flour, then gradually add white flour until dough is firm. Knead 5 to 8 minutes. Place in buttered bowl, turn once, cover, and let rise until doubled (2 to 3 hours). Punch dough down and knead again. Cut in half. Shape into loaves and place on greased baking sheets, sprinkled with a little cornmeal, or in 2 greased 8½ × 4½ × 2½-inch loaf pans. Cover and let rise again until doubled. Bake at 350° for about 50 minutes.

Hint: Dough is very sticky. Allow it to rest for 5 minutes after it is turned out on floured surface to increase ease of kneading.

Preparation time: 35 minutes
Baking time: 50 minutes

Can be frozen

Yield: 2 loaves

Edith Anderson

WHOLE WHEAT BREAD

4 cups milk
4 pkgs. active dry yeast
½–1 cup brown sugar, packed, or honey
4 tsps. salt
¾ cup shortening, melted
11–12 cups whole wheat flour

Scald milk and cool to lukewarm. Dissolve yeast in milk; add brown sugar or honey, melted shortening, and salt. Gradually add flour until the dough is workable. This dough is sticky even when thoroughly kneaded. Turn out on floured surface and knead 5 to 8 minutes, until smooth and elastic. Place in a greased bowl, turn once, cover, and let rise until doubled. Punch dough down; divide into 4 equal parts; shape into loaves. Put in well-greased 8½ × 4½ × 2½-inch loaf pans. Cover and let rise until doubled. Bake at 375° for 45 minutes. Cool completely on wire racks before wrapping.

Preparation time: 20–25 minutes
Baking time: 45 minutes

Can be halved

Yield: 4 loaves
Can be frozen

Kay Jones

COLONIAL BREAD

½ cup yellow cornmeal
⅓ cup molasses
1½ tsps. salt
2 cups boiling water
¼ cup vegetable oil
2 pkgs. active dry yeast
½ cup water (105°–115°)
¾ cup whole wheat flour
½ cup rye flour
4¼–4½ cups flour, unbleached

Thoroughly combine cornmeal, molasses, salt, boiling water, and vegetable oil. Cool to lukewarm. Dissolve yeast in ½ cup warm water; stir into cornmeal mixture. Add whole wheat and rye flours; mix well. Stir in enough white flour to make a moderately stiff dough. Turn out on a lightly floured surface, and knead until smooth and elastic—6 to 8 minutes. Place in a greased bowl, turn once, cover, and let rise in a warm place until doubled—about 50 to 60 minutes. Punch down, turn onto a lightly floured surface and divide in half. Cover and let rest for 10 minutes. Shape into 2 loaves and place in greased 9 × 5 × 3-inch loaf pans. Let rise again until almost doubled—about 30 minutes. Bake at 375° for 45 minutes or until done.

Note: Preheat oven for at least 20 minutes.

Preparation time: 45 minutes
Baking time: 45 minutes

Easily doubled
Can be frozen

Yield: 2 loaves

Betty Maxwell

CHRISTOPSOMO
Greek Christmas bread

2¾–3 cups flour
1 pkg. active dry yeast
⅔ cup milk (105°–115°)
4 T. butter
3 T. sugar
½ tsp. salt
2 eggs

TOPPING:
1 egg, beaten
Sesame seeds

Stir together yeast and 1½ cups flour. In saucepan, heat milk, butter, sugar, and salt until warm and butter almost melts. Add to flour mixture. Add eggs and beat at low speed for ½ minute. Beat 3 minutes at high speed. Gradually add rest of flour. Knead on lightly floured surface for 3 to 5 minutes, adding more flour as necessary, until dough is smooth and elastic. Place in a greased bowl, turn once, cover, and let rise until doubled. Punch down, cover, and let rest 10 minutes. Cut off ¼ of dough and divide it into 8 equal pieces. Roll each piece into a rope 10 inches long. Twist 2 pieces together, repeat with remaining 6 pieces, for a total of 4 twists. Grease a 9 or 10-inch round pan; place 2 twists around inner edge. Place the large piece of dough, which has been shaped into a round, in the center of the pan, and push down edges overlapping braids. Cross the other 2 twists on top of the large piece of dough to form an "x." Brush the top of bread with beaten egg, and sprinkle with sesame seeds. Bake at 350° for 30 to 35 minutes. Cover loosely with foil after 15 to 20 minutes to avoid burning top twists. Makes delicious toast.

Preparation time: 20 minutes
Baking time: 30–35 minutes

Requires only
1 rising

Yield: 1 loaf
Can be frozen

Carole Hawk

OLD-FASHIONED WHITE BREAD
Delicious plain or toasted

2 pkgs. active dry yeast
¾ cup water (105°–115°)
2⅔ cups water (105°–115°)
¼ cup sugar
1 T. salt
3 T. shortening
9–10 cups flour

Dissolve yeast in ¾ cup warm water. Add 2⅔ cups warm water, sugar, salt, shortening, and 4 cups flour. Beat with wooden spoon until smooth (may also be done with electric mixer). Gradually add enough remaining flour to make a workable dough. Knead until smooth and elastic—about 10 minutes. Place in a greased bowl, turn once, cover, and let rise until doubled (1 to 1½ hours). Divide into 3 equal parts, shape into loaves, and place in greased 8½ × 4½ × 2½-inch loaf pans. Let rise until doubled (1 to 1½ hours). Bake at 425° for 30 minutes. Remove from pans immediately and brush with melted butter. Cool completely before wrapping.

Note: Two very large loaves may be made by using 9 × 5 × 3-inch pans.

Preparation time: 30 minutes
Baking time: 30 minutes

Easy
Can be frozen
Can make ahead

Yield: 2–3 loaves

Deborah Klerk

OATMEAL BREAD
Try it with honey or molasses

2 cups boiling water
1 cup rolled oats, quick or regular
2 T. butter or margarine
⅓ cup water (105°–115°)
2 pkgs. active dry yeast
2½ tps. salt
½ cup honey or dark molasses
5–6 cups flour

Pour boiling water over rolled oats. Stir to blend, and let cool to lukewarm (110°). Dissolve yeast in water. Let stand 5 minutes. Add yeast mixture to rolled oats, then stir in salt and molasses. Gradually add enough flour to form a stiff dough. Knead 7 to 10 minutes. Place dough in a greased bowl, turn once, cover, and let rise until doubled (2 to 2½ hours). Punch dough down. Divide in half and place in 2 well-greased 9 × 5 × 3-inch pans. Cover and let rise until doubled. Bake 4 inches from oven bottom at 350° for 50 minutes.

Preparation time: 30 minutes
Baking time: 50 minutes

Can be frozen

Yield: 2 large loaves

Greeta Douglass
Chris Oosterbaan

SOURDOUGH STARTER

1 qt. water or milk,
  lukewarm
1 pkg. dry yeast
2 T. sugar
4 cups flour

Dissolve yeast in water or milk; stir in sugar. Gradually stir in flour; mix until smooth. Cover; let rise at room temperature at least 24 to 48 hours. Cover loosely in a container that allows room for expansion, and store in refrigerator. Don't let supply of starter get below 1 cup. To replenish starter, "feed" with 1 cup flour, 1 cup cool water or milk, and ¼ cup sugar; allow to stand at room temperature 3 to 4 hours before returning to the refrigerator.

Hint: Starter can be frozen indefinitely. NEVER use a metal container to store sourdough.

SOURDOUGH PUMPERNICKEL
Well worth the wait

½ cup coffee, boiling
2 T. caraway seeds,
  chopped in blender
2 cups rye flour
1½ cups sourdough starter
½ cup molasses
  (unsulfured preferred)
¼ cup powdered milk
2 tsps. salt
1 pkg. active dry yeast
3 T. butter or margarine,
  melted
½ cup milk, warm
2¾ cups whole wheat flour
½–1 cup unbleached white
  flour

Pour boiling coffee over caraway seeds. Set aside to cool. Put rye flour and sourdough starter in a large bowl. Add cooled coffee mixture, and stir until well blended. Cover bowl with plastic wrap, and let stand overnight. The next morning, add molasses, powdered milk, salt, dry yeast, butter, and milk. Gradually add whole wheat flour. Turn dough onto a floured surface and knead 5 to 8 minutes, adding more flour when dough becomes too sticky. This dough is very firm. Place in a greased bowl, turn once, cover, and let rise until doubled. Punch dough down, and divide into 2, 3, or 4 pieces and shape into loaves. Place on greased baking sheets which have been sprinkled with cornmeal. Cover and let rise until doubled (2 to 3 hours). Bake at 350° for 30 minutes, or until loaves sound hollow when tapped on the bottom. Cool on racks.

Preparation time:
  35–40 minutes
Baking time: 30 minutes

Must start the
night before

Yield: 2–4 loaves
Can be frozen

Ann Paulson

CINNAMON-OATMEAL BREAD
Delicious served warm or toasted

2 cups milk, scalded
1 cup rolled oats
2 tsps. salt
¼ cup vegetable oil
½ cup brown sugar, packed
1 tsp. cinnamon
¼ cup water (105°–115°)
2 pkgs. active dry yeast
2 eggs, lightly beaten
¼–½ cup wheat germ
6–7 cups flour

FILLING:
4 T. brown sugar
2 tsps. cinnamon
4 T. pecans, chopped

Pour scalded milk over rolled oats; add salt, vegetable oil, brown sugar, and cinnamon. Cool to lukewarm. Dissolve yeast in warm water and add to oat mixture. Stir in eggs and wheat germ. Gradually stir in flour until dough is stiff; knead 10 minutes. Place in a greased bowl, turn once, cover, and let rise until doubled. Divide dough in half. Roll each piece into a 6 × 18-inch rectangle. Mix filling ingredients together and sprinkle ½ this mixture on each rectangle. Roll up dough, starting with narrower side, and place in 2 well-greased 9 × 5 × 3-inch pans. Cover and let rise until doubled. Bake at 350° for 1 hour.

Preparation time: 30 minutes
Baking time: 60 minutes

Can be frozen

Yield: 2 loaves

Lucy Welch

CHALLAH
Serve with honey

2 pkgs. active dry yeast
2 T. sugar
2 cups water (105°–115°)
1 egg, beaten
1 T. salt
2 T. oil
6 cups flour (approximately)

TO BRUSH ON LOAF:
1 egg yolk
1 tsp. cold water

Dissolve yeast and 1 tablespoonful of the sugar in ½ cup warm water and let stand 5 minutes. Put remaining 1½ cups warm water and 1 tablespoonful sugar in a large bowl. Stir in yeast mixture, beaten egg, salt, oil, and flour. A little more than 6 cups may be needed. Knead dough until smooth and elastic. Coat inside of a bowl with a light film of oil; put dough in bowl, turn once, cover, and let rise until doubled. Punch down and briefly knead again. Shape into loaves or braid. Makes 2 braided or 2 plain loaves.

(continued)

CHALLAH (continued)

To braid: Divide dough in half; divide each half into 3 equal parts. Roll each piece of dough into a rope (14 to 16 inches long), then loosely braid 3 ropes together. Put on a greased baking sheet which has been sprinkled with cornmeal. Cover. Let rise again until doubled. Grease only the area of the baking sheet on which the bread will be. Brush loaves with egg yolk mixture and sprinkle with poppy seeds. Bake at 400° for 15 minutes; lower heat to 350° and continue baking for 30 to 40 minutes.

Preparation time: 45 minutes
Baking time: 45–55 mlnutes

Makes excellent toast
Can be made ahead

Yield: 2 loaves
Can be frozen

Mira Stulberg Halpert

SWEDISH LIMPA
You need a bread mixer to make this

3 cups milk
⅔ cup margarine
2 pkgs. active dry yeast
1½ tsps. sugar
¼ cup water (105°–115°)
3 cups water (105°–115°)
1½ cups light molasses
   (Golden Label preferred)
1½ cups dark brown sugar,
   packed
2½ tsps. salt
4 lbs., 2 ozs. flour
   (16½ cups)
1 lb., 3 ozs. rye flour
   (5 cups)

OPTIONAL:
2 T. fennel seed, crushed
3 T. orange rind, grated

Scald milk. Add margarine and let it melt. Dissolve yeast and 1½ teaspoonfuls sugar in lukewarm water. First place all liquids in the bread mixer; then add all the dry ingredients and optional ingredients. Mix for approximately 3 minutes. Cover. Let rise in warm place for 2½ to 3 hours, or until dough rises to the top of mixer. Mix again until dough forms a ball. Working on a floured board, shape into 6 to 9 loaves, depending on the size of the pans. Place in greased pans, cover, and let rise until doubled. Bake at 325° for 30 to 40 minutes.

Note: Recipe may be halved and made in an electric mixer with dough hooks. Add the rye flour first, then about half of the white flour. Stir remaining flour by hand. Mix well, cover, and proceed as above.

Preparation time: 45 minutes
Baking time: 35–45 minutes

Yield: 6–9 loaves
Can be frozen

Ethelyn Pearson

HOPPING BUNNIES
Little children love these

1 pkg. active dry yeast
¼ cup water (105°–115°)
1 cup milk, scalded
⅓ cup sugar
½ cup shortening
1 tsp. salt
5–5½ cups flour, sifted
2 eggs, beaten
¼ cup orange juice
2 T. orange peel, grated

Soften yeast in warm water. Combine milk, sugar, shortening, and salt; cool to lukewarm. Stir in 2 cups flour; beat well. Add beaten eggs; mix well. Stir in yeast, orange juice, orange peel, and enough remaining flour to make a soft dough. Turn out on a lightly floured surface and knead until smooth and elastic—about 5 to 10 minutes. Place dough in a greased bowl, turn once, cover, and let rise until doubled—about 2 hours. Punch down. Cover and let rest 10 minutes.

To shape rolls: On a lightly floured surface, roll dough into a rectangle ½ inch thick. Cut dough into strips ½ inch wide. Roll each strip into a smooth rope. Each bunny requires a 5-inch strip for the body and a 2½-inch strip for the head. On a lightly greased baking sheet, make a loose swirl of the strip for the body. Swirl strip for the head and place close to the body (they'll grow together as dough rises). For ears, pinch off 1-inch strips of dough and roll between hands until smooth and cigar shaped. Let point make tip of ear; snip off opposite end and place next to head. Pinch off a bit of dough and roll into a ball for the tail. Let the bunnies rise until almost doubled—about 45 to 60 minutes. Bake at 375° for 12 to 15 minutes. Frost while warm with sugar glaze.

(continued)

HOPPING BUNNIES (continued)

Note: This dough may be used to make filled orange rolls. Divide dough in half; roll each piece into a 20 × 12-inch rectangle. Spread with orange filling. Roll up, jelly-roll fashion; pinch edges to seal. Cut into 1 to 1½-inch slices and place close together on greased baking pans or in individually greased muffin tins. Cover and let rise until almost doubled. Bake at 350° for 20 to 25 minutes.

SUGAR GLAZE:
2 cups powdered sugar, sieved
¼ cup hot water
1 tsp. butter or margarine

To make sugar glaze: Add hot water and butter to sugar; mix until well blended. Brush over warm bunnies.

ORANGE FILLING (Optional):
6 T. butter, softened
3 cups powdered sugar, sieved
4 T. orange juice
2 T. orange rind, grated

To make orange filling: Beat about 1½ cups powdered sugar into softened butter. Gradually add rest of sugar and orange juice, then stir in orange rind. This may also be used to frost rolls.

Preparation time: 1½ hours
Baking time: 12–15 minutes

Yield: 30 bunnies
Can be frozen

Norma Stancati

GLAZES AND ICINGS

THIN GLAZES:
Stir 1 tablespoonful softened butter into 1 tablespoonful hot water; stir in 4 tablespoonfuls powdered sugar and ¼ to ½ teaspoonful vanilla.

Stir ¾ cup powdered sugar into 1 tablespoonful hot milk or cream; add ¼ to ½ teaspoonful vanilla.

THIN BUTTER ICING:
In a warm bowl, put 2 tablespoonfuls softened butter. When butter is melted, add 1 cup sieved powdered sugar alternately with 1½ tablespoonfuls milk. Add ½ teaspoonful vanilla.

MAPLE ICING:
Stir 2 to 3 tablespoonfuls cream into 1½ cups powdered sugar; add ¼ teaspoonful maple flavoring.

Hint: Instead of sifting powdered sugar, stir through a sieve with a spoon.

KHACHAPURI
Delicious as an hors d'oeuvre

2 pkgs. active dry yeast
1 cup milk (105°–115°)
3½ tsps. sugar
½ cup butter, unsalted
2 tsps. salt
4 cups flour

FILLING:
2 lbs. Muenster cheese, shredded
2 T. butter, unsalted, softened
1 egg

Dissolve yeast in ½ cup lukewarm milk; stir in sugar. Add butter to remaining ½ cup milk and stir until it melts. Add salt and 2 cups flour. Add yeast mixture and enough flour to make a workable dough. Knead until smooth and elastic—about 10 minutes. Place in a greased bowl, turn once, cover, and let rise until doubled. Punch down and let rise again for 45 minutes. Meanwhile, grate cheese in a food processor fitted with shredding disc. In a large bowl, beat egg; add softened butter and grated cheese and mix thoroughly. In food processor fitted with steel blade, puree the cheese mixture in 4 to 5 small batches. When dough has risen, punch down and divide in half. Roll 1 piece into a 12-inch circle; drape over an 8 or 9-inch greased cake pan. Put half the cheese into the middle of the dough. Starting at any point in the circle, gather the dough into 1½-inch pinch pleats. Gently squeeze the pleats together at the top and twist to make a topknot. Allow to rest for 10 to 15 minutes, then bake at 375° for 1 hour.

Note: This bread is best baked early in the day and reheated at 275° for 20 minutes before serving. Reheat unwrapped for a crusty bread and wrapped in foil for a soft bread. When bread is frozen, allow it to thaw overnight in the refrigerator before reheating.

Preparation time: 50 minutes
Baking time: 60 minutes

Best made ahead
May be frozen for
up to 2 weeks

Yield: 2 loaves

Sally Shipman Early
Jean Patt

FRESH SPINACH SALAD

GEINSING SALAD DRESSING:

¼ cup vinegar
1 cup salad oil
1 small onion, chopped
1 tsp. Worcestershire sauce
¾ cup sugar
⅓ cup catsup
Salt and pepper to taste

Mix together all ingredients in the blender. Dressing may be made 1 or 2 days prior to using.

SALAD:

1 lb. fresh spinach
1 can (20 oz.) bean sprouts, drained
1 can (8 oz.) water chestnuts, sliced
½ lb. bacon, fried crisp, drained, crumbled
4 eggs, hard cooked, sliced
1 cup seasoned croutons

Clean spinach; remove stems and dry well. Place all ingredients in salad bowl. At serving time, toss with dressing.

Variations that may be used with Fresh Spinach Salad:
1 pt. cherry tomatoes
1 cup cucumbers, sliced
Cheesy Poppy Seed Dressing (see page 100) may be substituted for Geinsing Salad Dressing.

Preparation time: 30 minutes

Serves: 6–8

CHRIS' STUFFED TOMATO SALAD

½ cup cottage cheese
½ cup cucumbers, diced
1 T. onion, chopped
1 T. catsup
½ tsp. salt
½ tsp. celery salt
½ cup mayonnaise
4 tomatoes
Parsley sprigs (for garnish)

Mix together first 7 ingredients. Stuff tomatoes with mixture. Garnish with parsley. Serve immediately.

Preparation time: 10 minutes

Serves: 4

Barbara Brandt

HEARTS OF PALM SALAD

¼ cup salad oil
1 T. onion, chopped
1 T. parsley, snipped
1 T. white vinegar
1 tsp. lemon juice
¼ tsp. salt
⅛ tsp. dry mustard
1 tsp. chervil
1 egg, hard cooked,
  chopped
½ T. pimiento, chopped
Bibb lettuce
1 can (14 oz.) hearts of
  palm, drained, cut in
  strips

Dressing: Combine oil, onion, parsley, vinegar, lemon juice, salt, dry mustard, and chervil in jar with top. Shake vigorously. Add egg and pimiento and stir. Line salad plates with lettuce and top with hearts of palm. Top with dressing.

Preparation time: 30 minutes

Serves: 4

Sally Shipman Early

SUMMER BROCCOLI SALAD
Good as a substitute for potato salad

1 medium bunch broccoli
1 cup celery, chopped
½ cup onion, chopped
3 eggs, hard cooked,
  chopped
1 jar (2 oz.) stuffed olives
½ tsp. lemon juice
1 cup mayonnaise
  (Hellmann's preferred)
Lettuce

Parboil broccoli in salted water. Cool and drain. Chop into ½-inch lengths. Add remaining ingredients. Mix and chill. Serve on lettuce.

Note: Two 10-ounce packages frozen broccoli may be substituted for fresh.

Preparation time: 20 minutes   Refrigerate   Serves: 4–6

Jan Wright

COBB SALAD
A nice change for tossed salad lovers

1 head Romaine lettuce, finely chopped
1 head iceberg lettuce, finely chopped
6 strips bacon, fried crisp, drained, crumbled
¼ lb. Roquefort cheese, crumbled
3 eggs, hard cooked, finely chopped
2 tomatoes, peeled, seeded, chopped
2 avocados, chopped
¼ lb. Swiss cheese, chopped
½ cup parsley, chopped

Arrange the lettuces in the bottom of a large, shallow salad bowl. Place the next 6 ingredients in rows across the top of the greens. Sprinkle with parsley. At the table, add ½ cup French dressing and toss.

FRENCH DRESSING:
1 tsp. salt
½ tsp. cracked pepper
¼ tsp. dry mustard
1 tsp. Worcestershire sauce
½ cup wine vinegar
1 T. water
⅔ cup olive oil

Combine all ingredients and shake well.

Preparation time: 30 minutes

Serves: 8

Mary Keyser

SOUR CREAM DRESSING

1 cup sour cream
Dash of salt
1½ tsps. sugar
¼ tsp. ginger
⅛ tsp. nutmeg

Mix and chill. May be served on gelatin salad molds or fresh fruit.

Preparation time: 5 minutes   Refrigerate   Yield: 1 cup

Aaron Riker

GREEN MEDLEY
A great combination of greens

1 pkg. (10 oz.) frozen
   chopped broccoli
1 pkg. (10 oz.) frozen cut
   asparagus
1 pkg. (10 oz.) frozen
   French-style green beans
1 can (14 oz.) artichoke
   hearts, drained
1 can (8 oz.) water
   chestnuts, drained, sliced
Red onion, sliced in rings
3 T. fresh parsley, chopped
2 T. garlic vinegar
1 cucumber, chopped
2 T. lemon juice
1½ cups mayonnaise

Cook broccoli, asparagus, and green beans according to package directions; drain well. Add the remaining ingredients. Mix well and refrigerate for 24 hours. Good with broiled meats.

Preparation time: 20 minutes

Must be made
day ahead
Refrigerate

Serves: 8

Linda Brown

PARMESAN DRESSING
Great with spinach salad

¾ cup salad oil
¼ cup lemon juice
2 T. Parmesan cheese
¾ tsp. salt
¼ tsp. sugar
Dash of pepper
Dash of paprika
1 clove garlic, chopped

Combine all ingredients. Refrigerate to blend flavors.

Preparation time: 10 minutes

Yield: 1 cup

Chris Garrett

GARDEN MARINADE
Refreshing and colorful

1 qt. Italian oil and vinegar
  dressing
1¼ cups sugar
⅛ tsp. garlic salt
1 tsp. salt
1 tsp. cracked pepper
Juice of 8 lemons
1 lb. raw mushrooms, sliced
2 bunches green onions,
  sliced (cut tops into
  1-inch pieces)
2 green peppers, sliced
2 cucumbers, sliced
2 tomatoes, cut in wedges,
  or cherry tomatoes

Mix together first 6 ingredients with wire whisk. Add mushrooms, onions, and green peppers in that order. Marinate for 7 hours in refrigerator; add cucumbers and tomatoes the last half hour to prevent breakdown from overmarination.

To serve: Gently mix vegetables and pour off marinade. Place marinated vegetables in lettuce-lined bowl and serve.

Preparation time: 45 minutes

Must make ahead
Refrigerate

Serves: 4–6

Mardee Mott

THOUSAND ISLAND DRESSING

½ cup mayonnaise
1 T. chili sauce
1 T. olives, chopped, or
  relish
1 tsp. chives, chopped
1 egg, hard cooked,
  chopped
½ tsp. paprika

Blend together all ingredients until well mixed.

Preparation time: 15 minutes

Refrigerate

Yield: 1 cup

Greeta Douglass

TOMATO-ZUCCHINI SALAD
Pretty and delightfully crunchy

⅓ cup salad oil
2 T. red wine vinegar
¼ tsp. salt
⅛ tsp. pepper
1 pt. cherry tomatoes,
  halved
2 small zucchini, thinly
  sliced
1 small onion, thinly sliced
⅓ cup blue cheese,
  crumbled
Lettuce

Mix oil, vinegar, salt, and pepper. Add tomatoes, zucchini, onion, and cheese. Toss lightly. Cover and chill several hours. Serve on lettuce.

Preparation time: 15 minutes   Must make ahead   Serves: 4-6
                                  Refrigerate

Esther Struck

FRESH FRUIT FANTASIA
As attractive as it is delicious

1 large lettuce leaf
2 sections grapefruit
2 slices cantaloupe
2 slices honeydew
1 slice orange
2 slices pineapple
2 cubes watermelon or
  a few slices plums,
  nectarines, or peaches
3 fresh strawberries or
  cherries

Wash and dry lettuce leaf. Tear in half lengthwise and put the halves together inside each other to form a cup. Peel fruit and put in cup in order listed, starting with grapefruit and ending with strawberries. Top with Poppy Seed Dressing and garnish with strawberries.

Suggestion: May be topped with raspberry ice or cottage cheese. Serve with banana bread sandwiches and grapes. Garnish with parsley.

POPPY SEED DRESSING:
1½ cups sugar
2 tsps. dry mustard
2 tsps. salt
⅔ cup vinegar
3 T. onion juice
2 cups salad oil
3 T. poppy seeds

Mix together sugar, mustard, salt, and vinegar in blender; add onion juice and blend thoroughly. With blender running, add oil slowly and continue blending until mixture is thick. Add poppy seeds and whirl for a few more seconds. Store, covered, in a cool place. Makes 1 quart.

Preparation time: 30 minutes   Serves: 1

Jill Berglund

TUNA ASPIC SALAD
A light meal for a hot summer day

FIRST LAYER:
1 pkg. (3 oz.) lemon gelatin
1 cup hot water
½ cup cold water
1 T. vinegar
½ cup mayonnaise
1 cup celery, chopped
¼ tsp. salt
¼ cup stuffed olives,
  chopped
1 tsp. onion, grated
1 can (7 oz.) tuna, drained,
  flaked

SECOND LAYER:
1 env. unflavored gelatin
½ cup cold tomato juice
⅛ tsp. pepper
1 tsp. Worcestershire sauce
1 T. lemon juice
1¼ cups hot tomato juice

Mix together all ingredients for first layer and let set in 9 × 9-inch pan. To make second layer, sprinkle gelatin into cold tomato juice to soften. Add pepper, Worcestershire sauce, lemon juice, and hot tomato juice. Stir until dissolved. Cool; pour over first layer and let set.

Note: Shrimp, salmon, or chicken may be substituted for tuna.

Preparation time: 30 minutes   Refrigerate   Serves: 8

Marian Klein

ROQUEFORT DRESSING

1 cup sour cream
½ tsp. garlic powder
¼ tsp. white pepper
Dash of vinegar
12 ozs. blue cheese
1 large wedge Roquefort
1 small onion, shredded
1 qt. mayonnaise
  (Hellmann's preferred)

Mix all ingredients and add mayonnaise. Mix by hand so that cheese is chunky.

Preparation time: 10 minutes   Can make ahead   Yield: 5 cups
                                 Refrigerate

Joan deMink

GREEK SALAD

DRESSING:
¾ cup olive oil
⅓ cup tarragon vinegar
1–2 T. lemon juice
½ cup onion, finely chopped
½ tsp. garlic, minced
1 tsp. peppercorns, crushed
½ tsp. rosemary
½ tsp. basil
½ tsp. oregano

Mix together dressing ingredients. Store for at least 24 hours in refrigerator. Combine salad ingredients. Toss with dressing.

SALAD:
1 large head iceberg lettuce
   or an equivalent amount
   of leaf lettuce
2 tomatoes, chopped
½ cucumber, chopped
1 green pepper, chopped
1 medium onion, sliced
¼ lb. feta cheese, crumbled
¼ lb. Greek olives

Preparation time: 15 minutes

Serves: 8

Greeta Douglass

GOURMET DRESSING

7 T. sugar
1 tsp. prepared mustard
   (French's preferred)
Butter, size of walnut
1 egg
5 T. vinegar
2 T. water

Beat together sugar, mustard, butter, and egg until well mixed. Add vinegar and water and cook over low heat, stirring constantly, until slightly thickened. Store in refrigerator and stir before using.

Preparation time: 15 minutes

Refrigerate

Yield: 1 cup

Pauline Solomon

99

CAESAR SALAD
Your emperor will love it

½ cup salad oil
¼ cup red wine vinegar
1 clove garlic, crushed
2 tsps. Worcestershire
   sauce
¼ tsp. salt
Dash of pepper
1 medium head romaine
   lettuce
½ cup Parmesan cheese,
   grated
¼ cup blue cheese,
   crumbled
Croutons
1 egg
Anchovies (optional)

The day before serving, combine oil, vinegar, garlic, Worcestershire sauce, salt, and pepper.

Before serving, wash lettuce and pat dry. Place lettuce in bowl. Sprinkle with cheeses. Toss. Add croutons. Toss. Add egg to dressing. Shake until mixed. Add dressing. Toss and serve.

Preparation time: 15 minutes

Serves: 6

Betsy Morren
Jackie Schaefer

CHEESY POPPY SEED DRESSING
Destined to be a favorite

¼ cup sugar
1 tsp. salt
1 tsp. dry mustard
1 T. onion juice or onion
   powder
⅓ cup cider vinegar
1 cup salad oil
1 T. poppy seed
1½ cups cottage cheese

Mix all ingredients in a jar and shake vigorously. Pour over salad and toss.

Preparation time: 10 minutes

Can make ahead
Refrigerate

Yield: 3 cups

Diane Basso

GERMAN POTATO SALAD

12 medium to large
  potatoes
1 lb. bacon
1 large onion, chopped
1 cup water
⅛ cup white vinegar
¼ cup brown sugar, packed
½ tsp. celery seed
Salt and pepper to taste
1 pt. sour cream

Boil potatoes with skins on until done but still firm. Cool. Peel and cut into ¾-inch pieces. Fry bacon until crisp. Drain on paper towel. Pour off all but ⅓ cup bacon grease; add chopped onion and cook slowly until tender. Add water, vinegar, and sugar; cover and cook over low heat for 5 minutes. Add potatoes and crumbled bacon to mixture. Cover and cook over low heat for 15 minutes. Add celery seed, salt, and pepper. Stir in sour cream.

Note: Vinegar and/or sugar may be increased or decreased to achieve correct sweet-and-sour taste before potatoes and bacon are added. After potatoes are boiled, the rest can be done in an electric skillet. Can be made in the morning and reheated in casserole at 350° until hot.

Preparation time: 30 minutes   Can make ahead   Serves: 8–10

Leatha Linders

RUSSIAN DRESSING

½ cup honey
2 T. catsup
1 tsp. mustard
1 T. horseradish
2 tsps. salt
½ tsp. celery seed
1 T. dried (or 2 T. fresh)
  parsley, chopped
1 clove garlic, quartered
¼ cup wine vinegar
¼ cup lemon juice
1 cup vegetable oil

Mix all the ingredients in a tightly closed jar or bottle. Refrigerate. Shake occasionally to mix. Serve over a tossed salad.

Preparation time: 15 minutes   Make a day   Yield: 2 cups
                                 or 2 ahead
                                 Refrigerate

Greeta Douglass

SOUR CREAM POTATO SALAD
Very creamy and worth preparation time

2 cups mayonnaise
⅓ cup Dijon mustard (Grey
  Poupon preferred)
¼ cup cider vinegar
1½ T. sour cream
4 large dill pickles, finely
  chopped, well drained
2 medium Spanish onions,
  finely chopped
6–8 large potatoes, boiled,
  cubed, chilled
6 eggs, hard cooked, sliced,
  chilled
Salt and pepper to taste
Radishes, sliced (for
  garnish)
Fresh parsley (for garnish)
1 cup celery, chopped
  (optional)

Combine first 6 ingredients. Refrigerate several hours to blend flavors. Add potatoes and eggs; toss lightly. Season to taste with salt and pepper. Garnish with radish slices and parsley.

Option: 1 cup chopped celery may be added.

Preparation time: 1 hour

Must make ahead
Refrigerate

Serves: 6–8

Maureen Abueva
Ann Paulson

AFRICAN BANANA SALAD

2 T. raisins
2 large bananas, sliced in
  rounds
2 T. grated coconut
2–3 slices ham, diced
Juice of 1 lemon
6 T. salad oil

Soak raisins in water to soften; drain and dry. Mix together all ingredients and let stand for 1 hour. Serve with any exotic dish.

Preparation time: 15 minutes

Serves: 4

Ellen Korstange

102

HEAVENLY ORANGE FLUFF

2 pks. (3 oz. each) orange
  gelatin
2½ cups boiling water
1 can (13½ oz.) crushed
  pineapple, undrained
1 can (6 oz.) frozen
  concentrated orange juice
2 cans (11 oz. each)
  mandarin oranges,
  drained
1 pkg. (3¾ oz.) instant
  lemon pudding
1 cup cold milk
1 cup whipping cream,
  whipped
Sharp cheddar cheese,
  grated

Dissolve the gelatin in the boiling water. Add pineapple and orange juice. Chill until partially set. Fold in mandarin oranges. Pour into 9 × 13-inch pan. Chill until firm. Beat together pudding mix and milk until smooth. Fold in the whipped cream. Spread over gelatin. Chill. Sprinkle with grated sharp cheddar cheese. Cut into squares.

Preparation time: 20 minutes   Refrigerate   Serves: 10–12

Leatha Linders
Geri Penniman

SUN-AND-SNOW SALAD

1 pkg. (3 oz.) lemon gelatin
½ cup hot water
1 lb. cottage cheese
½ cup mayonnaise or salad
  dressing
1 small cucumber, chopped
1 medium onion, finely
  chopped
1 T. vinegar

Dissolve gelatin in ½ cup hot water. Mix together cottage cheese and mayonnaise. Combine all ingredients. Pour into molds.

Preparation time: 20 minutes   Must be made   Serves: 8
                                day ahead
                                Refrigerate

Barbara Beardsley

SMASHED SALAD
A favorite with children

1 head romaine lettuce
1 head iceberg lettuce
2 avocados, cut into chunks
¼ cup onion, grated
1 cup cheddar cheese,
  grated
½ cup black pitted olives,
  sliced
½ cup walnuts, chopped
½ cup Parmesan cheese,
  grated
2 cups Doritos, smashed
  (not too fine)
1 cup Catalina dressing
2 tsps. chili powder

Wash and tear lettuce. Mix in next 6 ingredients. Add Doritos at serving time. Combine Catalina dressing and chili powder. Pour over salad at last minute. Toss well.

Optional: Green peppers and tomatoes may be added for extra flavor.

Preparation time: 20 minutes

Serves: 8–10

Sally Cassell
Alice Ripley

LETTUCE-CAULIFLOWER SALAD

1 head lettuce, torn into
  bite-sized pieces
1 onion, chopped
1 head cauliflower, raw, in
  bite-size pieces
1 lb. bacon, fried crisp.
  drained, crumbled
2 cups mayonnaise
⅓ cup sugar
¼ cup Parmesan cheese,
  grated
Salt and pepper to taste

In a very large bowl, layer lettuce, onion, cauliflower, and bacon. Mix together mayonnaise, sugar, and cheese. Season to taste with salt and pepper. Pour this dressing over salad; cover tightly. Refrigerate overnight. Toss before serving.

Preparation time: 20 minutes

Must be made
day ahead
Refrigerate

Serves: 8–12

Susie Sefton

104

TOSSED ITALIAN SALAD
Good with Italian food

1 head lettuce
1 red onion, sliced into
  rings
1 pkg. slivered almonds,
  toasted
1 avocado, sliced
½ can (16 oz.) pitted small
  black olives
3–4 ozs. blue cheese,
  crumbled
1 pkg. cheese and garlic
  salad dressing mix
  (Good Seasons preferred)
Cherry tomatoes (optional)

Prepare salad dressing according to package directions. Combine salad ingredients; add dressing and toss.

Preparation time: 10 minutes

Serves: 6–8

Jan Wright

MOLDED SUMMER SPINACH SALAD
Unique use of spinach

1 pkg. (3 oz.) lemon gelatin
1 cup hot water
½ cup cold water
1½ cups mayonnaise
¼ tsp. salt
Dash of pepper
1 cup raw spinach, chopped
  (washed thoroughly and
  finely cut with scissors)
¾ cup cottage cheese
⅓ cup celery, diced
1 T. onion, grated

Dissolve gelatin in hot water. Add cold water, mayonnaise, salt, and pepper and blend in blender. Refrigerate until firm around the edges but soft in center. Blend again; add spinach, cottage cheese, celery, and onion. Pour in 1-quart mold and chill until set.

Preparation time: 30 minutes   Refrigerate   Serves: 6–8

Jan St. John

WHITE WINE-APRICOT MOLD

2 envs. unflavored gelatin
½ cup sugar
¼ tsp. salt
2 cups apricot nectar
¾ cup water
1 cup dry white wine
1 cup sour cream (room
  temperature)
Lettuce
Fresh fruit of choice:
  grapes, peaches,
  raspberries, strawberries,
  bananas, etc.

Combine gelatin, sugar, and salt in medium saucepan. Stir in nectar and water. Stir over low heat until gelatin dissolves. Remove from heat and stir in wine. Gradually blend in sour cream. Pour into 5½-cup ring mold and chill until firm. Unmold on lettuce-covered plate and fill center with fresh fruit.

Preparation time: 15 minutes   Refrigerate   Serves: 8–10

Susan Ordway

CURRIED FRUIT SALAD
A warm and spicy salad you'll love

1 can (20 oz.) pears
1 can (20 oz.) peaches
1 can (20 oz.) apricot halves
1 can (20 oz.) pineapple
  chunks
1 bottle (6 ½ oz.)
  maraschino cherries

SYRUP:
½ cup water
¼ cup butter
¾ cup brown sugar, packed
2 tsps. curry
  (more if desired)

Drain thoroughly pears, peaches, apricots, pineapple chunks, and cherries. Mix ingredients for syrup and boil for 10 minutes. Pour over fruit in low dish. Bake at 350° for 45 minutes. Serve warm.

Preparation time: 30 minutes   Serves: 8

Sharon Cerovski
Maggie Hotop

PINEAPPLE SALAD
Rich enough for a dessert

½ cup butter
1 cup sugar
3 egg yolks, beaten
1 pkg. (3 oz.) lemon gelatin
1¾ cups boiling water
1 cup crushed pineapple, drained
½ cup nuts, chopped
½ cup graham cracker crumbs
Lettuce leaves
Whipping cream, whipped (for garnish)
Maraschino cherries (for garnish)

Cream together butter and sugar. Add beaten egg yolks. Dissolve gelatin in boiling water; cool at room temperature. Add pineapple, nuts, and butter mixture. Place in 8 × 8-inch pan. Top with graham cracker crumbs. Refrigerate until firm. Serve on lettuce; top with whipped cream and maraschino cherry. Could also be served as a light dessert.

Preparation time: 20 minutes   Refrigerate   Serves: 6–8

Joan deMink

CRANBERRY RING
Pretty holiday mold

1 pkg. (3 oz.) strawberry gelatin
1 cup boiling water
1 pkg. (10 oz.) frozen cranberry relish
1 pkg. (3 oz.) lemon gelatin
1 cup boiling water
2 cups miniature marshmallows
½ cup whipping cream, whipped
1 pkg. (3 oz.) cream cheese, softened
½ cup mayonnaise
1 can (13½ oz.) crushed pineapple, drained

Dissolve strawberry gelatin in 1 cup boiling water. Add cranberry relish and stir until well blended. Pour into large ring mold and refrigerate. In a separate bowl, dissolve lemon gelatin in 1 cup boiling water, then add marshmallows and stir to dissolve. Refrigerate until cool and slightly jelled. Blend together whipping cream, cream cheese, and mayonnaise. Add pineapple and cream cheese mixture to lemon gelatin mixture. Pour this over molded strawberry gelatin and refrigerate until set.

Preparation time: 30 minutes   Refrigerate   Serves: 12

Eleanor Allen

SALAD OF GOLD

1 pkg. (3 oz.) lemon gelatin
⅔ cup very hot water
⅔ cup pineapple juice (reserved from crushed pineapple)
2 T. vinegar
⅔ cup evaporated milk
2 pkgs. (3 oz. each) cream cheese, cut in 1-inch cubes
1 cup carrots, cut in pieces
⅔ cup crushed pineapple, drained

Oil a 1-quart mold. Put gelatin and hot water in the blender and process on low speed. Add juice, vinegar, and evaporated milk. With blender on chop setting add cream cheese cubes, 1 at a time. Remove cover and add carrot pieces and pineapple; process on chop until carrots are grated. Pour into mold and chill until set.

Preparation time: 15 minutes

Refrigerate

Serves: 6–8

Jan Cornell

WAIT-A-DAY SALAD
Fresh and tangy

2 eggs, beaten
Juice of 1 lemon
4 T. sugar
2 T. butter
1 cup whipping cream, whipped
1 can (20 oz.) white cherries, drained
2 cups pineapple tidbits, drained
2 fresh oranges, peeled, sectioned
2 cups miniature marshmallows

In a double boiler, over hot water, heat and whisk eggs, lemon juice, and sugar until smooth and thick. Remove from heat. Add butter. Cool mixture; fold in whipped cream, fruit, and marshmallows. Refrigerate for 24 hours.

Preparation time: 30 minutes

Refrigerate

Serves: 10–12

Virginia DeHaven

CHILIES RELLENOS SANTA FE
Excellent Mexican Dish

5 cans (4 oz. each) whole
    green chilies
1 lb. Monterey Jack or
    Muenster cheese
5 eggs
¼ cup flour
1¼ cups milk
½ tsp. salt
Black pepper, freshly
    ground, to taste
½ tsp. oregano
Tabasco sauce to taste
Paprika to taste
½ lb. cheddar cheese,
    grated

Carefully rinse seeds from chilies in cold water and dry on paper towels. Cut Monterey Jack cheese into strips about 3 inches long × ¾ inch wide × ½ inch thick. Carefully slip a piece of cheese into each chili. Beat eggs; gradually add flour until smooth. Add milk, salt, pepper, oregano, Tabasco sauce, and paprika. Beat thoroughly. Arrange half the stuffed chilies in well-greased shallow baking dish. Spread half the grated cheddar cheese on top; repeat, ending with cheese and paprika. Carefully pour egg mixture over all. Bake, uncovered, at 350° for 45 minutes.

Preparation time: 15 minutes
Baking time: 45 minutes

Serves: 8

Sally Shipman Early

BROCCOLI AND BLUE CHEESE

2 T. butter
2 T. flour
1 pkg. (3 oz.) cream cheese,
    softened
¼ cup blue cheese,
    crumbled
1 cup milk
2 pkgs. (10 oz. each) frozen
    broccoli spears, cooked,
    or 1 bunch fresh broccoli,
    cooked
⅓ cup Ritz crackers,
    crushed

Blend butter, flour, and cheeses in pan. Add milk; cook and stir until mixture comes to a boil. Stir in broccoli. Place in 1-quart buttered casserole. Top with cracker crumbs. Bake at 350° for 30 minutes.

Microwave: Follow above procedure and then microwave on high for 2 to 3 minutes, or until heated through.

Preparation time: 15 minutes
Baking time: 30 minutes

Serves: 8–10

Dottie Early

PEARLED ONIONS IN SWEET-AND-SOUR BACON SAUCE

This sauce delicious over other vegetables, too

1½ lbs. small onions or
  equivalent amount frozen
  pearled onions
½ lb. bacon, diced
¾ cup sugar
⅓ cup vinegar
2 cups mayonnaise
  (Hellmann's preferred)

Cook onions until tender. Fry and drain bacon. Add sugar and vinegar to bacon and bring to boil. Cool. Add mayonnaise; stir. Serve over cooked onions or any favorite vegetable.

Preparation time: 20 minutes

Easy
Can make ahead

Serves: 6–8
Easily doubled

Jane Todd

SPINACH-STUFFED TOMATOES

A touch of elegance for that special dinner

6 large tomatoes, firm
2 pkgs. (10 oz. each) frozen
  chopped spinach
1 cup sour cream
3 T. flour
⅓–½ cup Parmesan cheese
½ pkg. Italian dressing mix
  (Good Seasons preferred)
½ cup soft bread crumbs
2 T. butter

Wash tomatoes; cut off top ¼. Scoop out seeds and pulp. Turn upside down to drain. Cook spinach. *Drain well;* squeeze dry. Place cooked spinach in a saucepan. Mix sour cream with flour, Parmesan cheese, and salad dressing mix; add to spinach. Cook mixture over medium heat until thickened. Place tomato shells in casserole with sides to support them. Fill shells with spinach stuffing. Top with bread crumbs sautéed in butter. Bake at 350° for 20 minutes.

Microwave: Prepare according to directions above, using glass casserole. Microwave stuffed tomatoes on high for 4 to 5 minutes, or until heated through.

Preparation time: 20 minutes
Cooking time: 20 minutes
Microwave: 4–5 minutes

Serves: 6

Barbara Beardsley

Please note: Microwave directions in this book are for use with units having 600–700 watts (and above). If unit with lower wattage is used, baking times will need to be lengthened.

FESTIVE SPINACH RING
Lovely for a holiday dinner or buffet

2 lbs. fresh spinach or
  2 pkgs. (10 oz. each)
  frozen spinach
1 cup sour cream
¼ cup sherry
3 eggs, beaten
2 T. onion, grated
¼ tsp. nutmeg
Salt
Pepper

Cook spinach. Rinse, drain, and squeeze dry. Combine with remaining ingredients. Pour into greased 1½-quart ring mold. Place mold in jelly roll pan in which there is ¼ to ½ inch water. Bake at 350° for 40 to 45 minutes. Let set for 5 to 10 minutes. Unmold. Fill center with Sherried Onions (see below).

Preparation time: 20 minutes
Baking time: 40–45 minutes

Serves: 8–10

Greeta Douglass

SHERRIED ONIONS

20 small or 5 medium
  onions
3 T. butter
3 T. flour
1½ cups milk
Salt and pepper to taste
½ tsp. nutmeg
1½ ozs. sherry
Paprika

Cook onions until tender—about 10 to 15 minutes. Do not overcook. Slip onions out of skins. If using medium onions, quarter them. To make a roux, melt butter and blend in flour. Gradually add milk, stirring until thick. Add salt, pepper, nutmeg, and sherry. Pour mixture over onions. Serve in middle of Festive Spinach Ring. Sprinkle with paprika.

Preparation time: 20 minutes

Serves: 6

Greeta Douglass

EASY HOLLANDAISE
Delicious over asparagus or broccoli

½ cup sour cream
½ cup mayonnaise
1 tsp. prepared mustard
2 tsps. lemon juice

Combine all ingredients and cook over low heat, stirring constantly until just heated.

Preparation time: 5 minutes   Easy   Yield: 1 cup
Easily doubled

Sharon Garside

112

ASPARAGUS WITH TARRAGON HOLLANDAISE
A unique and versatile sauce

2 lbs. fresh asparagus,
  cooked, or equivalent
  amount of frozen
  asparagus
¼ lb. butter or margarine
¼ tsp. basil
¼ tsp. tarragon
¼ tsp. thyme
1 tsp. Worcestershire sauce
Juice of 1 lemon
3–4 T. Miracle Whip or
  mayonnaise
1 egg

Steam asparagus until tender and serve hot with the following sauce.

Sauce: Melt butter or margarine and add remaining ingredients except Miracle Whip and egg. With a wire whisk or beater, blend in Miracle Whip. Remove from heat and add egg just before ready to serve. If sauce is too thin, add a little more Miracle Whip. Bring to room temperature before serving over asparagus. Sauce is also good over cauliflower or Brussels sprouts or as a dip for artichokes.

Preparation time: 20 minutes   Easy   Serves: 8–10

Greeta Douglass

CLARE'S ONION TART
Marvelous not only for a luncheon but as an accompaniment for beef

1 (10-inch) or 2 (8-inch)
  pastry shells, baked
2 cups onions, sliced
6 T. butter
4 T. flour
2½ cups half-and-half
Salt and pepper to taste
Dash of nutmeg
5 eggs, beaten
½ cup sour cream
1 cup Swiss cheese, grated
4 T. Parmesan cheese

Sauté onions in 2 tablespoonfuls butter until soft and translucent. Make a roux by melting remaining butter and stirring in flour. Gradually add half-and-half, stirring over low heat until smooth and thickened. Add salt, pepper, and nutmeg. Cool slightly. Add eggs. Mix in sour cream and Swiss cheese. Place onions in pastry shell or shells; pour in cheese-cream mixture. Sprinkle with Parmesan cheese. Bake at 350° for 30 to 45 minutes, or until set.

Preparation time: 30 minutes   Can make ahead   Serves: 8
Baking time: 30–45 minutes   and reheat
                                 Can freeze

Susan Brown

113

EGGPLANT TOWERS

1 small eggplant, sliced
    into ½-inch pieces
Butter
Olive oil
2 medium onions, thinly
    sliced
2 medium tomatoes, sliced
3 T. mayonnaise
1 tsp. oregano
½ tsp. garlic salt
Parmesan cheese

Place eggplant slices on buttered baking sheet in a single layer. Brush both sides of slices with olive oil. Bake at 325° for 15 minutes. Top each eggplant slice with a slice of onion; bake for 5 minutes more. Place a tomato slice on top of each onion slice; spread with mixture of mayonnaise, oregano, and garlic salt. Bake for an additional 10 minutes. Sprinkle with Parmesan cheese and broil until cheese melts.

Preparation time: 10 minutes
Baking time: 30 minutes

Serves: 4

Sally Shipman Early

SAUTÉED ARTICHOKES AND TOMATOES
Beautiful served in center of a crown roast

¼ cup butter or margarine
½ cup onion, minced
1 clove garlic, minced
2 pts. cherry tomatoes,
    hulled, washed
2 cans (8½ oz. each)
    artichoke bottoms,
    drained, quartered
½ tsp. salt
¼ tsp. pepper
2 T. fresh parsley, chopped

Heat butter in large skillet over medium heat. Add onion; sauté for 2 minutes. Add garlic, tomatoes, artichokes, salt, and pepper. Cover. Cook for 2 to 3 minutes, or just until tomatoes are soft, stirring occasionally. Arrange around roast on serving platter or turn into serving dish. Sprinkle with parsley.

Preparation time: 15 minutes

Serves: 6–8

Sharon Garside

EUROPEAN-STYLE CARROTS

2 T. butter
1 medium onion, finely
   chopped
2 T. flour
1–2 T. fresh parsley,
   chopped
8 medium carrots, coarsely
   grated
Salt and pepper to taste
⅓ cup water

Melt butter in saucepan. Add onion and cook until transparent. Stir in flour and chopped parsley. Add grated carrots; mix well. Add salt, pepper, and water. Simmer, covered, until carrots are cooked (water should be absorbed)—about 15 minutes.

Preparation time: 10 minutes
Cooking time: 15 minutes

Easy

Serves: 6–8

Louisa Paulson

BROCCOLI AND ARTICHOKE CASSEROLE

1 can (8 oz.) artichoke
   hearts, rinsed, drained
2 pkgs. (10 oz. each)
   frozen chopped broccoli,
   cooked, drained
1 pkg. (8 oz.) cream
   cheese, softened
¼ cup butter, melted
1 tsp. lemon juice
Salt and pepper to taste
3 slices white bread,
   buttered, cubed

Grease 8-inch pie plate and arrange artichoke hearts on bottom. Combine all other ingredients and spread over artichokes. Top with buttered bread cubes. Bake at 350° for 30 minutes.

Microwave: Prepare as above except brown bread cubes in butter. Top casserole with browned bread cubes; microwave on high for 3 to 4 minutes, or until hot.

Preparation time: 20 minutes
Baking time: 30 minutes

Serves: 6

Linda Brown

BAKED MUSHROOMS

1 cup milk
4 ozs. cheddar cheese,
  grated
1 T. onion, grated
1 tsp. salt
¼ tsp. mustard
1 egg, beaten
1½ lbs. fresh mushrooms
1 pkg. (10 oz.) frozen
  spinach

Combine milk with cheese, onion, salt, mustard, and egg. Add mushrooms; pour into shallow baking dish. Bake at 375° for 30 minutes, or until set firm. While mushrooms are baking, prepare spinach according to package directions. Drain well. Before serving, arrange spinach around edge of mushroom dish.

Preparation time: 15 minutes
Baking time: 30 minutes

Serves: 4–6

Jeanne Miller

MORNAY SAUCE
Turns any vegetable into a gourmet delight

¼ cup butter
¼ cup flour, sifted
2 cups half-and-half
¼ cup Parmesan cheese
½ tsp. salt
Pinch of nutmeg
Pinch of thyme
⅛ tsp. garlic salt
2 T. white wine or sherry

To make a roux, melt butter and stir in flour. Add half-and-half and stir until thickened. Add cheese, seasonings, and wine. Stir until thick. Pour over any combination of vegetables.

Preparation time: 20 minutes   Can make ahead   Yield: 2 cups

Mary Jo Garling

VEGETABLES SUPREME

1 fresh whole cauliflower
  or 1 pkg. (10 oz.) frozen
  cauliflower
1 bunch fresh broccoli or
  1 pkg. (10 oz.) frozen
  broccoli spears

Steam vegetables until almost done. Put into 2-quart buttered baking dish. Cover with soup, Parmesan cheese, and onions. Bake, covered, at 350° for 15 minutes; remove cover and bake for 15 minutes longer.

(continued)

VEGETABLES SUPREME (continued)

1 can (10¾ oz.) condensed
  cream of mushroom soup
½ cup Parmesan cheese,
  freshly grated
1 can (3 oz.) French fried
  onions

Microwave: Follow above directions, using 2-quart glass baking dish. Microwave on high for 4 to 5 minutes, or until heated through.

Preparation time: 20 minutes
Cooking time: 30 minutes
Microwave: 4–5 minutes

Easy
Can make ahead

Serves: 6–8

Betty Van Kley

ASPARAGUS WITH ORANGE HOLLANDAISE

4 T. butter or margarine
2 egg yolks
¼ tsp. orange peel, grated
1 tsp. orange juice
Dash of salt
Dash of white pepper
¼ cup sour cream
16 oz. fresh asparagus,
  cooked, drained
Orange peel, shredded
  (for garnish)

Cut butter or margarine into 3 portions. In small heavy saucepan, combine egg yolks and ⅓ of the butter. Cook and stir over low heat until butter melts. Add ⅓ more of the butter and continue stirring. As mixture thickens and butter melts, add remaining butter, stirring constantly. When butter is melted, remove from heat; stir in orange peel, orange juice, salt, and white pepper. Return to heat and stir constantly until thickened—2 to 3 minutes. Remove from heat at once. Blend hot egg yolk mixture into sour cream. Spoon over each serving of asparagus. Garnish with shredded orange peel, if desired.

Preparation time: 30 minutes

Serves: 4–5

Sharon Garside

Hint: To make garlic potatoes, peel and shred 8 large potatoes. Place in ovenproof serving dish. Pour about 3 pints whipping cream (unwhipped) over potatoes until covered and approximately ¼ inch above the potatoes. Stir about ¼ bottle (3½ oz.) garlic salt into potato-cream mixture. Bake, uncovered, at 350° for 1 hour, or until brown. Serves 6 to 8.

Susan Holley

SPINACH WITH ARTICHOKES

4 pkgs. (10 oz.) chopped
  frozen spinach
11 ozs. cream cheese
5 T. butter or margarine,
  melted
Juice of 1 lemon
Salt
Pepper
Seasoned salt
Several dashes of ground
  nutmeg
2 cans (16 oz. each)
  artichoke hearts, drained
  thoroughly

Cook spinach according to package directions only until completely thawed; drain. Bring cream cheese to room temperature; soften well, then blend in melted butter until smooth. Add lemon juice; combine with spinach. Stir in all seasonings; blend well and check taste. Place artichoke hearts in 8 × 16-inch baking dish. Spoon spinach over artichokes. Cover with aluminum foil. Punch a few holes in foil and bake at 350° for 30 minutes.

Note: May be assembled in morning and refrigerated. Remove from refrigerator 1 hour before baking.

Preparation time: 15 minutes
Baking time: 30 minutes

Serves: 8–10

Barbara Long

SPINACH TART

1 lb. fresh spinach
2 T. butter, melted
3 eggs
6 T. whipping cream,
  unwhipped
2 cups Parmesan cheese,
  grated
1 cup ricotta cheese
½ tsp. salt
½ tsp. nutmeg
½ tsp. pepper
8 or 9-inch pie shell,
  unbaked
Dijon mustard (optional)
1 tsp. lemon juice (optional)

Wash and trim spinach; do not dry. Place spinach in covered pan with a little water. Cook about 3 minutes, or until wilted. Drain and chop. Blend butter into spinach; set aside. In another bowl, lightly beat eggs; add whipping cream, cheeses, and seasonings to eggs. Blend in the spinach mixture. Pour into pie shell. Bake at 350° for 35 to 40 minutes, or until mixture is set. For a spicy tang, spread pie shell with Dijon mustard, add spinach, and sprinkle with lemon juice.

Preparation time: 10 minutes
Baking time: 35–40 minutes

Serves: 8

118

PRYSNIC-BROCCOLI PUFF

3 pkgs. (10 oz. each)
  frozen chopped broccoli,
  cooked, drained
6 T. flour
¼ lb. margarine
½ lb. cheddar cheese,
  shredded
1½ lbs. small curd cottage
  cheese
Salt, pepper, and oregano
  to taste
6 eggs, beaten

Place broccoli in buttered 2½-quart casserole dish. Mix the flour, margarine, and cheeses and cook over low heat just until blended. Stir in spices. Add eggs. Mix well and pour over broccoli. Bake at 350° for 1 hour.

Preparation time: 20 minutes
Baking time: 1 hour

Serves: 8–10

Nancy Maza

VEGETABLE FANTASIA
A gourmet delight

4 pkgs. (10 oz. each) frozen
  chopped broccoli
½ lb. mushrooms, sliced
¼ cup + 2 T. butter (divided)
½ cup mayonnaise
½ cup sour cream
½ cup Parmesan cheese
1 can (8 ½ oz.) artichokes,
  drained
Salt and pepper to taste
3 tomatoes
½ cup dry bread crumbs

Cook broccoli according to package directions. Drain. Sauté mushrooms in 2 tablespoonfuls butter. Combine mayonnaise, sour cream, and Parmesan cheese. Stir in artichokes, broccoli, and mushrooms. Season to taste with salt and pepper. Pour into greased 9 × 13-inch baking dish. Slice tomatoes ½ inch thick; place on broccoli. Sauté bread crumbs in ¼ cup butter until browned. Sprinkle over casserole. Bake at 325° for 20 minutes.

Preparation time: 15 minutes
Baking time: 20 minutes

Easy
Can make ahead

Serves: 6–8

Susan Brown

Hint: Mix equal parts mashed cooked cauliflower and potatoes (approximately 2 cups each). Add 2 tablespoonfuls whipping cream, ½ cup butter, and salt and pepper to taste. Serve in casserole dotted with butter and sprinkled with chives, parsley, and paprika, or pipe around roast. Serves 6.

Sharon Garside

VEGETABLES IN ITALIAN BEER BATTER

12 ozs. beer
Vegetable oil (for frying)
1⅓ cups flour, sifted
2 T. Parmesan cheese,
  grated
1 T. parsley, snipped
1 tsp. salt
Dash of garlic salt or
  powder
1 T. olive oil
2 egg yolks, beaten
2 egg whites, stiffly beaten
Choice of vegetables:
  Zucchini; green pepper,
  cut in strips; cauliflower
  buds; small whole
  mushrooms; onion rings;
  eggplant, peeled, diced

Open beer and let stand at room temperature until flat—about 45 minutes. Preheat oil in deep fryer to 375°. In mixing bowl, combine flour, Parmesan cheese, parsley, salt, and garlic salt. Stir in olive oil, egg yolks, and flat beer; beat until smooth. Fold in egg whites. Dip vegetables in batter and fry in oil for 2 to 5 minutes, or until brown.

Preparation time: 15 minutes
Cooking time: 30 minutes

Serve immediately

Serves: 8

Ann Paulson

ARTICHOKES WITH PIQUANT CHEESE SAUCE

4 artichokes
2 pkgs. (3 oz. each) cream
  cheese, softened
1 T. water
2½ tsps. Beau Monde
  seasoning (Spice Islands)
¼ tsp. thyme
¼ tsp. marjoram
¼ tsp. summer savory
4 T. parsley
Dijon mustard to taste

Prepare artichokes for cooking by removing outer 2 or 3 rows of leaves and cutting off stem flush with bottom so that it will set upright in pan. Next cut off top third. Place artichoke in a pan with about 2 inches of water; steam for about 45 minutes, or until leaves pull apart easily. Remove from pan and cool. With a spoon, scoop out choke (the feathery purplish center leaves). Serve with sauce which has been prepared by combining cream cheese with water and spices until blended. Fill center of each artichoke with sauce. May also be served warm.

Preparation time: 20 minutes
Cooking time: 45 minutes

Can make ahead

Serves: 4

120

EGGPLANT PARMESAN
Especially good with lamb

1 large (about 1¼–1⅓ lb.)
  eggplant
2 eggs, beaten
1 cup dry Italian-seasoned
  bread crumbs
¾ cup salad oil
½ cup Parmesan cheese
2 tsps. dried oregano
1½ cups tomato sauce
½ lb. mozzarella cheese,
  sliced

Pare and slice eggplant. Dip each slice in egg and then in crumbs. Sauté in oil until brown on both sides. Place eggplant in a buttered 2-quart casserole. Sprinkle with Parmesan cheese and oregano. Cover well with tomato sauce. Repeat layers until all eggplant is used. Top last layer with mozzarella cheese. Bake at 350° for 30 minutes.

Microwave: Prepare eggplant as directed above, using glass casserole. Do not add the mozzarella cheese. Microwave on high for 14 to 16 minutes. Add mozzarella cheese and microwave on high for 1 minute, or until cheese melts.

Preparation time: 30 minutes
Baking time: 30 minutes
Microwave: 14–16 minutes

Serves: 6–8

Joy Hecht

CHEESE-PUFFED POTATOES

5 medium potatoes
⅓ cup sour cream
1½ cups small curd cottage
  cheese
1 T. onion, minced
½ tsp. salt
½ tsp. pepper
2 T. butter, melted, or 4 ozs.
  cheese, grated

Peel potatoes. Boil until tender. Drain; mash with sour cream. Add cottage cheese, onion, salt, and pepper. Place in 1½-quart casserole. Drizzle with melted butter or grated cheese. Bake, uncovered, at 350° for 30 to 35 minutes.

Microwave: Prepare as for above, using 1½-quart glass casserole. Microwave, covered and without cheese, on high for 6 to 8 minutes. Sprinkle with cheese after removed from oven.

Preparation time:
  20–25 minutes
Baking time: 30–35 minutes
Microwave: 6–8 minutes

Easy
Can make ahead

Serves: 6–8

Diane Basso

121

RUSSIAN VEGETABLE PIE

PASTRY:

1¼ cups flour
1 tsp. salt
1 tsp. sugar
3 T. butter
4–6 T. cold water

FILLING:

1 pkg. (3 oz.) cream cheese,
  softened
3 eggs, hard cooked, sliced
1 small head cabbage,
  shredded
1 onion, sliced
4 T. butter (divided)
⅛ tsp. salt
⅛ tsp. pepper
⅛ tsp. basil
⅛ tsp. marjoram
⅛ tsp. tarragon
½ lb. fresh mushrooms,
  sliced

Sift together flour, salt, and sugar. Cut in butter until well blended and particles are size of small crumbs. Add water; mix quickly and gently. Turn onto lightly floured board and knead lightly 9 to 10 times. Roll out pastry and fit ⅔ into bottom of 9-inch pie plate.

Spread cream cheese over crust. Top with layer of hard-cooked eggs; layer of grated cabbage, onion, and seasonings sautéed in 3 tablespoonfuls butter; and layer of mushrooms sautéed in 1 tablespoonful butter. Add top pie-crust. Slit crust and bake at 400° for 15 minutes; lower to 350° and bake for 25 minutes longer.

Preparation time: 30 minutes
Baking time: 40 minutes

Serves: 8

Jan Wright

SQUASH PIE

Pastry for double crust
2 lbs. (or larger) butternut
  squash
4 tsps. brown sugar
½ cup butter or margarine
3 egg yolks, slightly beaten
½ tsp. nutmeg
½ cup onion, finely chopped
1 T. lemon juice
Dash of salt
Dash of flour
1 cup apples, chopped
3 egg whites, stiffly beaten

Line 2-quart baking dish with pastry. Pierce squash in 2 to 3 places and put on baking sheet. Bake at 350° for 45 minutes, or until tender. Remove seeds. Scoop out meat and place in large mixing bowl. Set aside. In another bowl blend sugar and butter. Add egg yolks; blend. Add nutmeg, onion, lemon juice, salt, and flour; blend. Add squash; blend. Stir in apples and then egg whites. Place in pastry-lined dish. Bake at 375° for approximately 1 hour, or until a silver knife inserted near center comes out clean. Let stand before serving.

Preparation time: 1 hour
Baking time: 1 hour

Serves: 6

Gerald deMink

GOURMET GREEN BEANS

1 pkg. (10 oz.) frozen
  French-cut green beans
3 T. butter (divided)
2 T. flour
¼ tsp. salt
¼ tsp. pepper
¼ tsp. Aćcent
1 cup sour cream
1 tsp. prepared mustard
½ cup Swiss cheese,
  shredded
2 T. minced onion
¼ cup bread crumbs

Cook beans according to package directions; drain. Melt 1 tablespoonful butter; add flour, salt, pepper, and Aćcent. Heat until bubbly. Remove from heat; gradually add sour cream and mustard. Heat, stirring constantly, but DO NOT BOIL. Add beans, cheese, and onion to sauce. Put in casserole. Sauté bread crumbs in 2 tablespoonfuls butter. Top mixture with buttered crumbs. Bake at 350° for 15 minutes.

Microwave: Microwave green beans for 6 to 7 minutes on high in a covered glass casserole. Drain. Microwave 1 tablespoonful butter and bread crumbs on high for 1 to 2 minutes, or until golden. Melt 2 tablespoonfuls butter in microwave on high for 30 seconds. Stir in flour, salt, pepper, and Aćcent until smooth. Gradually stir in sour cream and mustard. Microwave, uncovered, on high for 2 to 3 minutes. Combine beans, cheese, and sauce in casserole. Top with toasted bread crumbs. Heat in microwave on high until hot.

Preparation time: 15 minutes	Can make ahead	Serves: 4
Baking time: 15 minutes		Easily doubled
Microwave: 10–15 minutes		

Linda Brown

ZUCCHINI CASSEROLE ITALIENNE

4 medium zucchini, peeled,
  sliced
½ green pepper, chopped
2 ripe tomatoes, sliced
6 slices bacon, chopped,
  fried
1½ cups Parmesan cheese,
  grated
⅓ cup onion, chopped
1½ tsps. salt
½ cup fine bread crumbs
2 T. butter, melted

Parboil zucchini. Drain. In buttered 1-quart casserole, layer zucchini, green pepper, tomatoes, bacon, cheese, onion, and salt. Cover top with bread crumbs mixed with melted butter. Bake at 375° for 35 minutes.

Preparation time: 30 minutes	Can make ahead	Serves: 6
Baking time: 35 minutes		

Wendy Field

POJOAQUE CHILI PEPPER PIE
Marvelous with Mexican dinner

4 cans (4 oz. each) chopped
  green chilies
2 cups cheese (cheddar,
  colby, or Monterey Jack),
  grated
2 eggs, beaten

Empty chilies into 9 or 10-inch pie plate. Cover peppers with cheese (should cover by about ½ inch). Pour eggs over all. Bake at 350° for about 20 to 25 minutes, or until melted and slightly browned on top.

Preparation time: 10 minutes
Baking time: 20–25 minutes

Easy

Serves: 8

Frances Shipman

WILD RICE IN CREAM

1 lb. fresh mushrooms,
  sliced
6 T. butter
4 T. flour
½ cup half-and-half
4 T. Worcestershire sauce
Salt and pepper to taste
2 pkgs. (8 oz. each) cream
  cheese, softened
2 cups cooked wild rice

Brown mushrooms in 4 tablespoonfuls butter. To make cream sauce, melt 2 tablespoonfuls butter. Blend in flour; gradually add half-and-half. Cook until thickened. Add Worcestershire sauce and salt and pepper to taste. Add cream cheese to cream sauce; stir until melted. Add mushrooms and wild rice. Put into a buttered casserole. Bake at 350° for 20 minutes.

Preparation time: 20 minutes
Baking time: 20 minutes

Serves: 8–10

Susan Brown

GREEN CHILIES AND RICE

4 cups cooked rice
1½ pts. sour cream
1 or 2 cans (4 oz. each)
  green chilies
Salt and pepper to taste
½ lb. Monterey Jack cheese,
  sliced
⅓–½ cup cheddar cheese,
  shredded

In a large casserole dish, layer rice, sour cream, chilies, salt, pepper, and Monterey Jack. Repeat layers 2 more times. Omit Monterey Jack from top layer. Bake at 350° for 20 to 25 minutes. Sprinkle cheddar cheese on the top for the last 5 minutes of baking.

Preparation time: 20 minutes
Baking time: 25 minutes

Serves: 10–12

Ginny Scott

ZUCCHINI-SOUR CREAM CASSEROLE

3 medium zucchini
¼ cup sour cream
1 T. butter
½ cup + 3 T. sharp cheese,
  grated (divided)
½ tsp. salt
1 egg yolk, beaten
½ onion, finely chopped
¾ cup bread crumbs,
  buttered

Slice zucchini horizontally; simmer, covered, in small amount of water for 6 to 8 minutes. Drain well. Combine sour cream, butter, 3 tablespoonfuls cheese, and salt. Stir over hot water in double boiler until cheese melts. Stir in egg yolk and onion. Add all this to zucchini; turn into buttered 3-quart casserole. Sprinkle top with buttered bread crumbs and ½ cup cheese. Bake at 350° for 20 minutes.

Preparation time: 20 minutes
Baking time: 20 minutes

Serves: 4–6

Barbara Beardsley

EGGPLANT-MUSHROOM CASSEROLE
Excellent—deserves a 5-star rating

2 medium (about 1 lb. each) eggplants, cut in 1½-inch cubes
1 large onion, thinly sliced
½ cup butter or margarine
½ lb. fresh mushrooms (larger ones, quartered; smaller ones, halved)
2 cloves garlic, minced
1 can (28 oz.) Italian tomatoes, sliced lengthwise, seeds removed, well drained
⅛ tsp. aniseed
1½ tsps. salt
¼ tsp. pepper
2 T. dry sherry
2 T. ruby port
⅓ cup Romano cheese, freshly grated

Cover eggplant and onion with water and simmer for about 15 minutes, or until done, stirring several times to cook evenly. Drain well; squeeze out excess liquid. While eggplant is cooking, sauté mushrooms and garlic in butter until golden and water from mushrooms is evaporated. Add tomatoes, aniseed, salt, pepper, sherry, port, and cooked eggplant and onion. Mix well. Spoon into 2½-quart casserole; top with Romano cheese. Bake at 350° for 30 minutes.

Microwave: Place eggplant, onion, and 2 tablespoonfuls water in covered 2½-quart glass casserole. Microwave on high for 12 to 14 minutes per pound, or until tender. Stir occasionally. Drain well; squeeze out excess liquid. Sauté mushrooms, garlic, and butter in microwave on high for 1 minute, stirring after 30 seconds. Add mushrooms, garlic, tomatoes, aniseed, salt, pepper, sherry, and port to cooked eggplant. Mix well; cover. Microwave on high for 5 to 7 minutes, or until hot. Sprinkle with Romano cheese. Serve immediately.

Preparation time: 30 minutes
Baking time: 30 minutes
Microwave: 30–35 minutes

Serves: 6

Nan Goldenthal

VEGETABLE SAUCE

¼ cup sharp cheese, grated
½ cup butter or margarine
¼ tsp. dry mustard

Cream together all ingredients and spread over hot cooked vegetables. Especially good with Brussels sprouts, broccoli, and cauliflower.

Preparation time: 5 minutes

Easy
Can make ahead

Yield: ¾ cup

Ann Paulson

BRAISED BROCCOLI PARMESAN
Deliciously simple

2 bunches fresh broccoli or 3 pkgs. (10 oz. each) frozen chopped broccoli, thawed
1 T. butter
1 Spanish onion, cut into lengthwise strips
½ cup chicken broth, boiling
½ cup Parmesan cheese, grated

Trim the broccoli stems, cutting them off about ½ inch from the ends. Discard. Chop the broccoli coarsely. Melt butter in heavy pan. Cook onion strips in melted butter until limp, but not browned. Add broccoli and toss lightly to coat well with butter and mix with onion strips. Pour boiling broth over vegetables; cover tightly and simmer for 8 minutes. Drain well. Sprinkle with Parmesan cheese and serve at once.

Preparation time: 20 minutes
Cooking time: 8 minutes

Easy

Serves: 8

Shirley Weiss

GREEN NOODLES SUPREME
A delightful departure from regular noodles

1 pkg. (7 oz.) spinach noodles
2 cups yellow onions, thinly sliced
2 cups fresh mushrooms, sliced
½ cup butter
1 cup whipping cream, unwhipped
1 cup sour cream
1 cup Parmesan cheese, freshly grated

Cook noodles according to package directions. Drain; rinse in cold water. Brown onions and mushrooms in butter. Add whipping cream and sour cream to this mixture. Mix in a large bowl with noodles. Pour into a 1-quart casserole. Cover with Parmesan cheese. Bake at 350° for 20 minutes.

Preparation time: 30 minutes
Baking time: 20 minutes

Can make ahead

Serves: 8–10

Susan Brown

Hint: To cook wild rice, place ¾ cup wild rice, 1 can consommé or chicken broth, and ½ soup can water in a casserole. Bake at 350° for 1½ hours, or until done.

Susan Brown

HASH BROWNS AU GRATIN

2 lbs. frozen hash brown
  potatoes
1 tsp. salt
¼ tsp. pepper
½ cup onion, chopped
2 cups sharp American
  cheese, grated
¾ cup butter or margarine,
  melted (divided)
1 pt. sour cream
1 can (10¾ oz.) condensed
  cream of chicken soup
2 cups corn flakes, crushed
  (optional)

Thaw potatoes; add salt, pepper, onion, and cheese. Melt ½ cup butter or margarine; add sour cream and soup. Pour over potato mixture and mix gently. Put in 3-quart buttered casserole. If desired, melt ¼ cup butter or margarine; add corn flakes and sprinkle over top. Bake at 350° for 45 minutes.

Preparation time: 15 minutes
Baking time: 45 minutes

Easy
Can make ahead

Serves: 8

Jan Orwin

MUSHROOMS ST. MORITZ
Wonderful as an appetizer, too

1 lb. fresh mushrooms
3 T. butter
2 T. flour
½ tsp. salt
½ tsp. pepper
½ tsp. tarragon
1 clove garlic, crushed
¼ cup sour cream
1 cup Swiss cheese, grated
1 tsp. chopped parsley

Wash, dry, and quarter mushrooms. Sauté in butter for 5 minutes. Add flour; stir and cook for 1 minute. Add seasonings and sour cream; blend and cook until bubbly. Combine mushroom mixture with grated cheese. Spoon into baking dish. Bake at 350° until cheese has melted and mushrooms are hot. Sprinkle with parsley; serve immediately.

This can also be served in individual dishes topped with a slice of cold liver pâté.

Preparation time: 20 minutes
Baking time: 15 minutes

Easy
Can make ahead
Serve immediately

Serves: 4–6

Sue Kilgore

GRILLED MUSHROOM SANDWICHES

Delicious for luncheon served with chilled cucumber soup

1 large onion, finely
  chopped
1 T. butter
1 lb. fresh mushrooms,
  finely chopped
1 tsp. salt
½ tsp. pepper
12 ozs. cream cheese,
  softened
1 tsp. Worcestershire sauce
½ tsp. garlic powder
1 large loaf thin-sliced
  bread (Pepperidge Farm
  preferred)

Sauté onion in butter. Add mushrooms; sauté for 2 minutes. Remove from heat; season with salt and pepper. Add cream cheese; mix until smooth. Stir in other seasonings. Cool. Spread mixture on 1 slice of bread and top with another. Grill in butter until bread is golden.

Preparation time: 15 minutes

Can be frozen
before being grilled

Yield: 12 or more
sandwiches

Susan Brown

OUTDOOR STEAK SANDWICH SUPREME

Ideal for a backyard barbecue

2–3 lbs. flank steak
10 ozs. vegetable oil
1 bottle (10 oz.) A.1. Steak
  Sauce
1 T. Worcestershire sauce
¼ tsp. pepper
½ tsp. dry mustard
1 T. sugar
¼ tsp. garlic salt
¼ tsp. onion salt
1 T. soy sauce

Cut steak into ½-inch strips. Combine remaining ingredients; mix well. Marinate steak strips in mixture all day or overnight. Stir occasionally so that marinade reaches all strips. Grill over coals until done—doesn't take long. Serve in elongated buns or Crusty White Rolls (see page 70). If grilled ahead, drizzle a little more marinade over steak and keep warm by wrapping in foil.

Preparation time: 15 minutes
Cooking time:
About 5–10 minutes

Must make
day ahead

Serves: 8–12

Jackie Schaefer

STROGANOFF STEAK SANDWICH
Ideal for a Sunday supper

⅔ cup beer
⅓ cup cooking oil
1 tsp. salt
¼ tsp. garlic powder
¼ tsp. pepper
2 lbs. flank steak, 1 inch
  thick
2 T. butter
½ tsp. paprika
Dash of salt
4 cups onion, sliced
12 slices French bread,
  toasted
1 cup sour cream, warmed
½ tsp. prepared horseradish

In shallow dish, combine beer, oil, salt, garlic powder, and pepper. Place flank steak in marinade; cover. Marinate overnight in refrigerator; drain. Broil steak 3 inches from heat for 5 to 7 minutes on each side for medium rare.

In the meantime, melt butter in saucepan. Blend in paprika and salt. Add onion; cook until tender but not brown. Thinly slice meat on the diagonal across the grain. For each serving, arrange meat slices over 2 slices of bread or Crusty White Rolls (see page 70). Top with onions. Combine sour cream and horseradish; spoon onto each sandwich. Sprinkle with paprika, if desired.

Preparation time: 20 minutes
  plus marinating time
Cooking time: 5–7 minutes

Must make
day ahead

Serves: 6

Sue Kilgore

BEEF STICK
Easy and fun to make

5 lbs. hamburger
5 tsps. Morton Tender Quick
  salt
2½ tsps. mustard seed
2 T. black pepper, ground
2½ tsps. garlic salt
1 tsp. hickory smoked salt
  or 1 tsp. liquid smoke

Combine all ingredients in bowl; refrigerate. Knead once a day for 3 days. On fourth day, knead and shape into 4 to 6 rolls; work with until solid. Place on rack in broiler pan to catch grease. Bake at 150° for 10 hours. Cool; refrigerate or freeze.

Preparation time: 4 days
Baking time: 10 hours

Easy
Must make ahead
Can freeze

Makes: 4–6
sticks

Nancy Jacobs

SLOPPY JOES

1 T. flour
1 T. Chili con Carne
  seasoning (Spice Islands)
1 tsp. garlic salt
1 tsp. salt
¼–½ tsp. cumin seed,
  crushed
1 tsp. sugar
Pepper, freshly ground, to
  taste
1 can (6 oz.) tomato paste
1¼ cups water
1 tsp. Worcestershire
  sauce (Lea & Perrins
  preferred)
2 T. margarine
2–3 T. celery, finely
  chopped
2–3 T. onion, finely
  chopped
1 lb. ground chuck
1 can (4 oz.) sliced
  mushrooms, drained

In small bowl, mix together first 7 ingredients. In 2-cup measuring cup, mix together tomato paste, water, and Worcestershire sauce. In margarine, sauté celery and onions. When soft, turn up heat. Add ground chuck; brown. Drain off fat; stir in dry mixture. When they are thoroughly mixed, add tomato paste mixture and mushrooms. Bring to a boil, lower heat to simmer, cover, and cook for 10 to 15 minutes more. Serve open-faced on toasted hamburger buns.

Note: Chili powder may be substituted for Chili con Carne seasoning. Mushroom may be omitted.

Preparation time: 30 minutes
Cooking time: 10–15 minutes

Can make ahead

Serves: 4

Ann Paulson

Devilish Hamburger Hint: To 1 pound ground beef, add 3 tablespoonfuls chili sauce, 1 tablespoonful minced onion, 1 teaspoonful Worcestershire sauce, 2 teaspoonfuls horseradish, 1 teaspoonful spicy mustard, ¼ cup bread crumbs, 1 clove pressed garlic, a dash of mace, 3 tablespoonfuls red wine, and salt and freshly ground pepper to taste. Shape into patties and broil to your preference.

GREEK-STYLE SANDWICHES

1 cup dry red wine
2 T. oil
1 small clove garlic, minced
½ tsp. oregano
½ tsp. salt
Dash of pepper, freshly
  ground
1¼ lbs. sirloin steak, ½ inch
  thick
1 T. butter

ACCOMPANIMENTS:
Lettuce, chopped
Tomato, chopped
Cucumber, chopped
Sour cream with chives dip
Horseradish dip

Combine first 6 ingredients for marinade. Cut steak into strips 2 inches long and ¼ inch wide. Pour marinade over beef; let set at room temperature for 1 hour (as long as 24 hours in refrigerator). Drain meat; cook half at a time in butter. Stir to brown on all sides—about 2 to 3 minutes. Serve in Syrian pocket bread or Arabic Bread (see page 78). Accompany with lettuce, tomato, cucumber, and sour cream with chives dip or horseradish dip.

Preparation time: 20 minutes
  plus marinating time
Cooking time: 20 minutes

Can marinate
night before

Serves: 4

Kathie Shellenbarger

NEW MEXICO OPEN-FACED SANDWICH

4 slices rye bread
2 T. mayonnaise
1 ripe avocado, thinly sliced
1 onion, thinly sliced
1 can (4 oz.) whole green
  chiles, cut in strips
1–2 tomatoes, sliced
8 slices bacon, fried crisp
8 ozs. cheddar cheese,
  thinly sliced

Spread rye bread with mayonnaise. Cover each bread slice with avocado slices, onion slices, green chile strips, tomato slices, and 2 strips bacon. Top with cheddar cheese slices. Broil until cheese is melted.

Preparation time: 15 minutes
Cooking time: 5 minutes

Easy

Serves: 4

Frances Shipman

PIZZA
The long and the short of pizza making

**REGULAR PIZZA DOUGH
(2 PIZZAS):**

1 pkg. active dry yeast
**¼ cup warm water
(105°–115°)**
1 cup skimmed milk
1½ T. shortening
1 tsp. salt
1 T. sugar
3 cups flour

Soften yeast in warm water. Scald milk; add shortening, salt, and sugar. Cool to lukewarm. In large bowl, combine yeast with milk. Add enough flour to make stiff dough; mix thoroughly and turn out on floured board. Knead for 5 to 10 minutes. Place dough in greased bowl; brush with shortening or olive oil. Cover with waxed paper and towel. Let rise in warm place until doubled (about 1 hour). Punch down. Fold over so that smooth side is on top.

Lightly oil top. Cover as before. Let rise again (1 hour). Punch down. Turn out on floured board. Divide in half. Allow to rest for 10 minutes. Roll out dough into a circle. Fit into pizza tin, pushing edges up a bit. If making only 1 pizza, freeze other half of dough for later use.

**QUICK 'N EASY PIZZA
DOUGH (1 PIZZA):**

1 pkg. active dry yeast
**1 cup warm water (105°–
115°)**
1 tsp. sugar
1 tsp. salt
2 T. salad oil
2½ cups flour

Dissolve yeast in warm water. Stir in remaining ingredients. Beat vigorously. Knead dough with hands. Let dough rest in bowl covered with damp towel. When sauce is ready, roll out dough in a circle to fit into greased 10-inch pizza tin. Press up edges a bit.

**JIFFY PIZZA DOUGH
(1 PIZZA):**

1 loaf frozen bread dough
Olive oil or vegetable oil

Take frozen bread dough out of freezer in morning to defrost. Put in pan or bowl; brush thoroughly with oil. Cover. During the day, periodically brush with oil so that dough doesn't dry out. When ready to make crust, press loaf into a ball and roll out just as for any other pizza crust. Place in greased and floured pizza tin or 9 × 13-inch pan.

(continued)

PIZZA (continued)

SAUCE (2 PIZZAS):
1 large onion, finely
  chopped
Olive oil
2 cans (8 oz. each) tomato
  sauce
½ tsp. basil
½ tsp. oregano
2 bay leaves
½ tsp. garlic salt or to taste
Pepper to taste

Brown onion in olive oil. Combine all ingredients in saucepan. Simmer for at least 30 minutes—preferably for 2½ hours. Sauce may be cooked while dough is being made—30 minutes for Quick 'n Easy dough; 2½ hours for regular dough.

TRIM (1 PIZZA):
8 ozs. mozzarella cheese,
  coarsely grated
Any of the following
  toppings:
½ stick pepperoni or polish
  sausage, thinly sliced
4 ozs. fresh or canned
  mushrooms, sliced,
  sautéed
½ green pepper, diced
½ can anchovies
½ lb. bulk sausage or
  hamburger, cooked,
  crumbled

To assemble pizza:
1. Brush prepared dough very lightly with olive oil.
2. Spread 1 recipe sauce on pizza.
3. Sprinkle mozzarella cheese over sauce.
4. Add favorite toppings.
5. Sprinkle lightly with about 1 table-spoonful olive oil.
6. Bake at 400° for about 20 minutes.

Preparation time: 40 minutes–
  2½ hours
Baking time: 20 minutes

Can freeze

Jan Cornell
Gary Ruoff
Suzanne Sellers

Hint: Make Italian beef sandwiches by pouring 1 bottle (8 oz.) Italian or French salad dressing over a 4 to 6-pound boneless rump roast. Cover. Bake at 300° for 6 to 8 hours, depending upon size of roast. Shred beef in juice after cooking. Serve on buns. Serves 12.

Sharon Garside

FRIED EGG ROLL

3 cups Chinese cabbage, very thinly shredded
1½ cups fresh or 1 can (16 oz.) bean sprouts
½ to 1 cup onion, chopped
4 T. peanut oil (divided)
1 can (8 oz.) water chestnuts, chopped
1½ cups fresh mushrooms, chopped
¼ lb. ground beef
¼ lb. ground pork
2 scallions, chopped
2 T. soy sauce
1 tsp. Aćcent
Pinch of salt, pepper, and red pepper
Egg roll skins (homemade or purchased)
Soy sauce
Hot mustard

Stir fry cabbage, bean sprouts, and onion in 2 tablespoonfuls hot oil for 4 minutes. Remove from heat and place on platter. Stir fry water chestnuts and mushrooms for 2 minutes. Remove from pan to platter. Add 2 tablespoonfuls oil and stir fry ground meats for 10 to 15 minutes. Add scallions, soy sauce, Aćcent, salt, pepper, and red pepper. Combine all ingredients and set aside.

EGG ROLL SKINS:
2 cups flour
½ cup cold water
Dash of salt
1–2 cups cooking oil

Mix together flour, water, and salt to make a smooth dough. Using extra flour to work with, roll out dough to a very thin sheet. Cut eight 5-inch squares. Fill each with about 1 tablespoonful stuffing. Roll up, taking care to fold ends into roll. Seal edges with a small amount of water. Fry egg rolls in hot cooking oil for 3 to 4 minutes on each side, or until golden brown. Serve with soy sauce and hot mustard.

Preparation time: 1 hour   Can make ahead   Serves: 8
                                                     Can freeze

Mrs. Young Hai Park

HOT CHINESE CHICKEN SALAD
Eaten happily by all ages

8 broiler fryer thighs,
skinned, boned, cut in
1-inch pieces
½ cup cornstarch
¼ cup corn oil
¼ tsp. garlic powder
¼ cup soy sauce
1 tsp. monosodium
glutamate (MSG)
1 large tomato, chunked
⅓ cup water chestnuts,
sliced
1 can (4 oz.) mushrooms,
sliced, drained, or 4 ozs.
fresh mushrooms, sliced
1 cup celery, bias cut
1 cup green onions,
coarsely chopped
2 cups lettuce, shredded

Roll chicken pieces in cornstarch. Heat oil in frying pan or wok over medium-high heat. Add chicken in small batches and brown quickly, adding more oil if needed. Remove browned chicken to a plate; sprinkle with garlic powder. Put water chestnuts, mushrooms, onions, and celery in wok. Stir to mix; add chicken and tomato. Sprinkle with MSG. Stir in soy sauce. Cover; reduce heat and simmer for 5 minutes. Remove from heat; add lettuce and toss. If desired, serve with rice.

Preparation time: 1 hour
Cooking time: 15 minutes

Serves: 4–5

Jill Berglund

SWEET-AND-SOUR MUSTARD SAUCE
Marvelous as sandwich spread or served with egg rolls

4 eggs
½ cup honey
1 T. flour
1 can (1½ oz.) dry mustard
(Colman's preferred)
¾–1 cup cider vinegar
1 cup sugar

Mix all ingredients in blender. Cook over medium heat until thickened, stirring constantly.

May store indefinitely in refrigerator.

Preparation time: 15 minutes   Can freeze   Yield: 2½ cups

Members of Service Club

137

SPANISH OMELET
The zesty sauce makes this omelet outstanding

Basic omelets (to serve 4–6)   Prepare omelets.

SPANISH SAUCE:
½ cup green pepper, chopped
¼ cup onion, chopped
1 clove garlic, crushed
⅓ cup celery, chopped
2 T. butter or bacon drippings
3 slices bacon
⅛ tsp. pepper
½ tsp. paprika
½ tsp. oregano
1 can (8 oz.) tomato sauce
1 can (3 oz.) mushrooms or equivalent amount of fresh mushrooms, sautéed
1⅓ cups fresh tomatoes, chopped

Fry bacon; crumble. Sauté green pepper, onion, garlic, and celery in bacon drippings for 5 to 10 minutes. Add bacon and remaining ingredients; simmer for 20 minutes longer.

Use this sauce to prepare Spanish Omelet. Before folding omelet, place ½ to ¾ cup Spanish Sauce in center; fold. Top with additional sauce.

Hint: This sauce may be used to make Eggs Ranchero. Prepare by frying corn tortilla in oil and draining on paper towel. Place tortilla on plate. Top with poached egg and about ¼ cup Spanish Sauce.

Preparation time: 10 minutes
Cooking time: 30 minutes

Serves: 4–6

Mabel Eyth

CURRIED EGGS WITH SHRIMP SAUCE
Elegant for a brunch buffet

8 eggs, hard cooked
1 tsp. salt
Dash of Worcestershire sauce
½ tsp. curry powder
½ tsp. paprika
¼ tsp. dry mustard
1½ T. lemon juice
2–3 T. sour cream

Cut eggs in half lengthwise and scoop out yolks. Mash yolks with salt, Worcestershire sauce, curry powder, paprika, dry mustard, and lemon juice; moisten with sour cream. Fill egg halves with mixture. Place in shallow greased baking dish. Cover and refrigerate for a few hours or until next day.

(continued)

CURRIED EGGS (continued)

CHEESE-SHRIMP SAUCE:
2 cups milk or half-and-half
2 T. butter
2 T. flour
1 tsp. salt
Pepper to taste
1 tsp. Worcestershire sauce
1 cup sharp cheddar
  cheese, shredded
2 cans (5 oz. each) shrimp
  or equivalent amount of
  fresh or frozen shrimp

To prepare sauce, heat milk. Melt butter and add flour to make a roux; blend in milk very slowly, stirring constantly. Cook and whisk until smooth and thick. Add salt, pepper, Worcestershire sauce, and cheese; heat until melted. Stir in shrimp (may be covered and refrigerated at this point). Pour sauce over deviled eggs. Bake, uncovered, at 350° for 20 to 30 minutes.

Preparation time: 45 minutes
Cooking time: 30 minutes

Must make ahead

Serves: 6–8
Easily doubled

Geri Penniman

HOT CHICKEN SALAD SUPERB

2 cups chicken, cooked,
  diced
2 cups celery, diced
½ cup hickory smoked
  almonds (Blue Diamond
  preferred)
2 T. onion, grated
2 T. lemon juice
¾ cup mayonnaise
1 cup mild cheddar cheese,
  grated (Cracker Barrel
  preferred)
1 cup potato chips, crushed

Mix together all ingredients except potato chips. Pour into greased 1½ to 2-quart casserole. Top with potato chips. Bake at 375° for 20 minutes.

Preparation time: 1 hour
Baking time: 20 minutes

Easy
Can make ahead

Serves: 8

Ruth Kasdorf

SHRIMP-ARTICHOKE CASSEROLE

3 T. butter
3 T. flour
1½ cups milk
1 tsp. salt
⅛ tsp. pepper
¼ tsp. Worcestershire
 sauce
½ cup Parmesan cheese,
 grated
Prepared mustard (optional)
Tabasco sauce (optional)
1 can (16 oz.) artichoke
 hearts
4 eggs, hard cooked, sliced
2 cups shrimp, cooked

In saucepan, melt butter; stir in flour to make a smooth paste. Gradually add milk. Season with salt, pepper, Worcestershire sauce, and ⅓ cup cheese. Add a little mustard and Tabasco, if desired. Drain artichoke hearts. Combine all ingredients. Pour into a 1½-quart casserole. Sprinkle with remaining Parmesan cheese. Bake at 350° for 30 minutes.

Note: Crab meat may be substituted for shrimp.

Preparation time: 20 minutes
Baking time: 30 minutes

Serves: 6–8

Linda Brown

HOT DAY SEAFOOD SALAD
Perfect for a light supper on a warm night

2 lbs. fresh or 2 pkgs.
 (10 oz. each) frozen
 asparagus, cooked,
 chilled
2 lbs. cod, scrod, or other
 white fish
6 ozs. frozen or canned
 crab meat
4 ozs. shrimp, cooked
Lettuce leaves
Salt and pepper to taste
Juice of 1 lemon
Mayonnaise or Zesty
 Mayonnaise (see below)
Lemon wedges

Poach cod in boiling salted water. When flaky, remove from water and refrigerate. Cook crab meat or drain (if canned). Refrigerate. Cook and chill shrimp. At serving time, remove bones from cod. Arrange on lettuce leaves; top with shrimp and crab. Arrange asparagus around salad. Sprinkle with salt and pepper; squeeze lemon juice over all. Smear lightly with mayonnaise or Zesty Mayonnaise. Pass extra mayonnaise.

(continued)

HOT DAY SEAFOOD SALAD (continued)

ZESTY MAYONNAISE:
⅓ cup mayonnaise
⅓ cup sour cream
½ tsp. dill
¼–½ tsp. tarragon
2 tsps. chives, minced
½ tsp. dried or 1 T. fresh
  parsley, minced

Prepare Zesty Mayonnaise by combining all ingredients and mixing well.

Note: This seafood salad is excellent served in the center of Cucumber Mousse (see page 150).

Preparation time: 30 minutes   Can make ahead   Serves: 6

Members of Service Club

CHICKEN SOUFFLÉ ROLL FLORENTINE

Butter
Flour
6 T. butter
½ cup flour
½ tsp. salt
⅛ tsp. white pepper
2 cups milk
5 eggs, separated
1 T. shallots, minced
½ cup mushrooms,
  chopped
1 pkg. (10 oz.) frozen
  chopped spinach,
  cooked, well drained
1 cup chicken, cooked,
  diced
1 T. Dijon mustard
¼ tsp. nutmeg
2 pkgs. (3 oz. each) cream
  cheese, softened
Parsley (for garnish)

Butter 15 × 10½ × 2-inch jelly roll pan. Line with wax paper. Butter wax paper. Dust with flour. In saucepan, melt 4 table-spoonfuls butter. Blend in flour, salt, and pepper. Over low heat, gradually add milk, stirring until smooth and thickened. Remove from heat. Beat egg yolks un-til thick and lemon colored. Add to white sauce, beating constantly. Cool slightly. Beat egg whites until stiff peaks form. Carefully fold egg whites into sauce. Pour into prepared pan. Bake at 400° for 25 minutes, or until puffed and brown. Turn out onto dish towel. Roll up like a jelly roll; let set for 1 or 2 minutes. Unroll. Spread with filling; roll up again. Place on platter, seam side down. Garnish with parsley. May serve immediately but is better the next day.

Filling: Sauté shallots in 2 tablespoonfuls melted butter. Add mushrooms; cook for 5 minutes more. Add spinach, chicken, mustard, nutmeg, and cream cheese. Mix well.

Preparation time: 1 hour   Best made ahead   Serves: 8
Baking time: 25 minutes   Can freeze and reheat

Evelyn Pryweller

141

BAKED SWISS FONDUE

1 clove garlic, crushed
1 tsp. dry mustard
⅔ cup butter, softened
1 large loaf French bread
3 T. onion, finely chopped
⅓ cup flour
1½ cups powdered
  non-dairy creamer
2 tsps. salt
1 tsp. paprika
3 cups boiling water
1 cup dry white wine
3 egg yolks, well beaten
12 ozs. natural Swiss
  cheese, grated

Blend garlic and ½ teaspoonful dry mustard with ⅓ cup butter. Cut bread into ¼-inch slices; spread with butter mixture. Line bottom and sides of 2½-quart casserole with some of bread, buttered side down.

In heavy saucepan, melt remaining ⅓ cup butter over low heat. Add onion; cook until tender. Blend in flour; cook and stir for 1 minute. Add non-dairy creamer, ½ teaspoonful dry mustard, salt, and paprika. Add boiling water; beat with whisk to blend. Cook and stir until sauce boils and thickens. Remove from heat; blend in wine and egg yolks. Return to heat; cook until heated through. In bread-lined casserole, alternate layers of grated cheese, bread slices, and sauce, ending with bread (buttered side up). Cover and refrigerate overnight. Bake at 350° for 50 minutes, or until cheese is bubbling and bread is brown. Must let set for 10 minutes before cutting. Great with green salad and cold beer.

Preparation time: 1 hour
Baking time: 50 minutes

Make night before

Serves: 8

Jean Dolbee

SAUSAGE-FILLED CREPES

16 crepes
1½ lbs. bulk sausage
¼ cup onion, chopped
½–⅔ cup processed cheese,
  shredded
1 pkg. (3 oz.) cream cheese
¼ tsp. dried marjoram
½ cup sour cream
¼ cup butter, softened

Make crepes (see page 168). To make filling, brown sausage and onion; drain. Add cheeses and marjoram. Place 2 tablespoonfuls filling in line down center of each crepe; roll up. Place in 11¾ × 7½ × 1¾-inch baking dish. May make to this point, cover, and chill. Bake, covered, at 375° for 40 minutes. Mix together sour cream and butter; spoon over top of each crepe. Bake, uncovered, for 5 minutes longer.

Preparation time: 40 minutes
Baking time: 40 minutes

Can make ahead

Serves: 8

Kelli Booth

CHICKEN QUICHE

2 cups chicken, cooked,
  boned, cubed
1 green pepper, diced
1 large onion, diced
2 cups Swiss cheese,
  shredded
2 (9-inch) pie shells,
  unbaked, or 2 frozen
  deep-dish pie shells
2 T. flour
4 tsps. butter, melted
5 eggs, well beaten
½ cup mayonnaise
1 can (13 oz.) evaporated
  mllk
⅛ tsp. nutmeg
⅛ tsp. garlic salt
⅛ tsp. white pepper
Dash of Tabasco sauce
Worcestershire sauce or
  soy sauce to taste

Divide chicken, green pepper, onion, and Swiss cheese between 2 pie shells. Top each with 1 tablespoonful flour and 2 teaspoonfuls butter. Mix together remaining ingredients and pour half over each quiche. Bake at 375° for 45 minutes.

Note: The extra quiche may be frozen.

Preparation time: 30 minutes   Can freeze   Serves: 8 or more
Baking time: 45 minutes

Barbara Long

SALMON SALAD

1 lb. piece of salmon
1 cup sour cream
½ cup chili sauce
1 T. lemon juice
4 tsps. horseradish
1–2 tomatoes
1 avocado
1 medium cucumber
½–1 cup cheddar cheese,
  shredded
Lettuce

Poach salmon; drain and chill. Combine sour cream, chili sauce, lemon juice, and horseradish; refrigerate. Peel and slice tomatoes, avocado, and cucumber. If preparing avocado ahead, sprinkle it with lemon juice and salt to prevent discoloration. At serving time, tear lettuce into bite-sized pieces; flake salmon into bowl. Add remaining ingredients and toss with sour cream mixture.

Preparation time: 30 minutes   Serves: 4

Carol VandenBerg

143

TARTE AUX ASPERGES

PÂTE BRISÉE:
1 cup flour
½ tsp. salt
¼ cup unsalted butter,
   chilled
1½ T. shortening
   (Crisco preferred)
2–3 T. ice water

TARTE:
⅔ cup fresh or frozen
   asparagus, cooked,
   chopped
2 eggs
Salt and white pepper to
   taste
¼ cup almonds, ground,
   toasted
⅔ cup half-and-half
½ cup Swiss cheese, grated
8 spears fresh or frozen
   asparagus, cooked

Combine flour, salt, butter, and shortening and work until crumbly. Add water and form ball. *Fraisage* dough—take small piece of dough, place on board or counter, and press and push with palm of hand to blend together fat and flour. Repeat procedure with remaining dough. Form into large ball, flatten, wrap in waxed paper, and chill for 2 or more hours. Remove from refrigerator 20 minutes before using. Roll out; line shallow 8 or 9-inch tart pan with lift-out bottom. Prick pastry; chill for 1 or more hours. Line shell with waxed paper; fill with rice, beans, or aluminum chips. Bake at 400° for 5 to 10 minutes, until partially done. Take out of oven and remove beans and paper; cool. Process asparagus, eggs, salt, pepper, almonds, and cheese in food processor or blender until well blended. Pour into tart shell and place whole spears on top in wheel effect. Bake at 375° for 25 minutes. Lift from pan and serve at once.

Preparation time: 3 hours
Baking time: 30–35 minutes

Serves: 6 to 8

Jean Patt

SWISS CHEESE PUFF WITH LOBSTER SAUCE
Outstanding!

9-inch pastry shell, unbaked
4 egg yolks, slightly beaten
1½ cups half-and-half
½ tsp. salt
⅛ tsp. ground nutmeg
⅛ tsp. allspice
Pinch of rosemary
4 egg whites
1½ cups Swiss cheese,
   grated

Bake pastry shell at 450° for 6 to 8 minutes. Reduce oven to 350°. Combine egg yolks, half-and-half, salt, nutmeg, allspice, and rosemary. Beat egg whites until stiff; fold into yolk mixture, then fold in cheese. Pour into pastry shell; bake at 350° for 40 minutes, or until knife comes out clean. Let stand for 5 to 10 minutes; serve with lobster sauce.

(continued)

SWISS CHEESE PUFF (continued)

SAUCE:

8 ozs. lobster, cut in chunks
2 T. butter, melted
2 T. flour
⅛ tsp. salt
White pepper, freshly
  ground
¾ cup half-and-half
¼ cup white wine
1 T. chives, snipped
1 T. parsley

Heat lobster in butter. Stir in flour, salt, and pepper. Add half-and-half, wine, chives, and parsley. Crab or shrimp may be substituted for lobster.

Preparation time: 30 minutes
Baking time: 40 minutes

Serves: 6–8

Sally Shipman Early

CHICKEN-AVOCADO CREPES

8 crepes
2 chicken breasts, cooked
8 slices bacon
1 large or 2 small avocados
1 recipe Mornay Sauce
½ lb. fresh mushrooms
2 T. butter
Paprika (for garnish)
Parsley (for garnish)

Make crepes (see page 168). Freeze extra crepes. Skin, bone, and dice cooked chicken. Fry and crumble bacon. Pit, peel, and mash avocado. Add bacon to avocado. Prepare Mornay Sauce (see page 116). Slice and sauté mushrooms in butter. When golden, mix with cooked chicken. Add 1 cup Mornay Sauce to chicken-mushroom mixture. Fill each crepe by spreading ⅛ avocado mixture in line down center. Spread ⅛ chicken-mushroom mixture over it. Fold edges of crepe toward center to make a cylinder. Place on heated plate, folded edges down. Top with more Mornay Sauce. Sprinkle with paprika and parsley. Crepes can be made and filled ahead, then warmed later. At serving time, top with Mornay Sauce and garnishes.

Preparation time: 1½ hours   Can make ahead   Serves: 8

Greeta Douglass

CURRIED CHICKEN SALAD

2 T. salad or vegetable oil
2 tsps. wine vinegar
1 tsp. curry powder
3 T. chutney, chopped
2 tomatoes, seeded,
  chopped
2 T. raisins
1 green pepper, cut in strips
1 stalk celery, chopped
2 T. parsley, chopped
1 cup chicken, cooked,
  cubed
2 T. cashews, broken
2 cups cold cooked rice
Salt and pepper to taste
Lettuce
2 eggs, hard cooked

Mix oil, vinegar, curry powder, and chutney. Combine with tomatoes, raisins, green pepper, celery, parsley, chicken, and cashews. Toss with rice; add salt and pepper. Serve in lettuce-lined bowls garnished with boiled eggs sliced or pressed into individual molds and unmold onto lettuce cups. When salad is served for luncheon, use chicken and cashews. They may be omitted when it is used as a dinner salad. All ingredients may be prepared and chopped in advance but should be combined only shortly before service.

Preparation time: 30 minutes

Serves: 6

Greeta Douglass

SAVORY CHICKEN ROLL-UPS

⅓ cup herb-seasoned
  croutons or herb-
  seasoned bread stuffing,
  crushed
¼ cup walnuts or pecans,
  crushed
1 pkg. (3 oz.) cream cheese,
  softened
2 T. butter, softened
1 T. dried onion
½ tsp. Worcestershire
  sauce
1 cup chicken, cooked,
  cubed
1 can (8 oz.) refrigerated
  crescent rolls
3 T. butter, melted

In a small bowl, combine crushed croutons and nuts. Set aside. In another bowl, combine cream cheese, 2 tablespoonfuls butter, onion, and Worcestershire sauce. Mix well. Add chicken; set aside. Separate crescent dough into 8 triangles. Spread each with a scant ¼ cup chicken mixture. Roll up, starting at shortest side of triangle and rolling to opposite point. Tuck sides and point under to seal completely. Gently roll back and forth to lengthen into uniform shape. Dip rolls in melted butter. Coat with crumb-nut mixture. Place on ungreased baking sheet. Bake at 375° for 15 to 20 minutes, or until golden brown. Serve with sauce.

(continued)

SAVORY CHICKEN ROLL-UPS (continued)

SAUCE:
2 T. butter
3 T. flour
2 cups chicken stock,
   boiling
¼–½ tsp. salt
White pepper, freshly
   ground
1 T. chives, chopped

In saucepan, melt butter; stir in flour to make a smooth paste. Gradually add chicken stock and seasonings, stirring constantly. Cook until smooth and consistency of gravy. Add chives.

Preparation time: 30 minutes
Baking time: 15–20 minutes

Can make ahead

Yield: 8 rolls

Marilyn Petzold

CRAB SOUFFLÉ
An elegant "make-ahead" brunch favorite

1 lb. crab meat
1 cup celery, chopped
2 tsps. onion juice or 1
   small onion, grated
2 tsps. prepared mustard
⅓–½ cup mayonnaise
Dash of Tabasco sauce
Dash of lemon juice
Butter, melted
12 slices bread, crusts
   removed
Sharp cheddar cheese,
   grated
5 eggs, slightly beaten
2 cups milk

Combine first 7 ingredients. Dip bread in melted butter. Make 6 sandwiches using crab mixture as filling; cut in fourths. Place layer of sandwiches in 9 × 13-inch baking dish. Cover with cheese; repeat sandwich layer and top with cheese. Beat eggs; add milk and pour over sandwiches. Cover and refrigerate for at least 2 to 4 hours—preferably overnight. Set dish in pan of hot water and bake at 325° for 1 hour.

Hint: Substitute equivalent amount of chicken for crab and create a chicken soufflé. For variety, make 1 of each for a large brunch.

Preparation time: 20 minutes
Baking time: 1 hour

Must make ahead

Serves: 8–10

Candy Woodruff

CHEESE STRATA
Make it today; bake it tomorrow!

12 slices white bread
8 ozs. sharp cheese, sliced
1 pkg. (10 oz.) frozen
  chopped broccoli,
  cooked, drained
4 cups ham, cooked, diced
6 eggs, slightly beaten
3½ cups milk
3 T. onion, minced
¾ tsp. salt
¼ tsp. dry mustard
Dash of paprika
1 can (10¾ oz.) condensed
  cream of mushroom soup,
  undiluted, heated

Cut 12 circles from bread. Fit scraps of bread in 9 × 13-inch buttered pan. Over bread, layer cheese, broccoli, and ham in that order. Arrange bread circles over ham. Combine next 5 ingredients and pour over bread until it's saturated. Add a dash of paprika; cover and refrigerate overnight. Bake, uncovered, at 350° for 55 minutes. Let stand a few minutes before cutting. Top with mushroom soup.

Variation No. 1: Substitute 3 pounds link sausage, browned and cut into pieces, for ham.

Variation No. 2: Substitute 3 cups chicken, cooked and cubed, for ham.

Variation No. 3: Substitute 3 cups seafood (shrimp, crab, lobster or a combination of any of them) for ham. May also substitute one 10-ounce package asparagus, cooked, for broccoli.

Preparation time: 30 minutes
Baking time: 55 minutes

Easy   Serves: 8
Must make a day ahead

Members of Service Club

SALMON PIE WITH CUCUMBER SAUCE

2 eggs, hard cooked
8 or 9-inch pie shell,
  unbaked
1 lb. salmon (fresh, frozen,
  or canned)
2 eggs, beaten
½ cup butter, melted
3 tsps. parsley, chopped
½ tsp. basil
½ tsp. salt

Slice hard-cooked eggs into pie shell. Flake salmon into bowl (fresh salmon should be skinned and boned). Add eggs, butter, herbs, and salt. Mix well; pour over eggs in crust. Bake at 425° for 20 to 25 minutes. Serve with cucumber sauce.

(continued)

SALMON PIE (continued)

CUCUMBER SAUCE:
1 medium cucumber,
  peeled, grated
1 tsp. onion, grated
¼ cup mayonnaise
2 tsps. vinegar
½ cup sour cream
2 tsps. parsley, chopped
Salt and pepper to taste

Press onion and cucumber through strainer to remove juice. Add remaining ingredients to drained cucumber and onion mixture. Serve at room temperature over hot pie.

Preparation time: 20 minutes
Baking time: 20–25 minutes

Can make ahead

Serves: 4–6

Greeta Douglass

SWEDISH SHRIMP BOWL

4 lbs. large shrimp, cooked
¾ cup tarragon vinegar
12 whole peppercorns,
  bruised
6 sprigs fresh dill or 1 T.
  dried dill
2 large bay leaves
1 sprig thyme or 1 tsp. dried
  thyme

Shell and devein shrimp. Marinate for 2 hours in refrigerator in tarragon vinegar seasoned with peppercorns, dill, bay leaves, and thyme. Serve on cracked ice with Russian dressing on the side.

RUSSIAN DRESSING:
3 T. chili sauce
1 tsp. pimiento, finely
  chopped
1 tsp. chives, finely
  chopped
1 cup mayonnaise

For the dressing, mix together all ingredients.

Preparation time: 1 hour

Serves: 6–8

Susan Balz

Hint: To make an open-faced chicken sandwich, layer a slice of Swiss cheese, some sliced chicken, lettuce, sliced tomato, and a sliced hard-cooked egg on a piece of rye bread. Top with Thousand Island Dressing (see page 96) and crisp crumbled bacon or bacon slices. Serves 1.

Eloise Vermeulen

CUCUMBER MOUSSE
Beautiful for a summer luncheon

2 cucumbers
1 env. unflavored gelatin
½ cup cold water
1 pkg. (3 oz.) lime gelatin
1¼ cups boiling water
½ cup lemon juice
2 tsps. onion juice
¾ tsp. salt
⅛ tsp. cayenne pepper
½ cup celery, chopped
¼ cup parsley, chopped
½ pt. whipping cream,
   whipped

Peel cucumbers. Remove seeds and grate coarsely. Soften unflavored gelatin in cold water. Dissolve lime gelatin in boiling water. Stir plain gelatin mixture, lemon juice, onion juice, salt, cayenne, and cucumbers into lime gelatin. Chill until somewhat thickened; fold in celery, parsley, and whipped cream. Pour into large oiled ring mold; chill until set. Unmold and fill center with Hot Day Seafood Salad (see page 140).

Preparation time: 20 minutes   Must make ahead   Serves: 6–8

Louise Ravenel

CHICKEN SALAD

4 cups chicken breasts,
   cooked, diced
2 cups seedless grapes
1 cup mandarin oranges,
   drained
¾ cup mayonnaise
¾ cup sour cream
2 bananas, sliced
Almonds, toasted
   (for garnish)

Combine chicken with grapes and oranges. Whip together cream and mayonnaise. Blend into chicken mixture. Dip bananas in juice drained from oranges to prevent discoloration. About 1 hour before serving, add the bananas. Garnish with toasted almonds, if desired.

Preparation time: 30 minutes   Serves: 6–8

Ann Block

FILET DE BOEUF EN VERMOUTH
Serve with sautéed mushroom and white rice

2 T. butter
4 filets of beef, 1 inch thick
¾ tsp. salt
¼ tsp. pepper
1 T. flour
¼ cup dry vermouth
½ cup whipping cream,
  unwhipped
2 T. parsley, chopped

Melt butter in skillet. Brown filets over high heat for 3 minutes on each side (shake pan a few times while cooking). Sprinkle meat with salt and pepper; stir flour into pan juice. Add vermouth and cream. Cook over medium heat for 4 to 6 minutes longer, or until done as desired, turning filets once. Arrange filets on hot serving dish; pour sauce over them. Sprinkle with parsley. Use combined juices from steak and mushrooms as gravy for rice.

Wine suggestion: California Cabernet Sauvignon.

Preparation time: 10 minutes
Cooking time: 10 minutes

Serves: 4

Mary Jo Garling

ALL ABOUT FLANK STEAKS
OR
FOUR FLANKLY FABULOUS FEASTS!

For all recipes, use a 2 to 2½-lb. flank steak. If broiling or grilling, place 3 to 4 inches from heat and allow 4 minutes per side for medium. Brush with extra marinade while cooking and pass extra marinade with servings. Always slice on diagonal.

LONDON BROIL:
½ cup orange marmalade
¼ cup soy sauce
¼ cup lemon juice

Combine ingredients and marinate steak for at least 30 minutes at room temperature or as long as 12 hours in refrigerator, turning frequently. Grill as directed above.

Preparation time: 5 minutes
  plus marinating time

Must make ahead

Serves: 4

Sharon Garside

LONDON BROIL WITH ROQUEFORT CHEESE:
1 cup salad oil
2 T. wine vinegar

Combine oil, vinegar, soy sauce, thyme, and garlic and marinate scored steak in

(continued)

FLANK STEAKS (continued)

1 tsp. soy sauce
⅛ tsp. thyme
1 clove garlic, minced
4 ozs. Roquefort cheese
2 T. whipping cream,
  unwhipped

Preparation time: 5 minutes
  plus marinating time

it for 12 to 24 hours in refrigerator. (May substitute one 8-ounce bottle Italian salad dressing for marinade.) Broil as directed above. Mash cheese with cream; spread over broiled steak. Broil for 2 minutes longer.

Must make ahead   Serves: 4

Claudia Lee

GARLIC PEPPER STEAK:

¼ cup oil
2 T. lemon juice
2 T. soy sauce
2 T. green onion, chopped
2 cloves garlic, pressed
1 tsp. black pepper,
  coarsely ground
1 tsp. celery salt

Preparation time: 5 minutes
  plus marinating time

Mix together all ingredients and marinate for 2 hours at room temperature or 6 hours in refrigerator. Turn frequently. Broil as directed above.

Must make ahead   Serves: 4

Claudia Lee

ROLLED LONDON BROIL:

1 medium onion, chopped
3 T. butter
2 cups fresh bread crumbs
½ cup ham, cooked, cut in
  small cubes
¼ cup parsley, chopped
½ tsp. basil
¼ tsp. savory
½ tsp. chervil
1 egg, beaten
Pinch of nutmeg
Pepper, freshly ground,
  to taste
3 slices bacon

Preparation time: 20 minutes
Cooking time: 25 minutes

Sauté onion in butter until golden. Combine bread, ham, parsley, basil, savory, chervil, egg, nutmeg, and pepper with onion. Score flank steak on both sides. Spread stuffing on top. Roll up and secure with toothpicks. Place bacon over top of rolled steak; tie each piece of bacon with string. Roast at 400° for 25 minutes. Turn off oven and let rest for 10 minutes. Remove from oven and slice in 1-inch slices.

Easy   Serves: 4–6
Can make ahead

Sally Shipman Early

153

CHINESE BEEF
Looks beautiful; tastes terrific

4 T. sugar
2 T. cornstarch
4 T. soy sauce
2 T. Burgundy
¾ cup cooking oil (divided)
1½–2 lbs. round steak, cut in thin strips
4 green peppers, cut in thin strips
4 celery stalks, cut in thin strips
2 onions, thinly sliced
2 scallions, thinly sliced
1 pt. cherry tomatoes

SAUCE:
3 T. cornstarch
6 T. sugar
6 T. catsup
3 T. soy sauce
3 T. Worcestershire sauce

Combine sugar, cornstarch, soy sauce, Burgundy, and ½ cup oil. Marinate meat in this for at least 30 minutes. Drain beef. Discard marinade. Cook strips in 4 tablespoonfuls oil for about 5 minutes. Remove beef; add green peppers, celery, onions, and scallions. Cook for about 5 minutes more. Keep vegetables crisp. Add beef and tomatoes. Combine sauce ingredients and pour over beef and vegetables. Cook for 1 minute. Serve with rice.

Hint: All vegetables can be chopped and the meat put in marinade the night before. Cook just before serving.

Preparation time: 20 minutes
Cooking time: 10 minutes

Serves: 8

Adrienne de Windt

SLOW ROAST METHOD FOR STANDING RIB ROAST
Insures a perfect roast every time!

In the morning, take rib roast from refrigerator. Wipe with damp paper towels and let stand for 1 to 1½ hours to reach room temperature. Preheat oven to 350°. Pepper roast (any size except a *very* large roast). Place in roasting pan, rib side down. Put in oven for exactly 1 hour. Turn off oven. DO NOT OPEN DOOR. About 1 hour before serving, turn oven to 375°. (At this point oven may be opened and another dish added. Restart oven.) Let roast cook for another 30 to 40 minutes. Rest 20 to 30 minutes before cutting to allow juices to set.

Wine suggestion: Good Red Burgundy or Bordeaux

Dottie Early

MARINATED ROAST SIRLOIN OF BEEF
Tender roast; terrific sauce

1 (3–4 lb.) boned sirloin
of beef
1 cup dry white wine
½ cup olive oil
2 shallots, sliced
1 small onion, sliced
2 bay leaves
4 sprigs parsley
Pinch of thyme
Salt and pepper to taste
1 T. wine vinegar

Trim fat (save) from meat. Mix together all remaining ingredients except vinegar. Marinate beef in mixture for 12 hours, turning several times. Place a strip of beef fat in roasting pan. Put shallots, onion, and seasonings on fat; top with meat. Put another strip of fat on meat. Insert meat thermometer in 1 end and add a little marinade. Roast at 350° for 16 to 18 minutes per pound, or until thermometer reads 135° for rare. Baste occasionally with marinade. Remove meat to a hot platter and let sit for 10 minutes before carving. Discard fat strips; add remaining marinade to pan, stirring in all the brown bits. Strain sauce into a small saucepan. Heat over high heat. Let stand a few minutes. Remove as much fat as possible from surface and add wine vinegar. Reheat sauce and serve with roast beef.

Wine suggestion: Zinfandel

Preparation time: 10 minutes
plus marinating time
Cooking time: 1 hour

Easy
Must make ahead

Serves: 8–10

Sharon Garside

INDIVIDUAL YORKSHIRES
Showy-great with roasts

2 eggs
½ tsp. salt
1 cup milk
2 tsps. butter, melted
1 cup flour
Beef drippings
(from standing rib roast)

Bring all ingredients to room temperature before beginning. Beat eggs until frothy. Stir in salt, milk, butter, and flour. Beat until just smooth. Heat a 12-muffin tin in a preheated 425° oven until very hot. Pour beef drippings into each cup—about ¼ inch deep. Return tin to oven until very hot again. Remove and fill each cup ⅔ full of batter; return to oven at once. Bake for 15 minutes at 425°. Reduce heat to 300° and bake for 15 minutes longer.

Note: Plan to take roast out of oven 30 minutes before serving to allow time for the Yorkshire puddings to bake and allow the roast juices to set.

Preparation time: 10 minutes
Baking time: 30 minutes

Serves: 12

Arlene Gardner

FONDUE COOKING WINE
An unusual calorie-saving twist to fondue

2½ cups red wine
2 cans (10 ¾ oz. each) beef broth or an equivalent amount of beef bouillon
1 medium onion, finely chopped
1 tsp. parsley flakes
1½ tsps. salt
¼ tsp. pepper
¼ tsp. garlic salt
1 bay leaf
½ tsp. marjoram

Mix together all ingredients in saucepan and heat for 15 minutes. Pour into fondue pot. May be used with meat, shrimp, and vegetables. Serve with fondue sauces.

Microwave: Microwave on high for 4 to 5 minutes, or until hot.

Preparation time: 5 minutes
Cooking time: 15 minutes
Microwave: 4–5 minutes

Easy

Yield: 5 cups

Sue White

FONDUE SAUCES

PIQUANT SAUCE:
½ cup sour cream
⅓ cup thick bottled French dressing
3 T. chutney

Combine all ingredients.

Yield: 1 cup

CHANTILLY SAUCE:
2 T. whipping cream, stiffly whipped
6 T. mayonnaise
Dash of lemon juice or to taste

Fold whipped cream into mayonnaise and season with lemon juice.

Note: Great on baked potatoes, too!

Yield: ½ cup
Can be doubled

(continued)

FONDUE SAUCES (continued)

CAPER BUTTER:
½ cup butter or margarine,
  softened
3 T. capers, undrained

Combine ingredients in blender or food processor. Cover and blend at high speed until smooth.

Yield: ½ cup

QUICK BÉARNAISE SAUCE:
2 tsps. dried tarragon
  leaves
2 T. tarragon vinegar
2 cups mayonnaise
6 green onions, peeled
¼ tsp. dry mustard
Dash of Tabasco sauce

Mix together tarragon leaves and vinegar; let stand for 30 minutes. Combine all ingredients in processor or blender and process for 30 seconds. Chill. Serve cold.

Yield: 2 cups

CREAMY GARLIC SAUCE:
4 ozs. cream cheese
½ cup sour cream
2–4 cloves garlic, pressed
Salt and pepper to taste

Blend cheese with sour cream; add garlic and salt and pepper.

Yield: 1 cup

Greeta Douglass
Jo Gager
Karen Teegarden

Hint: A good marinade for beef tenderloin may be made by mixing ¼ cup soy sauce, ¼ cup Worcestershire sauce, ½ teaspoonful garlic salt, and freshly ground pepper. Sprinkle tenderloin with mixture. Let stand for 3 hours at room temperature, basting frequently. Top with bacon strips and roast until rare or medium rare. Serve with béarnaise sauce (see page 208).

Priscilla Washburn

BEEF RAGOUT
Lamb or venison are equally good

2 lbs. round steak
2 cups Burgundy
6 sprigs or 1 tsp. dried
   rosemary
1 leaf sage
¼ tsp. pepper
1½ tsp. salt
Pinch of nutmeg
Flour
3 T. oil
1 carrot, diced
1 stalk celery, chopped
1 tsp. parsley, minced
2 cloves garlic, minced
2 T. tomato paste
1½ cups beef stock or 1 can
   (10¾ oz.) beef bouillon

Cut beef in cubes or strips. Marinate overnight in wine, rosemary, sage, pepper, salt, and nutmeg. Remove from marinade, reserving liquid, and dry with a towel. Dredge in flour. Brown in oil. Place in kettle. Add carrot, celery, parsley, and garlic. Pour in marinade. Add tomato paste and beef stock. Cover and cook gently for 2 hours, or until tender.

Wine suggestion: Burgundy

Preparation time: 20 minutes   Must make ahead   Serves: 4–6
Cooking time: 2 hours   Easily doubled

Greeta Douglass

BEEF WELLINGTON
Don't let the title scare you; this is easy!

1 (2½–3 lb.) beef tenderloin
1 pkg. (10 oz.) frozen pastry
   shells (Pepperidge Farm)
1 onion, finely chopped
2 carrots, finely chopped
2 stalks celery, finely
   chopped
3 T. cognac
Salt and pepper, freshly
   ground
4 slices bacon
2 cans (3½ or 5 oz. each)
   pâté de foie gras

Let beef tenderloin and pastry shells sit at room temperature for several hours. Put onion, carrots, and celery in bottom of roasting pan. Place fillet on top. Rub meat with cognac, salt, and pepper. Lay bacon strips over meat. Roast, uncovered, at 425° for 10 minutes per pound. Remove meat and cool to room temperature. Can be prepared ahead to this point.

Combine pastry shells; roll out pastry into a rectangle, making sure it will be wide enough to seal along bottom and ends of tenderloin. Spread top and sides of beef with pâté. Place beef, pâté side down, on pastry. Seal bottom and ends well.

(continued)

BEEF WELLINGTON (continued)

SAUCE:
1¾ cups beef stock
¼ cup dry white wine
4 T. pâté de foie gras
½ cup fresh mushrooms,
  thinly sliced

Turn over onto baking sheet. Make diagonal slits in pastry. Decorate with cutout pastry pieces, such as leaves and flowers. Bake at 425° until pastry is crisp and golden—about 30 minutes.

Sauce: Combine beef stock, wine, pâté and mushrooms; simmer for 10 minutes, stirring until pâté is smooth. Pass sauce separately.

Note: A Madeira sauce is also excellent.

Wine suggestion: Classified Red Bordeaux

Preparation time: 30 minutes
Baking time: 1 hour

Serves: 6

Amanda Clark Morrill

LOBSTER-STUFFED BEEF TENDERLOIN
Perfect combination of "land and ocean"

1 (3–4 lb.) beef tenderloin,
  trimmed
½ cup soy sauce
2 T. ginger, freshly grated
¾ cup sherry (divided)
2–3 lobster tails
1 onion, sliced
3 slices bacon
Parsley, chopped
4 T. butter, melted

Rub beef with a little soy sauce and ginger. Baste with ¼ cup sherry. Set aside. Drop lobster tails in pot of boiling salted water. Return to boil, reduce heat, and simmer for 5 minutes. Take from water, split tails, and carefully remove meat from shell. Baste with ¼ cup sherry. Split tenderloin ¾ of the way through; stuff with lobster meat. Tie tenderloin at 1-inch intervals. Place on bed of onion slices; lay bacon over top of meat. Mix remaining soy sauce and sherry and baste. Roast at 425° for 45 minutes for rare, basting often. Place on serving platter; sprinkle with parsley and butter. Slice and serve with juices.

Wine suggestion: Light Burgundy

Preparation time: 30 minutes
Cooking time: 45 minutes

Easy
Can make ahead

Serves: 6–8

Rowan Gregory

BEEF AND BARLEY
A fall and winter favorite

¾–1 cup onion, chopped
1 cup pearled barley, medium
2 T. butter
4 cups water
2 lbs. sirloin (or round) steak
⅓ cup fresh fine bread crumbs
1 T. sesame seeds
1¼ tsps. salt (divided)
1 tsp. paprika
¼ tsp. pepper
2 T. shortening
1 can (10 ¾ oz.) condensed cream of mushroom soup
1 can (4 oz.) button mushrooms, undrained
1 tsp. Worcestershire sauce
1 jar (2 oz.) pimientos, chopped

Sauté onion and barley in butter. Add 2 cups water. Cover and simmer for 15 minutes. Cut steak in strips and roll in mixture of bread crumbs, sesame seeds, 1 teaspoonful salt, paprika, and pepper. Brown in hot shortening. Combine barley and onion with soup, mushrooms, ¼ teaspoonful salt, Worcestershire sauce, pimientos, and remaining 2 cups water. Add browned steak. Pour into casserole. Cover and bake at 325° for 30 minutes. Uncover and bake for 30 minutes longer.

Note: Can add more meat. If round steak is used, it should be tenderized. Half sirloin and half round may be used.

Wine suggestion: California Burgundy

Preparation time: 30 minutes	Easy	Serves: 6–8
Cooking time: 1 hour	Can make ahead	Can freeze

Aaron Riker

Hint: Serve saffron rice as an accompaniment to your favorite curried dish. Mix ¼ teaspoonful chopped saffron with 1 tablespoonful hot water. Cook 1½ cups white rice and 1½ teaspoonfuls salt in 2 tablespoonfuls olive oil and 2 tablespoonfuls butter for 5 minutes, taking care not to burn it. Add saffron mixture and 3 cups water to rice. Bring to a boil; simmer covered for 20 minutes.

Sally Shipman Early

DILLED BEEF STRIPS
Keep meat pink for best flavor

2 lbs. sirloin steak
Salt and pepper
Flour
½ cup butter (divided)
½ lb. fresh mushrooms,
 wiped clean
4 green onions, chopped
2 cloves garlic, pressed
½ tsp. lemon juice
2 T. flour
1 cup hot beef stock
2 tsps. Dijon mustard
1 tsp. dried dill weed
½ cup sour cream
Rice or noodles (optional)

Cut sirloin into strips. Put salt, pepper, and flour in a bag; add meat and shake. In a skillet, melt 3 tablespoonfuls butter. Brown meat until pink. Remove and set aside. Add remaining butter to skillet. Add mushrooms, onions, garlic, and lemon juice. Sauté until onion is tender—about 4 minutes. Sprinkle with 2 tablespoonfuls flour. Stir and cook for 1 minute. Add beef stock and bring mixture to a simmer, stirring constantly until thickened—about 5 minutes. Stir in mustard and dill weed. Stir in browned meat and heat. Add sour cream just before serving.

Suggestion: Serve over rice or noodles.

Wine suggestion: Red Bordeaux

Preparation time: 30 minutes
Cooking time: 20 minutes

Serves: 4–6

Diane Basso

BARBECUED SHORT RIBS
This Oriental barbecue will be a family favorite

2 green onions, shredded
1 tsp. sesame seeds
1½ T. sugar
2 tsps. sesame oil or
 1 T. vegetable oil
¼ tsp. garlic powder
¼ tsp. pepper
3 tsps. white wine or sherry
 (optional)
¼ tsp. monosodium
 glutamate (MSG)
2 lbs. beef short ribs
 (boneless preferred)

In medium-size bowl, mix together all ingredients except beef. Trim off fat from short ribs and slice thin on meaty side. Marinate meat in marinade for about 20 to 30 minutes. Broil short ribs for 7 to 10 minutes on 1 side and about 5 minutes on the other.

Wine suggestion: Valpolicella or Zinfandel

Preparation time: 45 minutes
Cooking time: 15 minutes

Easy

Serves: 4

Mrs. Young Hai Park

STEAK ESZTERHAZY

2 lbs. round steak, ½ inch
   thick
Salt and pepper
Flour
3 T. butter
1½ onions, finely chopped
½ tsp. garlic, minced
½ carrot, finely chopped
3 T. flour
3 cups beef stock
½ tsp. ground allspice
3 bay leaves
4 peppercorns
⅛ tsp. thyme
1 strip lemon peel, ½ inch
   wide
2 T. parsley, chopped
4 slices bacon, chopped
¼ cup white wine vinegar
2 parsnips, julienne cut
1 carrot, julienne cut
¾ cup whipping cream,
   unwhipped
1 tsp. lemon juice
4 dill pickles, cut in strips

Cut steak into 6 portions; salt, pepper, and flour them. Brown in butter. Remove steaks. Add onions, garlic, and finely chopped carrot to skillet. Cook for 8 minutes. Stir in 3 tablespoonfuls flour. Gradually add beef stock, stirring until thickened. Add allspice, bay leaves, peppercorns, thyme, lemon peel, parsley, bacon, and vinegar. Return meat to the mixture. Bring to boil. Reduce heat to low. Partially cover. Cook 50 minutes, or until tender. In another pan, boil parsnips and carrots in salted water for 2 to 3 minutes, or until tender. Drain. Arrange steaks on platter and keep warm in 250° oven. Strain juice in skillet. Press vegetables through strainer. Whisk in cream and lemon juice. Add vegetable strips and dill pickle strips. Simmer for 2 to 3 minutes. Pour over steak.

Preparation time: 30 minutes
Cooking time: 1 hour

Can make ahead

Serves: 6

Mabel Eyth

TERIYAKI

Unusual way to prepare this dish

⅔ cup soy sauce
⅓ cup sugar
1 clove garlic, crushed
2–3 T. water
¼ cup red wine (optional)
2–3 lbs. round or sirloin
steak
3 ozs. fresh mushrooms,
sliced
2 hearts celery, sliced
horizontally
½ green pepper, cut in
strips
2 T. butter
1 T. soy sauce
(more, if desired)

In glass dish, combine soy sauce, sugar, garlic, water, and wine. Add steak and let stand for 2 to 3 hours, turning often. Take meat from marinade and cut in bite-sized pieces. Sauté mushrooms, celery, and green pepper in butter for a few minutes, keeping crisp. Add meat and cook until pink in middle. Pour in soy sauce before serving. Serve with Fried Rice.

Preparation time: 10 minutes   Easy   Serves: 4–6
Cooking time: 10 minutes   Must make ahead

Nancy Jacobs

VIENNESE GOULASH

1 lb. chuck (not stew meat),
cubed
1 large onion, sliced
1 green pepper, diced
¼ cup olive oil
1 can (6 oz.) tomato paste
2 bay leaves
1 T. paprika
2 T. sour cream
Baby lasagne or wide
noodles, buttered,
sprinkled with poppy
seeds

Sauté meat, onion, and green pepper in enough olive oil to cover bottom of pan. Add tomato paste, bay leaves, and paprika. Cover and bake at 350° for at least 1½ hours. Check for tenderness of meat. Refrigerate overnight (or freeze). Heat at 300° for 1 hour. Add sour cream. Toss noodles; top with goulash.

Preparation time: 20 minutes   Easy   Serves: 4
Cooking time: 2½ hours   Must make ahead   Can freeze

Millicent Penniman

SUKIYAKI
Add rice and your meal is ready

½ cup dried mushrooms
½ cup water (approximately)
6 T. consommé, undiluted
6 T. soy sauce
2 T. sugar
2 T. sake
1 Bermuda onion, sliced
8 green onions, cut in
  1½–inch pieces
1 cup green cabbage, sliced
1 cup Chinese cabbage,
  sliced
10 ozs. fresh mushrooms,
  sliced
1 cup bean sprouts
  (fresh preferred)
1 cup bamboo shoots
1 cup water chestnuts,
  sliced
½ lb. fresh spinach
1 lb. thinly sliced sirloin,
  cut into 2-inch strips

Boil dried mushrooms in water until tender. Reserve liquid. Combine 6 tablespoonfuls mushroom liquid with consommé, soy sauce, sugar, and sake. Sauté onion and green onions in butter in wok or large skillet for 1 to 2 minutes. Stir in green cabbage, Chinese cabbage, fresh mushrooms, dried mushrooms, and ¼ soy mixture. Cook for 3 to 4 minutes. Stir in bean sprouts, bamboo shoots, water chestnuts, spinach, and remaining soy mixture. Cook for 2 to 3 minutes. Add meat. Cook until it loses its red color. Serve immediately.

Note: Vegetables should be tender-crisp and can be sliced in the morning.

Preparation time: 20 minutes
Cooking time: 10 minutes

Serves: 4–6

Mabel Eyth

BEEF BARBECUE
Great for after-tennis suppers

5 lbs. lean beef roast (rump,
  brisket, etc.)
Salt and pepper
2 stalks celery, chopped
1 onion, coarsely chopped
1 bay leaf
⅓ cup brown sugar, packed
¼ cup prepared mustard
Dash of Worcestershire
  sauce

Pot method: Salt and pepper roast. Put meat in a 5-quart Dutch oven, covering halfway with 5 to 6 cups water. Add celery, onion, and bay leaf. Simmer for 5 to 6 hours. When meat falls apart, remove fat and pour broth into another pan. Add remaining ingredients to broth and pour back on meat. Continue simmering for 30 minutes.

Pressure cooker method: Salt and pepper roast. Put meat in a 6-quart pressure

(continued)

164

BEEF BARBECUE (continued)

1 cup catsup
1 can (15 oz.) tomato sauce
½ tsp. dry mustard
½ tsp. garlic salt

cooker; add 3 cups water, celery, onion, and bay leaf. Bring to pressure for 50 minutes. When meat falls apart, remove fat and pour broth into another pan. Add remaining ingredients to broth. Remove rack from cooker; add broth and 2 to 3 cups water. Continue simmering for 30 minutes.

Hint: For smoked flavor, brush roast with liquid smoke and let stand overnight.

Preparation time: 10 minutes
Cooking time: 5 hours
Pressure cooking time:
  1 hour 20 minutes

Easy
Can make ahead

Serves: 10–12
Can freeze

Kathryn Fields

DRUNKEN STEAK
Chuck made "choice" for picnics

Chuck roast (blade), 1¾–2
  inches thick
Meat tenderizer

Marinade:
½ cup bourbon
½ cup brown sugar, packed
2 T. lemon juice
2 T. Worcestershire sauce
10 ozs. soy sauce
2½ cups water

Rub roast generously with tenderizer on both sides. Combine marinade ingredients. Stir well and pour over meat. Marinate in refrigerator for 24 hours, puncturing roast often with a sharp fork. Turn roast at least 4 times while marinating. Place roast 5 inches from medium-hot coals. Turn roast every 5 minutes and baste generously with marinade at each turning. Grill for approximately 1 hour, puncturing roast with a sharp fork during grilling. There is enough marinade for 2 to 3 steaks.

Wine suggestion: California Burgundy

Preparation time: 5 minutes
Grilling time: 1 hour

Serves: 4

Janee Knapper

SOUTH SEAS BEEF AND PINEAPPLE

2 lbs. sirloin, cut into 1-inch cubes
1½ tsps. Aćcent
¼ cup salad oil
1 can (20 oz.) pineapple chunks
2 tsps. soy sauce
1 T. vinegar
2 cups rice, uncooked
1 can (13 oz.) chicken broth
¼ cup butter
½–¾ tsp. curry powder
1 medium onion, chopped
1 cup celery, diced
1 green pepper, cut in 1-inch cubes
1 cucumber, thinly sliced
1 tomato, peeled, cut in wedges
1 T. cornstarch mixed with 2 T. water

In large frying pan, sprinkle beef with 1 teaspoonful Aćcent; brown in oil. Drain pineapple, reserving syrup. Mix pineapple syrup, soy sauce, and vinegar; bring to boil. Add to beef; simmer for 20 minutes. Prepare rice according to package directions, substituting chicken broth for water. Stir in butter and curry powder. Sprinkle remaining Aćcent on vegetables. Add onion to beef mixture; simmer for 5 minutes. Add celery, green pepper, and cucumber; simmer for 5 minutes. Add pineapple and tomato; heat through. Add cornstarch-water mixture to beef mixture. Cook, stirring constantly, until it thickens and boils. Serve beef mixture over rice.

Wine suggestion: California Burgundy

Preparation time: 20 minutes
Cooking time: 30 minutes

Easy

Serves: 8

Kay Jones

MICHIGAN FARM PASTIES
Popular Michigan dish

PASTRY:
3 cups flour, sifted
1 cup lard
1 tsp. salt
½ cup cold water

Blend flour, lard, and salt with a fork until mixture is crumbly. Add water and work until the dough can be handled and is not sticky. Wrap in waxed paper and refrigerate while preparing meat filling.

(continued)

166

MICHIGAN PASTIES (continued)

FILLING:
1½ lbs. lean round,
　uncooked, cut into very
　small cubes
3 potatoes, cut in ½–inch
　cubes
½ cup carrots, grated
½ cup rutabagas, finely
　chopped
½ cup onion, finely chopped
½ tsp. salt
Dash of pepper
1 T. butter

In large bowl, combine first 5 filling ingredients. Add salt, pepper, and butter; blend well. Divide dough into 6 parts; roll out each to an 8 or 9-inch round. On half of each round, place ⅛ the filling. Fold over other half and press edges to seal. Slash top 4 times and bake at 325° for 1 hour, until lightly browned.

Preparation time: 1 hour
Baking time: 1 hour

Can make ahead

Serves: 6
Can freeze

Gerald deMink
Jan Shugars

BURGUNDY BRISKET

1 (3–4 lb.) beef brisket
3 T. bacon fat
2 medium onions, sliced
1 beef bouillon cube
　dissolved in 1 cup water
3 T. flour
1–2 T. catsup
1 tsp. salt
½ tsp. thyme
¼ tsp. garlic powder
1 cup Burgundy
2 T. sherry
Small potatoes (optional)
Carrots (optional)

In large kettle, brown beef in bacon fat. Remove beef. Add onions and sauté until transparent. Return meat to kettle. Mix prepared bouillon, flour, and catsup; pour over meat. Add seasonings, Burgundy, and sherry. Simmer for 3 hours, or until very tender.

Optional: Small potatoes and carrots may also be added.

Wine suggestion: California Burgundy

Preparation time: 30 minutes
Cooking time: 3 hours

Easy
Can make ahead

Serves: 6–8

Joann Data

MEAT SAUCE FOR CANNELLONI PARMESANI, MANICOTTI, AND SPINACH LASAGNE

2 pkgs. (12 oz. each)
   sausage links, cut into
   small pieces, or 1½ lbs.
   mild Italian sausage, fried,
   drained
1 large onion, chopped
¼ lb. fresh mushrooms
   (optional)
1 can (6 oz.) tomato paste
1 can (8 oz.) tomato sauce
2 cans (16 oz. each) stewed
   tomatoes
2 bay leaves
2 T. basil
2 T. oregano
1 T. Worcestershire sauce
1 T. sugar
2 cloves garlic

Brown meat and onion in skillet; drain. (If using mushrooms, add halfway through cooking time for meat.) In large pot, combine this mixture with remaining ingredients. Simmer for at least 3 hours.

Note: Best if made a day ahead so that flavors can blend.

Preparation time: 10 minutes
Cooking time: 3 hours

Should make ahead
Can freeze

Yield: 5 cups

CANNELLONI PARMESANI

3 eggs
⅔ cup flour
1 cup milk
1½ T. butter
1 T. garlic, minced
2 cups fresh parsley,
   minced, lightly packed
1½ lbs. Monterey Jack
   cheese, cut into sticks
1–1½ cups Parmesan
   cheese, grated
about 5 cups Meat Sauce
   (see page 168)

To make crepes, beat eggs slightly and add flour, beating until smooth. Blend in milk. Beat until smooth. In a lightly greased 6 to 8-inch skillet, pour 1 to 2 tablespoonfuls batter. Tip pan so that batter covers bottom. Cook over medium heat until top is shiny and edge brown. Flip crepe; brown lightly on other side. Cover crepes until ready to use (can freeze).

To prepare garlic-parsley, melt butter in skillet and add garlic and parsley. Cook and stir until parsley wilts or turns bright green.

(continued)

CANNELLONI PARMESANI (continued)

Assemble Cannelloni by placing a stick of Monterey Jack cheese in center of crepe (divide cheese equally among crepes). Sprinkle garlic-parsley (divided equally among crepes) over cheese stick. Fold crepe around cheese-parsley mixture to make a cylinder. In a 12 × 15-inch pan or two 6 × 15-inch pans, place about 1½ cups Meat Sauce. Arrange Cannelloni (seam side down) on top of sauce. Cover Cannelloni with remaining sauce (about 3½ cups). Sprinkle with Parmesan cheese. Bake at 450° for 12 to 15 minutes.

Wine suggestion: Barolo

Preparation time: 1 hour   Can make ahead   Serves: 8
Cooking time: 15 minutes   Can freeze

Greeta Douglass

MANICOTTI

FILLING:
⅓ cup Romano or Parmesan cheese, grated
1 cup ricotta cheese
1 lb. provolone cheese, grated
½ tsp. basil
¼ tsp. thyme
¼ tsp. oregano
2 eggs, slightly beaten
Salt and pepper to taste
Meat Sauce (see page 168)
1 pkg. (6 oz.) Manicotti noodles
8 ozs. presliced mozzarella cheese

To make filling, combine cheeses, herbs, eggs, and salt and pepper. Mix lightly. Parboil manicotti noodles according to package directions. Stuff with cheese mixtures. Place in 9 × 12-inch buttered baking dish so that they lie flat. Cover stuffed noodles completely with slices of mozzarella cheese. Top with enough Meat Sauce to cover. Bake at 350° for 30 to 40 minutes.

Wine suggestion: Barolo

Preparation time: 30 minutes   Can make ahead   Serves: 6–8
Cooking time: 30–40 minutes   Can freeze

Greeta Douglass

169

RAVIOLI

Worth the time it takes to make!

1 (3 lb.) pork butt
2 lbs. veal or beef
Salt and pepper
½ tsp. rosemary leaves
1–2 bay leaves
2–4 cloves garlic
6 or 7 cabbage leaves
7 eggs (divided)
4 T. water
3½ cups flour, sifted
2 T. Parmesan cheese,
  grated
Pinch of cinnamon
Pinch of nutmeg
Parmesan cheese,
  grated (for garnish)

Season meats with salt, pepper, rosemary leaves, and bay leaves; insert 1 or 2 garlic cloves into each. Roast at 325° for 2 hours. Remove from oven. Cool. Reserve drippings. Boil cabbage leaves until tender; drain well and set aside.

Beat 4 eggs well; add water and blend. Add flour gradually until dough can be handled. Knead on lightly floured board for about ½ hour. (This makes a medium-hard dough.) Place dough in lightly greased bowl. Cover. Let stand for 1 hour before rolling out. Rub dough with oil to prevent drying out.

Grind together both meats and cabbage. (Food processor is great for this, but do not grind meat too fine. It should have texture.) To ground meat mixture, add 3 eggs, Parmesan cheese, cinnamon, nutmeg, and about 3 tablespoonfuls warm drippings from roast. Mix together until meat is moist. If it is still too dry, add more gravy. Meat should be moist so that it can be shaped into balls a little smaller than a walnut. Set aside.

Take pieces of dough about the size of a baseball, and roll on lightly floured board into 4-inch-wide strips (about ⅛ inch thick). Work quickly so that dough doesn't dry out; keep extra dough covered. Place well-rounded teaspoonful filling in center of strip every 2 inches. Fold dough so that the 2 edges meet. With the side of hand, press down between each mound of filling. Seal outer edge and cut into squares with wheel-type ravioli cutter. Seal edges with fork. Repeat until all of dough and meat filling is used. When ready to cook, use an 8 or 10-quart kettle. Fill ⅔ full with water; add 1 tablespoonful salt and bring to a boil. Drop in ravioli; let simmer about 15 minutes. Cook about 3 dozen at a time—don't crowd. Lift out with slotted spoon; drain on paper towels. When all are cooked, reheat; place in heated dish. Pour sauce over them and garnish with grated Parmesan cheese.

Wine suggestion: Barolo

Preparation time: 5 hours
Cooking time: 15 minutes

Can make ahead

Serves: 8
Can freeze

Vi Anderson

TOMATO SAUCE FOR RAVIOLI

3 T. oil
1 small onion, chopped
1 lb. ground beef
Salt and pepper to taste
3 cans (8 oz. each) tomato
  sauce
¾ cup water
2 bay leaves
1 tsp. rosemary leaves
1 tsp. oregano
2–4 cloves garlic, pressed
1 can (6 oz.) tomato paste

Heat oil and sauté onion. When onion is brown, remove from oil. Add ground beef and brown. Add onion, salt and pepper, tomato sauce, water, bay leaves, rosemary, oregano, and garlic cloves. Simmer for 1 hour. Add tomato paste mixed with a little water. This will thicken the sauce. Simmer for about 2 hours. Stir occasionally so that sauce doesn't burn. If sauce is too thick, add a little water.

Preparation time: 20 minutes
Cooking time: 2 hours

Can make ahead

Serves: 8
Can freeze

Vi Anderson

DAUBE GLACE
Lovely for hot summer evening

STOCK:
4–5 lbs. veal shank and
    fresh pork hocks
1 small onion, sliced
1 small green pepper,
    chopped
3 stalks celery, sliced
2 carrots, sliced
2 tsps. (scant) salt
Dash of black pepper
Dash (generous) of cayenne
    pepper
¾ cup dry sherry
7–10 cups cold water
3 sprigs parsley

Brown shank and hocks in 400° oven for 20 minutes. Place all remaining stock ingredients in a large kettle of cold water and bring to boil. Skim surface, lower heat, and partially cover. Cook for 3 to 4 hours. Strain broth and reserve. Begin preparing meat 1½ hours before broth is finished.

MEAT:
2 strips bacon
1 bay leaf, crushed
½ tsp. thyme
½ tsp. marjoram
Dash of garlic powder
¼ tsp. sage
3 lbs. sirloin tip or beef
    round
2 T. butter
1 T. oil
2 T. brandy

Cut bacon into small pieces and roll in combined herbs. Insert bacon into slits which have been cut in the meat. Let stand for 1 hour. Melt butter and oil in a large skillet. Brown meat on all sides. Add brandy and ignite; let burn until flame dies. Place browned meat in kettle containing strained stock; pour in pan juices. Simmer, covered, until tender—approximately 2 hours. Remove meat. Cool. Reserve broth.

CLARITY BROTH:
1 egg white and eggshell
1 large lemon, very thinly
    sliced
Sprigs parsley (for garnish)

Beat egg white lightly and add with the eggshell to the boiling reserved stock. Boil for 5 to 10 minutes; strain through a cloth-lined sieve. Check for seasoning. Cool to lukewarm.

(continued)

DAUBE GLACE (continued)

To assemble: Pour ½-inch layer of broth in lightly greased 9 × 5-inch loaf pan. Let set in refrigerator. Place lemon slices dipped in broth over this layer and around sides of pan. Either trim the cooled meat to fit the pan or cut into bite-sized pieces. Place in pan. Add rest of broth and chill thoroughly or overnight. Chill any extra broth in square pan. Unmold loaf onto serving platter. Cube remaining chilled broth and place around loaf. Garnish with parsley sprigs.

Suggestion: Very good with cooked asparagus, rice salad, and French bread.

Wine suggestion: Cabernet Sauvignon

Preparation time: 6 hours	Must make ahead	Serves: 6–8

George Ann Castel

BEEF STEW IN RED WINE
Robust flavor

4 strips bacon, cut into
  1-inch pieces
2½ lbs. beef stew meat,
  cut into cubes
Salt and pepper to taste
½ lb. small onions
1 cup dry red wine
1½ T. brandy or cognac
2 cloves garlic, minced
⅛ tsp. marjoram
⅛ tsp. thyme
1 strip peel from large
  orange
1 T. beef stock base
  dissolved in 1½ cups
  water
1 medium onion, sliced
½ lb. mushrooms
2 T. butter or margarine
Parsley, finely cut

In heavy pan, brown bacon; remove. Season beef with salt and pepper. Add to bacon drippings; brown. Transfer to a 3-quart casserole. Add small onions and brown slightly. Remove from pan and set aside. Gradually stir in wine and brandy. Add garlic, marjoram, thyme, orange peel, prepared beef stock, and onion. Bring to boil; pour over meat. Cover casserole; bake at 325° for 2 to 2½ hours. Add browned onions and cook for 30 minutes longer. Quarter mushrooms or leave whole if small. Add mushrooms to meat for the last 10 to 15 minutes. Sprinkle with parsley.

Wine suggestion: California Burgundy or Zinfandel

Preparation time: 25 minutes	Can make ahead	Serves: 8
Cooking time: 2½ hours		

Eleanor Allen

SPINACH LASAGNE

1 box (16 oz.) lasagne
noodles
2 pkgs. (10 oz. each) frozen
chopped spinach, drained
(press out excess water)
1 egg
3 T. Parmesan cheese
1½ cups ricotta cheese
⅛ tsp. nutmeg
Salt and pepper to taste
Meat Sauce (see page 168)
½ lb. mozzarella cheese,
grated

In large pot of boiling water, cook noodles according to package directions. Combine spinach with egg, cheeses, and seasonings. In large baking dish, alternate layers of Meat Sauce, noodles, spinach mixture, and Meat Sauce, ending with Meat Sauce. Top with mozzarella cheese. Bake at 350° for 20 to 30 minutes, until bubbly. Let set for 10 minutes before serving.

Wine suggestion: Barolo

Preparation time: 40 minutes
Cooking time: 20–30 minutes

Can make ahead

Serves: 8
Can freeze

Bettina Rollins

STEAK AND MUSHROOMS ANYTIME!!
This will become a family favorite!

1 lb. ground beef
½ cup evaporated milk
1 T. onion, grated
½ tsp. salt
½ tsp. pepper
2 T. butter
2 T. flour
½ cup consommé
½ cup red wine
1 tsp. parsley, chopped
1 can (4 oz.) mushrooms,
undrained

Lightly mix meat with evaporated milk, onion, salt, and pepper. Shape into 4 large patties. Heat butter in 14-inch skillet; quickly brown patties. Remove. Add flour to butter and blend. Add consommé and remaining ingredients. Simmer sauce, stirring occasionally, until thick—about 10 minutes. Add patties and simmer until meat is medium rare—about 4 minutes. Serve over toast points, rice, noodles, or mashed potatoes.

Preparation time: 10 minutes
Cooking time: 15 minutes

Easy
Can make ahead

Serves: 4

Barbara Beardsley

STUFFED CABBAGE, FRENCH STYLE
This looks as lovely as it tastes

2 cups cooked brown rice
½ tsp. cumin
1 large cabbage
1½ lbs. ground beef
1 T. Dijon mustard
1 clove garlic, minced,
  or ¼ tsp. garlic powder
2 large tomatoes, diced
½ tsp. marjoram
¼ tsp. celery seed
2 eggs, beaten
2 cans (10 ½ oz. each)
  beef stock (bouillon)
½ cup red wine
½ tsp. ground cloves
⅓ cup cheddar cheese,
  grated
Carrots (optional)
Potatoes (optional)

Combine rice with cumin. Core and scoop out cabbage; keep large round shell intact. Sauté beef; drain fat. Add mustard and garlic. Mix meat and rice with tomatoes, marjoram, celery seed, and ¾ of the eggs. Stuff mixture into cabbage and place, open end up, in Dutch oven or crockpot. Mix stock and wine with cloves; pour over stuffed cabbage so that bottom half of cabbage rests in broth. Brush remaining egg over stuffing. Sprinkle with cheese. May add pared carrots and/or potatoes to side of pot. Simmer for 50 to 60 minutes. Serve cabbage in tureen; cut in sections to serve.

Preparation time: 45 minutes
Cooking time: 50 minutes

Can make ahead

Serves: 6–8

Mark Sutherlin

Hint: Change spaghetti night by making a spaghetti pie. To 6 ounces cooked spaghetti, add (and stir) 2 tablespoonfuls margarine, ⅓ cup Parmesan cheese, and 2 beaten eggs. Form this into a "crust" in a buttered 10-inch pie plate. Spread 1 cup cottage cheese over top of spaghetti and cover all with a generous amount of favorite spaghetti sauce. Sprinkle with ½ cup shredded mozzarella cheese; bake at 350° for 20 minutes. Can be frozen.

CHILI
Super midwinter treat!

2 lbs. (or more) ground beef
4 onions, chopped
5 cloves garlic, minced
1 cup celery (with leaves, chopped
1 green pepper, chopped
1 can (3 lb. 5 oz.) red kidney beans, undrained
1 can (28 oz.) tomatoes
2 cans (6 oz. each) tomato sauce or 6 ozs. tomato paste and 8 ozs. tomato sauce
2 beef bouillon cubes dissolved in 1 cup water
1 can (12 oz.) beer
1 tsp. Worcestershire sauce
2 T. chili powder
1 T. oregano
1 tsp. basil
1 tsp. cumin seeds or powder
2 tsps. salt
Pepper, freshly ground
Dash of Tabasco sauce
1 T. vinegar
1 T. brown sugar
¼ cup catsup

Sauté together meat, onions, garlic, celery, and green pepper until meat is no longer pink. Drain fat. In a large kettle, combine meat mixture with remaining ingredients. Bring to boil; lower heat and simmer, covered, for 2 to 3 hours.

Note: Better if made day before and reheated.

Preparation time: 30 minutes
Cooking time: 3 hours

Should make ahead

Serves: 10–12
Can freeze

Jessie B. Quinn

176

ENCHILADAS

1 can (10 oz.) mild or hot
    enchilada sauce
1 can (8 oz.) tomato sauce
Oil (for frying)
1 pkg. (12) corn tortillas
1 lb. ground beef, cooked,
    or 2 cups chicken,
    cooked, chopped
1 cup onion, chopped
1 can (4 oz.) green chili
    peppers, chopped (for
    extra spice, use jalapeño
    peppers)
2½ cups Monterey Jack
    cheese, grated (grated
    sharp cheddar will do)
1 cup black olives, chopped
    (optional)
½ pt. sour cream

In a skillet, mix enchilada and tomato sauces. In another small skillet, heat 1 inch oil. With tongs, place each tortilla in hot oil; slowly count to 3—tortilla should be just softened. Remove from oil and place on paper towels, stacking each on top of paper. Place softened tortilla in skillet with sauce briefly. Remove tortilla; lay flat. Place a line of meat, onion, chili peppers, cheese, and black olives in the middle of tortilla. Roll up and secure with toothpick. Place in 9 × 13-inch pan which has been spread with 6 to 8 tablespoonfuls sauce. When all 12 tortillas have been filled, sprinkle any remaining peppers and onion over enchiladas and pour remaining sauce over this. Top with remaining cheese. Bake at 375° for 20 to 30 minutes, or until sauce is bubbling and cheese is melted. Serve with sour cream. Can assemble in morning and bake later.

Beer suggestion: Carta Blanca

Preparation time: 30 minutes   Can make ahead   Serves: 6
Baking time: 25 minutes   Can freeze

Mary Godfrey

GATLETTA

½ cup milk
2 slices stale bread, cubed
1½ lbs. ground beef
1 egg
Salt and pepper
2–3 T. onion, chopped
1 egg, beaten
Cracker crumbs
2 T. margarine
1 cup sour cream (optional)

Combine milk and bread cubes; add to meat along with egg, salt, pepper, and onion. Mix all together. Shape into 8 oval (not round) patties. Dip each patty in beaten egg and cracker crumbs. In a skillet, fry in margarine until browned but pink in the middle. Sour cream may be mixed with pan drippings and served with meat.

Preparation time: 20 minutes   Easy   Serves: 6

Emma Born

177

CROWN ROAST OF PORK
(WITH 2 STUFFINGS)
Marvelous for holidays or dinner parties

½ lb. lean sausage
2 T. fat
¼ cup onion, chopped
½ tsp. salt
½ tsp. pepper
Poultry seasonings to taste
2 T. mustard pickle relish
3 cups soft stale bread
   crumbs
1 egg, beaten
½ cup white raisins,
   steamed
1 (6 lb.) crown roast of pork

Sauté sausage in hot fat; break with a fork until brown. Add onion and stir fry for 1 minute. Cool. Crumble large pieces of sausage; toss with remaining ingredients and moisten with hot water or broth if desired. Stand roast in oiled shallow roasting pan and fill center with stuffing. Roast at 325° for 2½ to 3 hours.

Adrienne de Windt

2 cups fresh bread crumbs
⅓ cup milk
½ cup onion, minced
2 T. butter
½ lb. pork sausage
¾ cup celery, chopped
¼ cup raisins
¼ cup raw cranberries
2 tart apples, peeled, diced
   (Granny Smith apples
   good for this)
Salt and pepper to taste
Sage to taste
Thyme to taste

In a small bowl, moisten bread crumbs with milk. Squeeze crumbs dry. Sauté onion in butter until soft but not colored. Add sausage and sauté lightly, breaking meat with fork. Add celery, raisins, cranberries, and apples. Cook for 5 minutes. Transfer to large bowl; combine with bread crumbs. Season stuffing with salt, pepper, sage, and thyme. Stuff and roast crown as directed above.

Wine suggestion: Beaujolais

Preparation time: 20 minutes
Roasting time: 3 hours

Can make ahead

Serves: 6–8

Julie Crockett

TART COUNTRY RIBS

Great for large parties!

3–4 lbs. Country-style ribs,
   cut into serving pieces
Salt and pepper
½ cup pineapple juice
Juice of 2 limes
¾ cup catsup
1½ tsps. soy sauce
2 T. instant minced onion
2 T. brown sugar
½ tsp. dry mustard
1 tsp. salt

Sprinkle ribs with salt and pepper and arrange in shallow baking pan. Cover and bake at 350° for 40 minutes. Pour off excess fat. Combine remaining ingredients to make marinade. Pour over ribs. Cover. Marinate in refrigerator overnight. Remove from marinade. Drain well. Grill on low coals for 10 minutes per side, or until meat is nicely browned; baste frequently with remaining marinade.

Preparation time: 10 minutes
   plus marinating time
Cooking time: 1 hour

Easy
Must make ahead

Serves: 4–6
Easily doubled

Jill Berglund

MAPLE-GLAZED HAM WITH SWEET POTATOES

½ smoked ham, butt end
   (about 6–7 lbs.)
Whole cloves
¼ cup butter or margarine,
   melted
1 cup maple syrup
Rind of 1 orange, grated
¼ tsp. ground cloves
1 cup brown sugar, packed
8–10 sweet potatoes,
   cooked until tender,
   peeled

With a sharp knife, cut fat of ham into diamonds. Press a whole clove into the center of each diamond. Place ham, cut side down, on foil-lined baking pan. In a bowl, mix butter, syrup, orange rind, cloves, and brown sugar. Place sweet potatoes around the ham. Spoon some of glaze mixture over ham and potatoes. Bake at 350° for 1 hour. Baste ham and potatoes with glaze every 15 minutes. Slice ham and serve some of pan juice over each serving (or serve in a gravy boat).

Wine suggestion: Vouvray or Chenin Blanc

Preparation time: 30 minutes
Baking time: 1 hour

Serves: 10–12

Marilyn Walker

BAKED HAM IN RYE CRUST

Working dough is easy and fun with a man's help

1 (8 lb.) ham
1 cup brown sugar, packed
1 cup honey
2 T. dry mustard
20 whole cloves
8 cups rye flour
2–3 cans (10 oz. each) beef bouillon
1–2 cans (12 oz. each) beer
½ T. each chives, chopped; tarragon; chervil; parsley; garlic, minced; green onion, chopped; oregano, chopped; and pinch of nutmeg (mixed together)
2 tsps. caraway seed

Remove skin, rind, and excess fat from ham; score surface. Make a thick paste of brown sugar, honey, and mustard. Spread over ham; stick cloves into top of ham. Mix rye flour with enough beef bouillon to make a thick dough. On a large floured breadboard, roll the dough out to ½-inch thickness. Brush surface with beer and sprinkle with mixed seasonings. Scatter caraway seed over dough. Place ham in middle of dough. Carefully pull dough up and around ham, forming a bottle-like opening at the top. Make a "stopper" of dough, roll in dry flour, and set lightly in the opening. Place on baking sheet and bake at 325° until dough has set hard—45 to 60 minutes. Take out of oven, remove "stopper," and pour in as much beer as the sugar-honey-mustard coating will absorb. Recork and bake for 50 minutes longer, or until crust is thoroughly baked and browned. Take from oven. Break crust from ham. Slice ham and serve.

Preparation time: 40 minutes
Cooking time: 2 hours

Can make ahead

Serves: 12–16

Ann Johnson

Hint: Marinate a 3-pound pork roast in 4 teaspoonfuls sugar, 4 teaspoonfuls honey, and 3 tablespoonfuls chicken broth for 1 to 2 hours at room temperature. Roast at 350° for 2½ hours. Slice. Provide the following condiments: 1 bowl soy sauce, 1 bowl sesame seeds, 1 bowl Mr. Mustard.

Nancy Wedd

GLAZED PORK ROAST

1 (4–5 lb.) pork roast
1 cup sugar
½ tsp. salt
½ cup water
½ cup vinegar
1 tsp. paprika
2 T. green pepper, chopped
2 tsps. cornstarch
1 T. water

Brown pork, uncovered, at 450° for 30 minutes. While roast is browning, mix sugar, salt, water, vinegar, paprika, and green pepper in small saucepan. Stir and bring to boil. Remove from heat; add cornstarch mixed with water. Drain fat from roast. Reduce oven to 300°. Baste roast with some of the glaze. Roast at least 2½ hours longer, basting frequently with fresh glaze. Roasting time depends upon size of roast.

Microwave: Combine sugar, salt, water, vinegar, paprika, and green pepper in a 4-cup glass measuring cup. Microwave on high for 2 to 3 minutes, or until mixture boils. Stir once. Add cornstarch-water mixture. Place pork roast in shallow glass or pyroceramic pan. Microwave on high for 15 to 20 minutes. Pour off fat. Baste roast with glaze. Microwave on high for 10 minutes per pound, or until microwave thermometer registers 170°. Baste with glaze and turn frequently during cooking. Wrap roast in aluminum foil until thermometer registers 185°—about 15 minutes.

Preparation time: 5 minutes   Easy   Serves: 8
Cooking time: 3 hours
Microwave: 1½ hours

Sally Mantle

TAIWANESE CABBAGE AND PORK
Add rice—dinner's ready!

1 lb. pork
3 T. oil
2 cups onion, diced
1 medium head purple
  cabbage, shredded
1 T. ginger root, chopped
1 tsp. sugar
1 green pepper, sliced

Cut pork into small pieces. Heat oil in pan and sauté pork until tender; add onion and sauté lightly. Add cabbage and stir in pan for a few minutes. Add ginger root, sugar, and green peppers. Heat thoroughly; serve at once over hot rice.

Note: Vegetables *must* be crisp. If much liquid forms, thicken with 1 tablespoonful cornstarch in ¼ cup water.

Preparation time: 15 minutes   Easy   Serves: 4
Cooking time: 20 minutes   Must serve immediately

Estelle Early

DEVILED PORK TENDERLOIN
Basting gives this its marvelous flavor

2 or 3 tenderloins
Flour
Dry mustard to taste
Soy sauce to taste
Paprika to taste
Onion powder to taste
Pepper to taste
3 T. margarine
1½ cups water
½ cup vinegar
1 T. beef stock base
1 can (16 oz.) pineapple
  slices
Prepared mustard (optional)

Dredge meat in flour; place in baking pan (with about 2-inch sides). Sprinkle dry mustard and soy sauce generously over tenderloins. Add some paprika, onion powder, and pepper. Dot with margarine. Pour water and vinegar around meat; add bouillon. Bake at 325° for 1 hour, basting 2 or 3 times. Top with pineapple. Cook for 15 minutes longer. Serve with pan juices and prepared mustard.

Preparation time: 5 minutes
Cooking time: 1½ hours

Easy

Serves: 6–8
Easily doubled

Candy Woodruff

PORK CHOPS CARAWAY

Salt and pepper
4 loin pork chops,
  1 inch thick
2 tsps. caraway seed
2 large onions, sliced
½ pt. sour cream
½ tsp. dill weed

Salt and pepper chops and place in broiler pan or similar baking dish. Sprinkle with caraway seed. Place sliced onions on chops. Bake for 1½ hours at 300°, or until tender. (May be covered with foil and oven reduced to 250°, if necessary.) For last 15 minutes of baking time, add a large teaspoonful sour cream to each chop. Before serving, sprinkle with dill.

Suggestion: Brussels sprouts are good with this.

Microwave: Place pork chops (about 2 pounds) in 9 × 13-inch glass dish. Sprinkle with pepper (DO NOT SALT) and caraway seed. Add sliced onions. Cover with waxed paper and microwave on high for 15 to 20 minutes, or until chops are tender. For last 5 minutes, add large tablespoonful sour cream to each chop. Sprinkle with dill before serving.

Wine suggestion: White Burgundy

Preparation time: 5 minutes
Cooking time: 1½ hour
Microwave: 15–20 minutes

Easy

Serves: 4

Judy Brown

PORK LOIN JAVANESE

4 lbs. pork tenderloin
12 Brazil nuts, ground
2 cups onion, minced
4 cloves garlic, minced
½ cup olive oil
½ cup lemon juice
½ cup soy sauce
4 T. brown sugar
4 T. coriander
½ tsp. crushed red pepper
1 large green pepper, cut
  into chunks
1 lb. fresh mushrooms
1 pt. cherry tomatoes
1 large onion, cut into
  chunks

Cut tenderloin into 1-inch cubes. Combine next 9 ingredients to make marinade. Marinate pork and mushrooms for at least several hours. Put pork on skewers; broil over coals for about 30 minutes. Turn and baste several times. At the same time, grill green pepper, mushrooms, tomatoes, and onion on skewers over coals. Vegetables require less cooking time, so place them on separate skewers and cook for a shorter period of time. Onion chunks may be put on skewer with pork, if desired.

Preparation time: 15 minutes
Broiling time: 30 minutes

Easy
Must make ahead

Serves: 8

Greeta Douglass

TASTY PORK CHOPS
Good family fare

4 pork chops, 1 inch thick
2 T. butter
1 can (10¾ oz.) condensed
  cream of mushroom soup,
  undiluted
1 can (1 lb.) mixed chop
  suey vegetables,
  undrained
½ cup rice, uncooked
½ tsp. curry powder

In skillet, brown chops on both sides in butter. Mix soup, vegetables, rice, and curry powder; place in casserole. Add chops and drippings to top of rice mixture. Bake at 350° for 1 hour.

Microwave: In skillet, brown chops on both sides in butter. Mix remaining ingredients; place in glass or pyroceramic casserole. Add chops and drippings to top of rice mixture. Microwave on high for 20 minutes.

Wine suggestion: Riesling

Preparation time: 20 minutes
Cooking time: 1 hour
Microwave: 20 minutes

Can make ahead

Serves: 4

Jane Todd

RIO GRANDE PORK ROAST
Spicy sauce really perks up this roast

1 (4–5 lb.) boneless rolled
pork loin roast
½ tsp. salt
½ tsp. garlic salt (use
1 clove garlic if
microwaving)
1 tsp. chili powder (divided)
½ cup apple jelly
½ cup catsup
1 T. vinegar
½ cup corn chips, crushed

Place roast, fat side up, on rack in shallow roasting pan. Combine salt, garlic salt, and ½ teaspoonful chili powder; rub into roast. Roast at 325° for 2 to 2½ hours, or until thermometer registers 165°. In small saucepan, combine jelly, catsup, vinegar, and ½ teaspoonful chili powder. Bring to boil. Reduce heat and simmer, uncovered, for 2 minutes. Drain excess fat from pan and brush roast liberally with glaze. Sprinkle top with corn chips and roast for 10 to 15 minutes longer, or until thermometer registers 170°. Remove roast from oven and place on serving platter. Let stand for 10 minutes. Measure pan drippings, including any corn chips, and add water to make 1 cup. Heat to a boil and pass with meat.

Preparation time: 30 minutes
Cooking time: 2 hours

Easy
Should serve immediately

Serves: 8

Sue Kilgore

PORK CHOPS MADEIRA
This may become habit-forming!

4 loin pork chops
2 T. butter or margarine
3 T. Madeira
⅓ cup sour cream
Salt and pepper to taste

Brown chops in butter; lower heat and cook gently for about 30 minutes. Remove from pan. Drain off excess fat, if any. Add Madeira and sour cream. Stir to loosen brown bits from pan. Season to taste with salt and pepper. Add chops and simmer for a few minutes to heat. Do not boil sauce.

Wine suggestion: White Burgundy

Preparation time: 5 minutes
Cooking time: 35 minutes

Easy

Serves: 4
Easily doubled

"H" and Betz Nevenzel
The Butler Pantry
Saugatuck

PORK IN MUSTARD SAUCE

8 pork medallions (¾-inch rounds cut from loin or tenderloin)
Salt and pepper
Flour
¼ cup oil
⅔ cup dry white wine
⅔ cup sour cream
1 T. Dijon mustard
¼ tsp. basil
1 egg, hard cooked, minced

Sprinkle pork medallions with salt and pepper and dust with flour. Sauté in oil for 8 minutes, or until browned. Transfer to heated serving dish. Keep warm. Add wine to the pan; bring to a boil, stirring in the brown bits clinging to the bottom; reduce heat for 1 minute. Stir in sour cream; boil and stir the mixture for 2 minutes, or until reduced and thickened. Remove from heat and stir in mustard and basil. Add salt and pepper to taste. Pour sauce over medallions and garnish with hard-cooked egg.

Wine suggestion: Riesling

Preparation time: 10 minutes
Cooking time: 10 minutes

Easy

Serves: 4
Easily doubled

Bettina Rollins

SCHNITZEL HOLSTEIN

2 lbs. veal scallops
Salt and pepper
¼ cup flour
1 egg, lightly beaten
½ cup fine dry bread crumbs
6 T. butter
6 eggs, fried
Anchovy fillets (optional)
Pickled beets, thinly sliced
Dill pickles

Sprinkle veal with salt and pepper and dip in flour. Then dip into egg and coat with bread crumbs. (Can coat scallops in the morning and refrigerate until ready to cook.) Sauté in hot butter over medium high heat for about 3 minutes on each side, or until the crumbs are golden. Arrange on a warm serving platter. Top each schnitzel with a fried egg and garnish the platter with anchovy fillets, pickled beets, and dill pickles.

Wine suggestion: Pouilly-Fumé or Orvieto.

Preparation time: 30 minutes
Cooking time: 6 minutes

Easy
Can partially make ahead
Serve immediately

Serves: 6

Frances Shipman

VEAL CHOPS PARMESAN WITH GNOCCHI
All will appreciate the effort

4 veal loin chops,
  1¼ inches thick
Juice of 1 lime
Salt
Pepper, freshly ground
¼ cup plus 2 T. butter
  (divided)
½ tsp. chervil
Flour
Parmesan cheese, freshly
  grated
1 egg, beaten
¾ cup dry white wine or
  chicken stock

Trim chops and brush with lime juice, salt, and pepper. Melt ¼ cup butter with chervil. Dip chops in butter, then flour, and then Parmesan cheese; let sit for 5 minutes. Dip chops in egg, flour, and Parmesan cheese; let stand in refrigerator for 2 hours. Sauté chops quickly in 2 tablespoonfuls butter until they are browned on both sides. Pour wine or stock into skillet and simmer for 30 to 40 minutes. Serve with Gnocchi.

GNOCCHI:
1 cup water
¾ cup butter (divided)
1⅔ cups flour
1 tsp. salt
4 eggs
1 tsp. dry mustard
¼ cup Parmesan cheese,
  grated
¼ cup parsley, chopped

Bring water and ½ cup butter to boil. Remove from heat and beat in flour and salt. Return to heat and heat for 5 minutes longer. (Mixture should form ball.) Remove from heat and add eggs, beating vigorously after each addition. Beat until mixture is shiny. Stir in mustard and Parmesan cheese. Bring 2 quarts water to a boil and then reduce to a simmer. Put ⅓ dough at a time into a pastry bag with a No. 8 tip (round tip with about ½-inch opening). Pipe mixture into simmering water, cutting into 2-inch "noodles" as it falls. They will rise to surface when cooked—about 3 to 5 minutes. Remove with slotted spoon. Drain on paper towels. Repeat process with second and third batches. Set aside. This can be done early in the day. When ready to serve, pour ¼ cup melted butter and parsley over them, heat through, and serve with the veal chops.

Wine suggestion: Bardolino

Preparation time: 1 hour   Must make ahead   Serves: 4
Cooking time: 40 minutes

Marcia Brocklebank

VEAL SMETANA

The flames will bring raves from all

**12 veal scallops (about
    8 × 4 × ½ inch thick)**
Salt
Flour
**6–8 T. butter or margarine
    (divided)**
1 cup onion, finely minced
**1 lb. mushrooms,
    thinly sliced**
¼ cup brandy
1 cup dairy sour cream
½ tsp. salt

Dry scallops, sprinkle with salt, and dredge with flour. Heat 2 tablespoonfuls butter in chafing dish until bubbly. Add a few scallops; take care not to crowd them. Cook for 3 minutes on each side. Remove to a warm plate. Add fresh butter for each batch of scallops. When all have been cooked, add onion to fat left in pan and sauté and stir with a wooden spoon for 2 to 3 minutes. Add 1 or 2 more tablespoonfuls butter to pan; add mushrooms and stir with onions. Cover pan and cook mixture for 5 to 8 minutes, or until mushrooms are tender, stirring occasionally. Add the brandy, shake pan (keep face turned away). If brandy does not flame, ignite it with a match. After flames subside, stir in sour cream and ½ teaspoonful salt. Bring just to the boiling point. Return scallops to pan; spoon sauce over them and let it come to a boil (can keep warm but do not boil).

Wine suggestion: Mâcon Blanc

Preparation time: 40 minutes   Can make ahead   Serves: 6

Sharon Garside

Please note: Microwave directions in this book are for use with units having 600–700 watts (and above). If unit with lower wattage is used, baking times will need to be lengthened.

VEAL SCALLOPINI

1 T. flour
½ tsp. salt
Dash of pepper
4 (about 1 lb.) veal cutlets
¼ cup cooking oil
½ medium onion, thinly
  sliced
¼ lb. fresh mushrooms,
  sliced
1 can (16 oz.) tomatoes
1 T. parsley, snipped
1 T. capers, drained
¼ tsp. garlic salt
¼ tsp. leaf oregano,
  crushed
Noodles, buttered (optional)

Dust veal lightly with mixture of flour, salt, and pepper. In medium skillet, brown meat slowly in hot oil. Remove meat to warm plate; add onion and mushrooms to same skillet. Cook until tender but not brown. Add meat, tomatoes, parsley, capers, and seasonings. Cover. Simmer for 20 minutes, or until veal is tender, stirring occasionally. Arrange veal on hot buttered noodles; top with sauce.

Wine suggestion: Soave or Bardolino

Preparation time: 10 minutes
Cooking time: 30 minutes

Can make ahead

Serves: 4

Sharon Garside

VEAL WITH ARTICHOKES
Serve with a nice green salad for blue ribbon dinner

½ lb. veal scallops
Flour
1 pkg. (10 oz.) frozen
  artichoke hearts
¼ cup sweet butter
⅓ cup dry white wine
Salt and pepper to taste
Lemon wedges

Pound veal; lightly flour. Slice into narrow strips. Boil artichoke hearts until tender. Drain; sauté in butter for 5 minutes (until lightly browned). Add veal and brown on both sides for about 5 minutes (don't overcook). Add wine and bring to a boil. Salt and pepper to taste. Lower heat and simmer for 1 minute. Serve with lemon wedges and linguine.

(continued)

188

VEAL WITH ARTICHOKES (continued)

LINGUINE:
16 ozs. linguine
⅓ cup sweet butter, melted
¼ cup Parmesan cheese,
  grated
Fresh parsley, chopped
Salt and pepper to taste

Boil and drain linguine according to package directions. Toss immediately with butter, Parmesan cheese, parsley, and salt and pepper.

Wine suggestion: Chianti

Preparation time: 15 minutes
Cooking time: 25 minutes

Easy
Must serve
immediately

Serves: 2
Easily doubled

Laurie DeHaven

ROLLED VEAL SCALLOPS

16 veal scallops
½ lb. sausage
1 cup stale bread crumbs,
  crumbled, soaked in hot
  milk, squeezed dry
2 eggs, beaten
2 T. parsley, minced
Black pepper to taste
4 T. butter
1 cup white wine or stock
⅔ cup hot stock
½ cup whipping cream,
  unwhipped (optional)
1 lb. mushroom caps,
  sautéed
Watercress

On chopping board, pound veal scallops quite thin; trim to even rectangles. Mince remaining scraps of veal, and mix with sausage, bread, eggs, parsley, and pepper. Spread on veal; roll and tie with string. Melt butter in large skillet and add veal rolls. Simmer, without browning, for 15 minutes—turn several times. Add wine or stock and braise slowly, covered, for 45 minutes, or until tender. Transfer to heated platter and cut and remove string. Deglaze skillet with ⅔ cup hot stock, stirring briskly over flame for 2 to 3 minutes. Pour sauce over veal rolls and garnish with sautéed mushroom caps and watercress.

Optional: Whipping cream may be added to sauce.

Wine suggestion: Valpolicella

Preparation time: 1 hour
Cooking time: 1½ hours

Easy
Must serve immediately

Serves: 8

Sharon Garside

MOCK VEAL CORDON BLEU
Very simple way to prepare Cordon Bleu

2 T. butter (divided)
½ cup seasoned bread
  crumbs
1 packet green onion dip
  mix
Generous ¼ cup whipping
  cream, unwhipped
1 lb. veal, cut very thin as
  for scallopini
3 thin slices boiled ham
3 slices Muenster cheese

Note: To make Chicken
Cordon Bleu, substitute
1 pound chicken breasts,
boned and skinned, for veal.

Coat bottom and sides of 9-inch pie plate with 1 tablespoonful butter; sprinkle with ¼ cup bread crumbs. Mix whipping cream with green onion dip mix. Dip ½ the veal slices in cream mixture and place on top of bread crumbs. Add ham and then cheese. Dip remaining veal in cream mixture. Place on top of cheese. Sprinkle with ¼ cup bread crumbs. Dot with 1 tablespoonful butter. Bake at 400° for 30 minutes.

Wine suggestion: Tavel Rosé or California Sauvignon Blanc

Preparation time: 10 minutes
Baking time: 30 minutes

Easy

Serves: 4
Easily doubled

Greeta Douglass

MUSHROOM-STUFFED LAMB CHOPS
Even those who do not appreciate lamb will love these

2 T. shallots, finely chopped
2 T. parsley, snipped
1 T. green pepper, chopped
1 T. fresh basil, chopped, or
  ½ tsp. dried basil
½ lb. mushrooms, chopped
3 T. butter, preferably
  clarified
⅔ cup soft bread cubes
¼ tsp. salt
Dash of pepper, freshly
  ground
6 loin lamb chops, 1½
  inches thick, with pocket

Sauté shallots, parsley, green pepper, basil, and mushrooms in butter for 5 minutes, or until golden. Remove from heat, stir in bread, salt, and pepper. Wipe chops and trim. Stuff each pocket with a rounded tablespoonful mushroom mixture; fasten with wooden picks. Place remaining stuffing in hollow of tails. Roll and secure with pick. Can do ahead and refrigerate to this point. Broil 4 inches from heat for 8 minutes; turn and broil for 8 minutes longer for medium rare. Serve with Savory Butter.

(continued)

MUSHROOM-STUFFED LAMB (continued)

SAVORY BUTTER:
¼ cup unsalted butter,
    softened
1 T. parsley, chopped
1 T. lemon juice
½ tsp. salt
Dash of cayenne pepper

Beat all ingredients until well blended. Refrigerate. This is good also with veal or pork chops.

Wine suggestion: Médoc

Preparation time: 25 minutes   Easy   Serves: 6
Broiling time: 16 minutes   Can make ahead   Easily doubled

Sally Shipman Early

LAMB CURRY
Authentic Indian dish

2½ lbs. lamb, diced into
    1-inch cubes, uncooked
    or cooked
1 T. olive oil
1 T. butter
2 onions, diced
2 cloves garlic, minced
2 bay leaves, crushed
⅛ tsp. paprika
⅛ tsp. cayenne pepper
⅛ tsp. thyme
¼ tsp. ginger
¼ tsp. turmeric
3 T. curry powder
2 T. tomato puree
Juice and rind, grated,
    of ½ lemon
½ cup seedless raisins
2 whole cloves
1 cup rich stock or gravy
1¼ cups yogurt
2 T. coconut, grated
3 T. chutney, chopped
1 large tart apple, chopped

Cook lamb in olive oil and butter—if uncooked, about 15 minutes; if cooked, about 4 minutes. Add onions, garlic, bay leaves, paprika, cayenne pepper, thyme, ginger, turmeric, and curry powder. Sauté for 10 minutes. Add tomato puree, lemon juice and rind, raisins, cloves, and stock; cook for 10 minutes more. Carefully stir in yogurt, coconut, chutney, and apple; heat thoroughly (DO NOT BOIL). Serve with rice. Chutney, coconut, salted peanuts, and chopped apple should be served as condiments.

Preparation time: 20 minutes   Can make ahead   Serves: 4
Cooking time: 35 minutes

Ellen Gauntlett

BRAISED LAMB SHANKS

4 lamb shanks
¼ cup flour
1 tsp. salt
3 T. butter
2 T. olive oil
1 large onion, sliced
2 cloves garlic, minced
Generous ½ cup red wine
1½ cups water or beef broth
½ tsp. oregano
Pepper, freshly ground

Dredge shanks in flour and salt. Brown on all sides in butter and olive oil. Place in casserole. Brown onion and add to casserole along with garlic, wine, water, oregano, and pepper. Cover and bake at 300° for 3 hours, or until tender.

Wine suggestion: Red Burgundy

Preparation time: 20 minutes
Baking time: 3 hours

Easy
Can make ahead

Serves: 4
Can freeze

Frances Shipman

GRILLED BUTTERFLIED LEG OF LAMB
(2 styles)
Both easy and great

1 (4–6 lb.) leg of lamb
2 jars (10 oz. each) mint jelly
½ cup brown sugar, packed
½ cup white sugar
1 cup white vinegar
Juice and rind, grated, of 1
  lemon
Dash of dry mustard
Salt and pepper to taste

Have butcher butterfly leg of lamb. Combine all other ingredients and heat until jelly melts. Cool. Pour marinade over meat. Grill over coals for 40 to 60 minutes, turning every 15 minutes and basting at each turn. Slice lamb and serve with remaining sauce.

Wine suggestion: Cabernet Sauvignon

Preparation time: 10 minutes
Broiling time: 40–60 minutes

Easy

Serves: 6–8

Adrienne de Windt

(continued)

GRILLED BUTTERFLIED LAMB (continued)

1 (4–6 lb.) leg of lamb,
   butterflied
Salt
Pepper
¼ tsp. garlic powder
Flour
¼ tsp. dry mustard

Rub salt, pepper, and garlic powder into leg of lamb. Sprinkle a little flour and the mustard over leg; grill 8 inches from heat for 40 minutes, fat side up. Turn and cook for 10 minutes more. Slice and serve

Wine suggestion: Cabernet Sauvignon

Preparation time: 5 minutes
Broiling time: 50 minutes

Easy

Serves: 6–8

Carolyn Shinnick

NOISETTES DES TOURNELLES
For that special evening with special friends

2 large onions, minced
11 T. butter (divided)
4 T. flour
1 cup half-and-half
¼ tsp. salt
¼ tsp. white pepper
2 egg yolks
2 T. flour
8 rib lamb chops,
   1½ inches thick, fat
   and bone removed
½ cup Madeira
¼ cup chicken stock
Salt and pepper to taste
1 tsp. parsley, chopped
8 artichoke bottoms,
   fresh or canned

In a covered saucepan, boil onions in water just to cover for 2 minutes; drain. Melt 4 tablespoonfuls butter in another saucepan. Whisk in flour; cook for 2 minutes without browning. Slowly add half-and-half, salt, and pepper. To the drained onions, add 2 tablespoonfuls butter. Cook slowly for 10 minutes. Add the white sauce to onions. Cover and cook for 10 minutes. Put in blender or food processor for 15 seconds; strain. Mix together egg yolks and 2 tablespoonfuls of both melted butter and flour in a saucepan. Add a little hot onion sauce to this paste; then add remaining onion sauce and cook slowly until thick. In a skillet, melt 1 tablespoonful butter. Sauté noisettes (lamb with bone removed) over high heat until pink (4 minutes on each side). Remove and keep warm. In same skillet, make Madeira sauce by adding Madeira and chicken stock to juices. Cook until reduced by half. Add 2 tablespoonfuls butter, salt and pepper, and parsley. Heat artichokes in simmering water. Place artichokes on ovenproof platter and fill with onion sauce. Top each with lamb and then 2 tablespoonfuls onion sauce. Broil until hot and slightly brown. Serve immediately with Madeira sauce on side.

Wine suggestion: Classified Red Bordeaux

Preparation time: 60 minutes

Serves: 4

Ellen Gauntlett

COSSACK LAMB KABOBS
Grilled for the gourmet

4 lbs. boned leg of lamb
¼ cup olive oil
1 large onion, finely
  chopped
1 T. parsley, chopped
1 T. Worcestershire sauce
1 bay leaf
1½ tsps. salt
½ tsp. pepper, freshly
  ground
1 clove garlic, crushed
2 cups red wine
1 pt. cherry tomatoes
1½ lbs. fresh mushroom
  caps, wiped clean
1 lb. thick-sliced bacon, cut
  in quarters

SAUCE:
½ cup butter or margarine
1 cup sour cream or yogurt
1 tsp. caraway seeds
¼ cup brandy
2 T. onion, chopped
2 T. parsley, chopped
Dash of cayenne pepper
Salt and pepper, freshly
  ground, to taste

Remove skin and fat from lamb; cut meat into 2-inch square pieces, 1 inch thick. Mix olive oil, onion, parsley, Worcestershire sauce, bay leaf, salt, pepper, and garlic; rub thoroughly into lamb. Place in bowl and add 2 cups red wine, or enough to cover the meat. Marinate, covered, for 24 hours.

To make sauce: Melt butter in saucepan; add sour cream or yogurt, caraway seeds, brandy, onion, parsley, cayenne pepper, and salt and pepper. Simmer *very gently* for 5 minutes.

Thread meat and vegetables onto skewers; be sure that a piece of bacon "sandwiches" each mushroom cap (thread in this order: bacon, lamb, tomato, bacon, mushroom, bacon, lamb, etc.) Roll each skewer in sauce and broil on grill for about 10 minutes. Baste with sauce and turn every few minutes. Serve with pilaf and salad.

Wine suggestion: Red Burgundy

Preparation time: 30 minutes   Must make ahead   Serves: 8
Broiling time: 10 minutes

Steven Early

CHICKEN TETRAZZINI
Great for a buffet

2 lbs. whole chicken
breasts, split
3 lbs. chicken legs and
thighs
3 celery tops
3 parsley sprigs
2 medium carrots, pared,
sliced
1 onion, quartered
2 tsps. salt
10 whole black peppercorns
1 bay leaf
1 lb. thin spaghetti
2 cans (6 oz. each) whole
mushrooms, drained
4 cups (6 oz.) sharp cheddar
cheese, grated

SAUCE:
¾ cup butter
¾ cup flour
3 tsps. salt
⅛ tsp. nutmeg
Dash of cayenne
1 qt. milk
4 egg yolks
1 cup whipping cream,
unwhipped
½ cup dry sherry

In the morning, wash chicken. Put in 6-quart kettle with 3 cups water, celery, parsley, carrots, onion, 2 teaspoonfuls salt, peppercorns, and bay leaf. Bring to boiling, reduce heat, and simmer covered for 1 hour until chicken is tender. Remove chicken from stock; remove bone and skin and set aside. Strain stock; return to kettle. Bring to boiling and boil uncovered until reduced to 2 cups—about 30 minutes. To make the sauce, melt butter in a large saucepan. Remove from heat. Stir in flour, salt, nutmeg, and cayenne until smooth. Return to heat and gradually stir in milk and 2 cups stock. Bring to a boil, stirring constantly. Boil gently, stirring constantly, for 2 minutes until slightly thickened. In a small bowl, beat egg yolks with cream. Beat in a little of hot mixture. Return to saucepan. Heat over low heat—DO NOT BOIL! Remove from heat and add sherry. Cook spaghetti according to package directions and drain. Add 2 cups sauce to spaghetti and toss well. Reserve 2 cups sauce, cover, and refrigerate. To remaining sauce, add large chunks of chicken and mushrooms. Divide spaghetti into two 12 × 8-inch baking dishes, arranging it around edges. Spoon half of chicken mixture into center of each. Sprinkle 2 cups cheese over spaghetti in each dish. Cover with foil and refrigerate. Bake covered at 350° for 30 to 45 minutes. Heat reserved sauce and spoon over spaghetti.

Wine suggestion: California Chardonnay

Preparation time: 2¼ hours
Baking time: 30–45 minutes

Can make ahead
Can freeze

Serves: 14–16
Can be halved

Sandra Wotta

KING RANCH CHICKEN
Some like it hot, and this is just spicy enough

1 fryer or 3 whole chicken breasts (about 4 lbs.)
2 tsps. salt
2 peppercorns
1 bay leaf
Celery leaves
Onion, chopped
1 can (10 oz.) tomatoes and green chilies (or plain tomatoes with a drop of Tabasco sauce)
1 can (10¾ oz.) condensed cream of chicken soup
1 can (10¾ oz.) condensed cream of mushroom soup
½ cup chicken broth
Salt and pepper to taste
1–2 tsp. chili powder to taste
1 doz. soft tortillas, torn into small pieces
1 cup green onions, chopped
2–3 cups cheddar cheese, grated

Poach chicken until tender with the following seasonings: salt, peppercorns, bay leaf, celery leaves, and onion. DO NOT BOIL! Or—place chicken in a greased pan, cover, and bake at 350° for 45 to 60 minutes. Bone and cut into large bite-size pieces. Combine tomatoes and chilies, soups, broth, and seasonings. Mix well. In a buttered 3-quart flat casserole, place ingredients in layers in the following order: tortillas, chicken, tomato mixture, green onions, and grated cheese. Repeat these layers 2 more times ending with cheese. Bake for 45 minutes to 1 hour at 350°. Allow extra time if casserole has been refrigerated.

Wine suggestion: Mexican Beer or Valpolicella.

Preparation time: 45 minutes
Baking time: 45–60 minutes

Can make ahead and refrigerate

Serves: 6–8
Can freeze

Dori Lawrence

CHEESY CHICKEN CASSEROLE

1 chicken (3 lbs.), salted and peppered
Water to cover chicken
1 cup onion, finely diced
1 cup celery, diced
1 cup green pepper, diced
½ cup margarine (can use bacon drippings)

Salt and pepper well 1 large chicken. Place in Dutch oven and cover ⅔ of chicken with water. Simmer for 1 hour, or until tender. Set aside to cool; reserve broth. Dice onion, celery, and green pepper. Sauté vegetables in ½ cup of margarine in large skillet for 20 minutes. Remove vegetables from skillet. Add flour

(continued)

CHEESY CHICKEN CASSEROLE (continued)

5 T. flour
2 cups milk
1 can (10¾ oz.) condensed
  cream of mushroom soup
8 ozs. processed cheese
  (Velveeta preferred), diced
8 ozs. wide noodles

to margarine; stir to blend. Add milk slowly to make a cream sauce. Add cream of mushroom soup and stir. Add cheese and stir until melted. Cut chicken into bite-sized pieces and add to sauce. Return vegetables to sauce and mix well. Cook noodles in chicken broth according to package directions. Serve chicken mixture over noodles or stir in noodles. Can also be served over chow mein noodles or rice.

Wine suggestion: Good White Jug Wine

Preparation time: 1 hour

Can be made ahead
and reheated

Serves: 6
Can be frozen

Patricia Ellwood

FOIL-BAKED CHICKEN
A family favorite

½ cup water
⅓ cup catsup
⅓ cup vinegar
¼ cup brown sugar, packed
4 T. butter or margarine,
  melted
2 T. lemon juice
2 tsp. salt
2 tsp. paprika
2 tsp. chili powder
2 tsp. dry mustard
2 broilers (2⅓–3 lbs. each),
  split or cut into pieces

To make sauce, blend first 10 ingredients in a bowl. Dip chicken pieces in sauce and place on pieces of foil. Pour 1 tablespoonful of sauce over each portion. Wrap each piece securely, leaving a small vent so packet doesn't expand and lose the marinade. Bake at 400° for 45 to 55 minutes. Open foil, brush with remaining sauce, and bake for 15 minutes more.

Wine suggestion: Chianti or Red Rioja

Preparation time: 10 minutes
Baking time: 60–70 minutes

Easy
Can do sauce ahead

Serves: 4–6

Susan Ordway

CHICKEN CORDON BLEU
The name is elegant—the flavor, too

2(3) boned chicken breasts, whole
2(3) slices Swiss cheese
4(6) slices Canadian bacon
¾ tsp. salt
¾ tsp. monosodium glutamate (MSG)
⅛ tsp. pepper
Flour
1(2) egg(s), beaten
3(4½) T. sesame seed
⅓ cup packaged dried bread crumbs
3(4½) T. butter

SAUCE: (optional)
½ (¾) tsp. shallots, finely minced
1(1½) tsp. butter
2(3) T. white wine
½(¾) tsp. beef extract
¾ tsp. paprika
Dash each of
  Worcestershire sauce and
  Tabasco sauce
¼ tsp. monosodium glutamate (MSG)
¼ cup commercial sour cream
Parsley (for garnish)

*Note: Measurements in parentheses are for
6 servings.

Preparation time: 35 minutes
Baking time: 10 minutes

Cut boned breasts into halves; fill pocket in each of the pieces with ½ slice Swiss cheese, folded twice, and 1 slice Canadian bacon. Sprinkle with salt, MSG, and pepper. Dip in flour, next in beaten egg(s), then in mixture of sesame seeds and bread crumbs. Can be made ahead to this point and refrigerated. Sauté chicken in butter until golden on both sides; then cook, covered, 10 minutes or until tender. To keep crispy: Cook uncovered 10 minutes on 1 side and 5 minutes on the other.

Sauce: While chicken is cooking, sauté shallots in butter until golden. Add wine, beef extract, and paprika. Cook until liquid is reduced to half. Stir in Worcestershire and Tabasco sauces, MSG, and sour cream. Heat. Serve over chicken. Garnish with parsley.

Wine suggestion: Chardonnay or Rheingau

Can be made ahead and cooked later

Serves: 4(6)

Suzanne Sellers

CHINESE CHICKEN
WITH SWEET-AND-SOUR SAUCE
You'll want to buy a wok for this one

4 oz. almonds, slivered
¾ cup reserved pineapple
  juice
2 T. cornstarch
2 T. vinegar
1 T. soy sauce
1 large clove garlic
¼ cup brown sugar, packed
2 whole chicken breasts,
  boned, skinned
2 tsp. cornstarch
¼ tsp. salt
1 egg white, unbeaten
2 T. vegetable oil
1 can (20 oz.) pineapple
  chunks in natural
  unsweetened juice,
  drained (reserve juice)
1 pkg. (10 oz.) peapods,
  thawed
1 can (6 oz.) bamboo
  shoots, sliced
1 can (8 oz.) water
  chestnuts, sliced
1 cup celery, sliced thin
1 cup fresh mushrooms,
  sliced
2 T. pineapple preserves or
  2 T. brown sugar, packed
  (optional)

Place almonds in a shallow pan. Toast in a 400° oven for 8 to 10 minutes. Combine reserved juice, cornstarch, vinegar, soy sauce, garlic, and brown sugar; set aside. Cut chicken in strips or cubes. Place in bag with cornstarch and salt; shake to coat. Heat oil in wok to 375°. Mix egg white with chicken and stir fry for approximately 3 minutes. Remove meat from work. Place vegetables in wok and stir fry for 2 minutes. Add meat, pineapple chunks, and pineapple-juice mixture. Heat thoroughly, stirring to coat meat and vegetables with sauce. Add preserves or brown sugar if a sweeter taste is desired.

Wine suggestion: Wan Fu or Tavel Rosé

Preparation time: 30–40 minutes

Serves: 4

Anne Rapp

HERB-BAKED CHICKEN WITH WINE

16 chicken legs
16 chicken thighs
Salt and pepper
6 T. clarified butter
2 T. oil
1 cup (or less) fresh bread
  crumbs
2 T. shallots, finely chopped
2 tsps. garlic, finely
  chopped
4 T. parsley, chopped
1 tsp. thyme, chopped
2 tsps. fresh rosemary,*
  chopped
½ cup dry white wine

*If dried herbs are used
decrease the amount.

Preparation time:
  5–10 minutes
Baking time: 65 minutes

Preheat oven to 425°. Sprinkle chicken pieces with salt and pepper. Put clarified butter and oil in a baking dish large enough to hold all the pieces in 1 layer. Add chicken legs and thighs and roll them in butter until well coated. Arrange pieces skin side down in 1 layer. Bake 30 minutes. Meanwhile, combine the bread crumbs, shallots, garlic, parsley, thyme, and rosemary. After 30 minutes, turn chicken pieces and sprinkle with bread crumb mixture. Bake 30 minutes more. Pour wine around, not on, the chicken and bake for 5 minutes longer.

Hint: Lower oven termpature by 25° whenever glass or Corning Ware dishes are used.

Wine suggestion: California Sauvignon Blanc or Fumé Blanc

Recipe can be   Serves: 12–16
halved or quartered

Ann Paulson

CHICKEN AND SCAMPI
Quite delectable

1 fryer (3½–4 lb.), cut up,
  or an equal amount of
  breasts and legs
1 T. salt
½ tsp. pepper
¼ cup butter
3 small onions, finely
  chopped
1 clove garlic, minced
3 T. parsley, snipped
½ cup light port wine
1 can (8 oz.) tomato sauce
1 tsp. dried basil

Rub chicken well with salt and pepper. Sauté in hot butter in a large skillet until golden on all sides. Add onions, garlic, parsley, wine, tomato sauce, and basil. Simmer, covered, about 30 minutes, or until chicken is tender. Remove chicken. Turn up heat so that sauce boils; add shrimp. Cook uncovered for 3 to 4 minutes, just until shrimp is pink and tender. It may be necessary to skim fat from surface of sauce before pouring over meat. Serve shrimp and sauce over chicken. Garnish with parsley. Good served over rice. Can do chicken and sauce ahead,

(continued)

CHICKEN AND SCAMPI (continued)

1–2 lbs. medium to large-sized shrimp, peeled, cooked

keep warm, add shrimp before serving, and heat.

Wine suggestion: Grey Riesling or Beaujolais

Preparation time: 10 minutes
Cooking time: 45 minutes

Can make ahead   Serves: 6

Maggie Hotop

CHICKEN 'N BISCUIT PIE

BISCUIT MIX:*
9 cups flour
1 T. salt
¼ cup baking powder
2 cups solid shortening

CHICKEN 'N BISCUIT PIE:
2 cans (10¾ oz. each) condensed cream of chicken soup
⅓ cup chicken broth
1 T. parsley, chopped
⅛ tsp. thyme leaves
Dash of pepper
2 cups chicken, cooked, diced
1 pkg. (10 oz.) frozen peas
1 pkg. (10 oz.) frozen carrots, fingerling or sliced
1 cup frozen small white onions
*1½ cups homemade biscuit mix
½ cup milk

Combine flour, salt, and baking powder. Using a pastry blender, cut shortening through dry ingredients until mixture is mealy. Store in tightly covered container in a cool area. Does not need refrigeration and remains good indefinitely.

Preheat oven to 425°. In a 2-quart rectangular casserole, combine chicken soup, broth, parsley, thyme, and pepper. Add chicken chunks. Cook peas, carrots, and onions. Drain and add to chicken mixture. Bake uncovered 20 minutes until bubbly. Meanwhile, combine biscuit mix and milk, stirring with a fork until all of the mix is moistened. Drop dough by tablespoonfuls on top of heated chicken mixture. Bake an additional 25 minutes.

Wine suggestion: French Colombard

Preparation time: 25 minutes
Baking time: 45 minutes

Serves: 4

Jan Cornell

CHICKEN-ARTICHOKE CASSEROLE
An irresistible combination

3 lbs. chicken pieces,
   breasts and thighs
6 T. butter
1½ tsp. salt
½ tsp. paprika
¼ tsp. pepper
1 can (8 oz.) whole
   mushrooms, drained
2 T. flour
1 cup chicken broth
¼ cup dry sherry or
   dry white wine
1 can (14 oz.) artichoke
   hearts, drained

Melt butter in a large skillet. Season chicken with salt, paprika, and pepper and brown on all sides. Place chicken in a casserole large enough to hold it in a single layer. Sauté mushrooms in drippings remaining in pan. Blend in flour and cook for about 2 minutes. Add chicken broth and wine and cook until thick. Place artichokes in casserole on top of chicken. Pour sauce over all. Bake uncovered at 375° for 45 minutes. Serve with fluffy rice and a crisp salad.

Microwave: Season chicken (DO NOT SALT). Brown chicken in butter in skillet. Place chicken in a glass or pyroceramic casserole. Pour drippings into a 4-cup glass measuring cup; add mushrooms. Microwave on high for 1 minute. Blend flour, chicken broth, and wine into drippings. Microwave on high for 2 to 3 minutes, or until thick and smooth. Pour sauce over chicken; microwave on high for 10 to 12 minutes. Add artichokes. Spoon sauce over artichokes and microwave on high for 4 to 5 minutes, or until chicken is tender.

Wine suggestion: Vouvray

Preparation time: 30 minutes
Baking time: 45 minutes
Microwave: 20 minutes

Can be made ahead
and refrigerated

Serves: 4–6

Ann Paulson

ORANGE CHICKEN
Only 200 calories per serving!

1 3 lb. fryer, cut into serving
   pieces
Salt and pepper
1 medium onion, sliced
½ tsp. paprika
½ cup frozen orange juice
   concentrate

Brown chicken under broiler. Place in casserole and season with salt and pepper. Cover chicken pieces with onion slices. Combine remaining ingredients and pour over chicken. Cover and simmer until chicken is tender. This can be done on top of the stove or in the oven at 375°. Bake approximately 40 to 50 minutes.

(continued)

ORANGE CHICKEN (continued)

2 T. brown sugar
2 T. chopped parsley
2 tsp. soy sauce
½ tsp. ground ginger
⅓ cup water

Microwave: Brown chicken under broiler. Place in casserole and season with pepper (DO NOT USE SALT). Cover chicken pieces with onion slices. Combine remaining ingredients and pour over chicken. Cover with waxed paper. Microwave on high for 20 minutes, or until tender

Wine suggestion: California Gamay

Preparation time: 10 minutes
Baking time: 40–50 minutes
Microwave: 20 minutes

Easy

Serves: 4–6

Pat Rooney

CHICKEN MARENGO

1 chicken, cut into serving
  pieces
Salt and pepper
Flour
2 T. oil
2 T. margarine or butter
1 cup white wine
3 T. brandy or Cointreau
Garlic to taste (2 cloves)
A bouquet garni
3 large tomatoes, peeled,
  quartered
4 oz. or more fresh
  mushrooms
Fresh parsley, chopped

Wipe chicken with a damp cloth; sprinkle with salt, pepper, and flour. Heat oil and margarine in skillet; brown chicken over high heat until golden, turning frequently. Remove chicken from pan. Remove all oil from pan. Add to pan the wine, brandy, garlic, and bouquet garni. Cook until all crusty particles are mixed into liquid. Add chicken and tomatoes. Cover skillet tightly. Lower heat to low and cook gently until almost tender—about 30 minutes. Taste for seasoning and add some quartered or sliced mushrooms. Cook 10 minutes longer, or until tender. Serve in skillet. Sprinkle with chopped parsley.

Wine suggestion: Pinot Noir

Preparation time: 30 minutes
Cooking time: 40 minutes

Serves: 4–6

Susan Balz

Hint: A bouquet garni is a small cheesecloth bag containing 1 large bay leaf, ¼ teaspoonful leaf thyme, ¼ teaspoonful dried basil, about 8 sprigs fresh parsley, ¼ teaspoonful dried tarragon, 3 chopped green celery tops, 6 whole peppercorns, and a slashed clove of garlic.

BREAST OF CHICKEN WITH WILD RICE
Exquisite dining

6 chicken breasts, boned, skinned
½ tsp. salt
Ground pepper
½ cup butter
1 lb. fresh mushrooms, whole
1 T. onion, grated
2 cups whipping cream, unwhipped
4 T. brandy
4 T. dry sherry
8 ozs. wild rice, cooked, or 1 pkg. (6 oz.) long grain and wild rice mix, prepared as directed on pkg.

Season chicken with salt and pepper. Sauté in butter over low heat for 20 minutes, or until rich brown. Remove chicken and keep hot. Add mushrooms and onion to butter remaining in pan and cook for 5 minutes, stirring constantly. Reduce heat and add cream slowly, stirring constantly. Simmer 5 minutes. Add brandy and sherry and simmer for 5 minutes.

Arrange chicken on top of wild rice and pour sauce over it.

Wine suggestion: Puligny-Montrachet

Preparation time: 35 minutes

Serves: 6

Alice Ripley

CHICKEN À L'ORANGE

8 chicken breasts
2½ tsps. salt
½ cup butter
6 T. flour
6 T. sugar
½ tsp. dry mustard
1 tsp. cinnamon
¼ tsp. ginger
3 cups orange juice (fresh squeezed)
Almonds, slivered
Orange slices

Sprinkle chicken with 1½ teaspoonfuls salt. Brown in butter. Remove. Add the following to drippings: flour, remaining salt, sugar, and spices. Stir into a paste. Gradually add orange juice. Cook, stirring constantly, until mixture comes to a boil. Add chicken and cover. Simmer over low heat until chicken is tender—about 40 minutes. Garnish with slivered almonds and orange slices.

Microwave: (About 3 to 4 pounds chicken breasts). DO NOT SALT chicken. Brown chicken in butter in a skillet. Place chicken in a glass or pyroceramic casserole. Pour drippings, flour, sugar, spices,

(continued)

CHICKEN À L'ORANGE (continued)

and 1 teaspoonful of salt into a 4-cup glass measuring cup. Stir into a paste. Gradually add orange juice. Microwave on high for 3 to 5 minutes, or until thick and smooth. Stir frequently. Pour over chicken; cover. Microwave on high for 20 to 25 minutes, or until chicken is tender. Garnish with slivered almonds and orange slices.

Wine suggestion: White Hermitage

Preparation time: 20 minutes
Cooking time: 40 minutes
Microwave: 30 minutes

Serves: 6–8

Greeta Douglass

CHICKEN ADOBO

Chicken fat or about 2 T. oil
6 cloves garlic, minced
2½–3 lbs. chicken parts
3 medium onions, sliced
3 T. soy sauce
1 T. vinegar

RICE:
1 cup long grain rice
2 cups water
½ cup butter
2 stalks celery, sliced
1 tsp. Jane's Krazy salt

Render chicken fat until pan is greased well or coat pan with oil. Sauté garlic. Turn up heat, add chicken parts, and brown lightly (10 to 15 minutes). Place onion slices over chicken. Sprinkle with soy sauce. Cover and simmer 30 to 40 minutes.

Rice: Bring rice, water, butter, Krazy salt, and celery to a boil. Stir until well mixed and immediately pour into a casserole. Cover and bake at 325° for 40 minutes. Fluff up rice before serving. Top with chicken parts. Pour sauce and onions over this. Just prior to serving, sprinkle with vinegar.

Wine suggestion: Beaujolais or White Rhône

Preparation time: 25 minutes
Baking time: 40 minutes

Serves: 4

Minnie Graf

Hint: To make chicken mozzarella, dip chicken breasts in a mixture of 1 egg and ½ cup milk. Roll in Italian bread crumbs. Brown in oil. Place in a casserole dish, cover with favorite spaghetti sauce, and bake for 1 hour at 350°. Before serving, add a slice of mozzarella cheese to each piece and cover with more sauce. Bake additional 15 minutes.

Carole Cupps

TARRAGON CHICKEN
Superb company dish and easy to prepare

2 whole large frying chicken breasts (1¼ lb.), boned, skinned
¾ tsp. salt
¼–½ tsp. fresh ground pepper
4 tsps. cornstarch
4 tsps. olive oil or other oil
1 egg white, unbeaten
¼ cup butter or margarine
4 tsps. tomato, finely diced, peeled, seeded
1½ tsps. mild white wine vinegar
1 cup whipping cream, unwhipped
1 tsp. dried tarragon
3 T. parsley, minced
Salt and fresh ground pepper

Slice chicken in strips no larger than 2½ × ½ inch. Sprinkle chicken with salt and pepper and let stand 20 minutes. Sprinkle with cornstarch and oil, turn to mix, and let stand 20 minutes. Mix in egg white and let stand 30 minutes.

In a large skillet over medium-high heat, sauté chicken in butter just until opaque throughout and a little golden—about 5 minutes. Remove chicken with slotted spoon and keep warm. Add tomato, vinegar, cream, and tarragon to pan. Increase heat to high and stir until mixture is blended and consistency of heavy cream. Put chicken back in pan with half the parsley and turn gently to mix. Heat through. Correct seasoning with salt and pepper. Sprinkle with remaining parsley. Serve with rice.

Wine suggestion: Gewürztraminer

Preparation time: 70 minutes
Cooking time: 15 minutes

Serve immediately

Serves: 4

Patricia Ellwood
Ann Paulson

THREE-CHEESE CHICKEN BAKE

8 ozs. wide noodles
½ cup onion, chopped
½ cup green pepper, chopped (optional)
3 T. butter
1 can (10¾ oz.) condensed cream of chicken soup
⅓ cup milk
1 can (6 oz.) sliced mushrooms, drained, or 1 cup fresh mushrooms, sliced

Cook noodles until tender in a large amount of salted boiling water. Drain. Rinse in cold water. To prepare mushroom sauce, sauté onion and green pepper in butter. Stir in soup, milk, mushrooms, pimiento, and basil.

Place half the noodles in a 3-quart greased baking dish. Cover with half of each of the sauce, cottage cheese, chicken, and cheeses. Repeat layers. Bake at 350° for 45 minutes.

(continued)

THREE-CHEESE CHICKEN BAKE (continued)

¼ cup pimiento, chopped
½ tsp. basil
1½ cups cream-style
  cottage cheese
3 cups chicken, cooked,
  diced
2 cups American cheese,
  shredded
½ cup Parmesan cheese,
  grated

Microwave: Cook noodles as directed above. Microwave onion and green pepper in butter on high for 1 to 2 minutes in a glass casserole; stir in soup, milk, mushrooms, pimiento, and basil. Place half the noodles in a 3-quart greased baking dish. Cover with half of each of the sauce, cottage cheese, chicken, and cheeses. Repeat layers. Microwave on high for 10 to 15 minutes, or until hot.

Wine suggestion: Sauvignon Blanc or White Bordeaux

Preparation time: 30 minutes
Baking time: 45 minutes
Microwave: 15 minutes

Can do ahead
and refrigerate

Serves: 8–10
Can be frozen

Martha Hilboldt

CHICKEN-WILD RICE CASSEROLE

2 whole chickens (2 lbs.
  each)
1 cup water
1½ tsps. salt
1 medium onion, chopped
1 cup dry sherry
½ tsp. curry powder
½ cup celery, sliced
1 lb. fresh mushrooms
¼ cup butter
2 pkgs. (6 oz. each) long
  grain and wild rice mix
1 cup sour cream
1 can (10¾ oz.) condensed
  cream of mushroom soup

Cook chickens in water, sherry, salt, curry powder, onion, and celery. Simmer 1 hour, or until tender. Refrigerate chicken in strained broth. When chicken is chilled, remove it from bone. Cut into bite-sized pieces. Reserve broth. Wash mushrooms; slice and sauté in butter. Cook rice according to package directions for a firm rice, using reserved broth for the liquid and adding water to broth if needed. Combine chicken, rice, and mushrooms. Blend sour cream and soup and toss gently with chicken mixture. Refrigerate. To serve, cover and bake at 350° for 1 hour in a 3½ to 4-quart lightly greased casserole.

Wine suggestion: White Hermitage or Muscadet

Preparation time: 1 hour
Baking time: 1 hour

Must be made ahead

Serves: 8–10
Can be frozen

Judy Brown

CHICKEN PONTALBA
Unforgettable

2 cups potatoes
Oil (for frying)
1½ cups white onions,
  thinly sliced
¾ cup green onions,
  chopped
3 medium-small cloves
  garlic, minced
Butter (for sautéing)
1 cup (about 6 oz.) fresh
  mushrooms, sliced,
  cooked
1½ cups (approximately
  ½ lb.) ham, cooked,
  chopped
¾ cup sauterne
3 T. parsley, minced
Salt and pepper to taste
8 large chicken breast
  halves
Seasoned flour
½–¾ cup bread crumbs,
  sautéed

BÉARNAISE SAUCE:
  (4 cups)
8 egg yolks
Juice of 2 lemons
2½ cups butter
Salt and pepper
1 T. tarragon vinegar

Peel and dice enough potatoes to measure 2 cups. In a frying basket, lower the potatoes slowly into a deep fryer of hot oil (375°) and fry until browned. Remove the basket and transfer potatoes to paper towels to drain. In a large skillet, sauté in butter all the onions and minced garlic cloves until they are soft. Stir in mushrooms, ham, and potatoes and sauté the mixture for 5 minutes. Stir in sauterne and parsley. Remove from heat; salt and pepper to taste and keep the mixture warm. Dredge the chicken breasts in seasoned flour and sauté until golden brown and tender. Keep warm while making the béarnaise sauce. Then arrange the chicken over the first mixture and cover with béarnaise sauce and bread crumbs.

Sauce: In the top of a double boiler, whisk egg yolks and lemon juice until the mixture is thick and creamy. Whisk in melted and cooled butter, 2 tablespoonfuls at a time, lifting the pan occasionally to let the mixture cool. Add tarragon vinegar and whisk the sauce until it is thick. Salt and pepper to taste. All but the chicken can be made ahead and reheated.

Hint: If sauce should curdle, add an ice cube and stir until dissolved.

Wine suggestion: Chassagne-Montrachet or Soave

Preparation time: 2½ hours

Can prepare ahead
and reheat

Serves: 8

Anne Rapp

CHICKEN CACCIATORE
Lively taste and easy, too

2½–3 lbs. chicken breasts
2 T. butter
Oregano
1 can (10¾ oz.) tomato
  puree
2–3 cloves garlic, minced
1 small hot pepper, chopped
½ tsp. celery seed
1 tsp. sage
1–1½ cups sauterne
1 large can (28 oz.)
  tomatoes, quartered
1 green pepper, chopped
1 can (8 oz.) mushrooms,
  sliced

In a large skillet, brown chicken in 2 tablespoonfuls butter. Sprinkle with oregano while browning. Combine remaining ingredients in a large bowl. Blend well and pour over chicken. Cover and simmer until tender—2 to 3 hours. Serve over spaghetti or with rice.

Wine suggestion: Orvieto Secco

Preparation time: 20 minutes
Cooking time: 2–3 hours

Can make ahead
and reheat

Serves: 4–6

Stephanie Wirt

CHUTNEY CHICKEN
Savory and simple

5–6 lbs. fresh boneless
  chicken breasts
Salt and pepper
1½ cups orange juice
½ cup white raisins
½ cup chutney, cut in small
  pieces
½ tsp. cinnamon
1 tsp. (or less) curry powder
Dash of thyme

Arrange chicken breasts (halved if large) in a greased shallow baking dish; sprinkle lightly with salt and pepper. Bake at 450° for 15 minutes. In the meantime, combine remaining ingredients in a saucepan and simmer for 10 minutes. Pour sauce over chicken; reduce temperature to 350° and continue baking for 1 hour, or until fork tender. Cover with foil after 30 minutes.

Wine suggestion: Chenin Blanc

Preparation time: 15 minutes
Baking time: 1¼ hours

Easy

Serves: About 8

Mary Ellen Godfrey

ALL-PURPOSE SAUCE FOR STEAK

3 T. butter
3 T. flour
2 tsps. Worcestershire sauce
2 tsps. prepared mustard
1 tsp. salt
1 can (10¾ oz.) consommé
1 cup Burgundy wine
4 green onions and tops, thinly sliced

Melt butter in a heavy pan. Blend in flour. Blend in Worcestershire sauce, mustard, and salt. Stir in consommé, a little at a time, until smooth. Stir in wine. Cook, stirring constantly, until thickened. Simmer gently for 10 minutes. Add onions and simmer for 5 minutes. If not thick enough, add some cornstarch mixed with water, or thicken entirely with cornstarch. Use for any steak or roast.

Preparation time: 30 minutes

Easy
Can make ahead

Yield: 2 cups

Dorrie Kelly

FRUIT CHILI SAUCE

30 ripe tomatoes, peeled, chopped
6 onions, ground
6 pears, peeled, ground
6 peaches, peeled, ground
6 green peppers, ground
2 cups celery, chopped
2 T. salt
1 qt. vinegar
4 cups sugar
1 tsp. allspice
1 tsp. nutmeg
1 tsp. cinnamon

In large heavy kettle, combine all ingredients and boil until fairly thick—1 to 2 hours. Stir occasionally with wooden spoon. Pour into pint jars and process in boiling water for 40 minutes.

Preparation time: 1 hour
Cooking time: 2 hours

Can make ahead
Can freeze

Makes: 12–15 pints

Mary Louise Sheehan Avery
Bertha Sheehan

SAUCE FOR SPARERIBS, CHICKEN, OR SLOPPY JOES

1 onion, chopped, sautéed
   in 3 T. butter
2 T. lemon juice
2 T. vinegar
1 tsp. salt
1 tsp. paprika
Dash of pepper
¼ tsp. Worcestershire
   sauce
1 T. dry mustard
3 T. brown sugar
¾ cup catsup
¾ cup water

Combine all ingredients and simmer until thick.

Preparation time: 20 minutes   Easy   Yield: 2 cups
                                  Can make ahead

                                  Joyce Melvin

SWEET-AND-SOUR PINEAPPLE SAUCE

2 T. butter
½ cup carrots, thinly sliced
¼ cup green pepper, thinly
   sliced
2 T. cornstarch
2 T. water
1 can (1 lb. 4 oz.) pineapple
   chunks
½ cup cider vinegar
¼ cup sugar
¼ cup light brown sugar,
   firmly packed
2½ T. soy sauce
2 T. catsup

In pan, melt butter; add carrots and green pepper. Sauté until slightly tender—about 3 minutes. Dissolve cornstarch in water. Drain pineapple; reserve syrup. Add syrup, vinegar, both sugars, soy sauce, and catsup to cornstarch mixture. Add to vegetables and cook, stirring over medium heat until thickened, for about 8 minutes. Add pineapple chunks and cook, stirring occasionally, for about 4 minutes longer.

Good served over baked ham, pork, chicken, shrimp, or rice. May be used as sauce on the side.

Preparation time: 20 minutes   Easy   Yield: 3½ cups
                                  Can make ahead

                                  Alice Ripley

RAISIN SAUCE FOR HAM

1 cup raisins
1¾ cups water
⅓ cup brown sugar, packed
1½ T. cornstarch
¼ tsp. cinnamon
¼ tsp. cloves
¼ tsp. dry mustard
½ tsp. salt
1 T. vinegar

Boil raisins in water for 5 minutes. Add sugar mixed with cornstarch, spices, mustard, and salt. Cook, stirring, until thickened. Blend in vinegar. Serve hot.

Preparation time: 15 minutes   Easy   Serves: 6–8
                                 Can make ahead

                                 Jan Wright

HAM SAUCE

1 cup sugar
1 T. (heaping) flour
2 T. (heaping) dry mustard
½ cup distilled vinegar
1 cup half-and-half
1 egg yolk, beaten

Mix sugar, flour, and mustard. Add vinegar, half-and-half, and egg yolk. Cook over medium heat, stirring constantly, until thick. Serve hot or cold.

Preparation time: 10 minutes   Easy   Serves: 12
                                 Can make ahead

                                 Jean Shaw

CRANBERRY SAUCE FOR
ROCK CORNISH GAME HENS

1 can (16 oz.) whole
  cranberries
1 bottle (8 oz.) French
  dressing
1 env. dry onion soup mix
2 T. sherry (optional)

Put all ingredients in small saucepan. Heat thoroughly, stirring constantly. Remove from heat and reserve.

Preparation time: 10 minutes   Easy   Yield: 3 cups
                                 Can make ahead

                                 Evelyn Pryweller

PLUM SAUCE CASSIS
Great with Rock Cornish game hen, duck, or pheasant

1 can (1 lb. 1 oz.) plums
2 T. butter
1 onion, minced
2 T. brown sugar
2 T. chili sauce
1 tsp. Worcestershire sauce
¼ cup Crème de Cassis
½ tsp. ginger
Juice of ½ lemon

Put all ingredients in saucepan and simmer for 10 minutes. Cool and remove pits from plums. Pour into processor or blender and puree. Baste game hens, game, or poultry with sauce. Serve sauce with meat.

Wine suggestion: Riesling or Tavel Rosé

Preparation time: 15 minutes   Can make ahead   Serves: 6–8

Sally Shipman Early

TACO SAUCE

30–40 ripe red tomatoes, chopped
1 cup celery, chopped
2–4 large onions, diced
1 T. chili powder
½ cup cider vinegar
2 cloves garlic, minced
Fresh basil
3 T. Tabasco sauce
2 T. ground cumin
1 T. beef bouillon
12–15 young fresh Hungarian peppers
2 T. sugar
½ T. oregano

Combine all ingredients and simmer until thick—3 to 4 hours. Sauce should be the consistency of catsup. Pack in half-pint or pint jars; adjust lids. Process in boiling water for 40 to 45 minutes.

Preparation time: 30 minutes   Must make ahead   Yield: 8–10
Cooking time: 3–4 hours   half-pints

Bea Coleman

PHEASANT IN WHITE WINE SAUCE
Elegant and delicious

3–4 pheasants, breasts only
Margarine
1 can (10¾ oz.) beef
  consommé
1 pt. half-and-half
½ bottle (1⅓ cups) dry white
  wine
2 T. cornstarch
2 T. water
Garlic salt to taste
Salt and pepper to taste
Mushrooms, freshly sliced
  (optional)
1 can (8 oz.) white grapes
  (optional)
1 can (16 oz.) artichoke
  hearts, halved or
  quartered (optional)

Brown pheasant in margarine. In another saucepan, mix consommé, half-and-half, and wine. Cook slowly for 5 to 10 minutes. Thicken sauce with cornstarch mixed with water. Add sauce to meat; cook on top of stove until pheasant is tender—30 to 45 minutes. Season with garlic salt and salt and pepper. Add mushrooms and/or grapes and artichoke hearts.

Suggestion: Serve over wild rice or white rice.

Wine suggestion: St. Émilion

Preparation time: 30 minutes
Cooking time: 30–45 minutes

Easy

Serves: 4–6
Easily doubled

Jean Vander Velde

DUCKLING WITH CURRANT JELLY SAUCE

SAUCE:
1 cup currant jelly
5 T. Grand Marnier
Dash of cayenne pepper
¾ cup orange juice
¾ tsp. lemon juice
1½ tsps. butter
Rind of 1 orange, grated
1 (5 lb.) domestic duckling
Wild rice (optional)

Melt currant jelly in small saucepan over low heat. Add remaining ingredients and heat until just warmed. Remove from heat and reserve.

(continued)

DUCKLING (continued)

Have butcher quarter duckling. Thaw if frozen and quarter. Place duckling in ovenproof pan. Bake at 425° for 15 minutes. Reduce temperature to 350° and bake for 45 minutes longer. Baste with sauce during last 15 minutes of baking time. Turn duckling once during total baking time.

Suggestion: Serve with wild rice. Heat remaining sauce and pass with duck.

Wine suggestion: Côtes du Rhône

Preparation time: 10 mintes   Easy   Serves: 4
Baking time: 1 hour   Can make ahead

Amanda Clark Morrill

ROAST VENISON, CONTINENTAL STYLE

1 (4–5 lb.) venison roast
  (any cut)
8 slices bacon
¼ tsp. pepper
2 large shallots, thinly
  shredded lengthwise
½ lb. fresh mushrooms
2 cloves garlic, crushed
2 cups dry white wine
½ tsp. salt
2 cans (10¾ oz. each)
  condensed cream of
  mushroom soup

Wash meat carefully and trim fat. Dice bacon into ½-inch cubes and brown in Dutch oven. Remove and reserve bacon. Brown meat over medium-high heat in bacon grease; add pepper. Remove meat and add shallots, mushrooms, and garlic. Sauté all lightly. Add 1 cup wine, meat, and bacon; cover. Roast at 350° for 35 minutes per pound, basting every hour. Add salt after first hour. After second hour, mix soup with 1 cup wine; add to meat and baste. Return to oven for 30 minutes.

Note: Length of roasting time varies according to age of venison—older roasts requiring extra wine and roasting time.

Suggestion: Serve with carrots, onions, and noodles cooked al dente.

Wine suggestion: Côtes du Rhône or California Pinot Noir

Preparation time: 30 minutes   Can make ahead   Serves: 6–8
Roasting time: 2–3 hours

Robert Campbell

215

GLAZED DUCKLING WITH PEANUT-RICE STUFFING

1 cup celery, finely chopped
½ cup onion finely chopped
½ cup margarine
2⅔ cups cooked rice
2 cups cocktail peanuts, chopped
¼ cup parsley, chopped
1 T. salt
½ tsp. thyme
½ tsp. rosemary
1 cup orange juice
1 cup fresh orange sections, cut into thirds
4 tsps. orange peel, grated
2 (4–5 lb.) ready-to-cook ducklings
¼ cup honey
2 tsps. soy sauce

Sauté celery and onion in margarine until tender. Toss together with rice, peanuts, parsley, salt, thyme, and rosemary. Add orange juice, sections, and peel. Stuff each duckling lightly with half of mixture; skewer opening and truss. Prick surfaces of ducklings generously with fork. Place on rack in roasting pan and roast at 350°, allowing 25 to 30 minutes per pound. Combine honey and soy sauce and brush over surface of ducklings ½ hour before removing from oven.

Wine suggestion: Bardolino

Preparation time: 30 minutes
Roasting time: 2 hours

Easy
Can make ahead

Serves: 8

RABBIT DELUXE

4 T. butter
1 large rabbit, cut into serving pieces
2–4 ozs. bourbon
1 T. butter
1 T. flour
1½ cups white wine
Salt and pepper to taste
1 T. Worcestershire sauce
Pinch of thyme
¼ cup parsley, chopped
1 bay leaf
10 small white onions

In skillet, melt butter. Brown rabbit on all sides; add bourbon and ignite. Set aside when flame burns out. In a saucepan, blend butter and flour; stir in wine. Cook, stirring until sauce is slightly thickened. Add salt, pepper, Worcestershire sauce, thyme, parsley, bay leaf, onions, and garlic. Pour sauce over rabbit. If this is not enough to cover, add some chicken broth. Cover and cook over medium heat for 30 minutes. Add bacon; cook over low heat for 30 minutes longer. Sauté mushrooms in butter and add to rabbit, heating through.

(continued)

RABBIT DELUXE (continued)

2 cloves garlic, crushed
Chicken broth
2 slices bacon, diced,
   cooked
¼ lb. small mushrooms
2 T. butter

Wine suggestion: Pommard

Preparation time: 30 minutes
Cooking time: 1 hour

Easy
Can make ahead

Serves: 4

Susan Balz

GLEN ACRES BRAISED DUCK

2 mallard ducks
2 T. cooking oil
2 T. sherry
2 T. tomato paste
3 T. flour
1½ cups strong bouillon,
   heated
½ cup dry red wine
Salt and black pepper,
   freshly ground, to taste
½ lb. mushrooms, thinly
   sliced
1 bay leaf or ¼ tsp.
   marjoram (preferred)
2 cups cooked wild rice
Red spiced crab apples
   (for garnish)

Cut ducks in half and snip out backbones. Remove and discard wings. Heat cooking oil in Dutch oven; brown ducks, turning often. Pour sherry over them. Turn ducks over for 2 minutes and remove from pan. Lower heat and stir in tomato paste. Sift in flour gradually, whisking until smooth. Gradually stir in bouillon and wine. Add salt and pepper to taste. Bring mixture to boiling point; return duck halves to pan. Add mushrooms and bay leaf or marjoram. Bake at 325° until tender—2 to 3 hours depending on size of ducks. Remove duck to serving platter and keep warm. Strain sauce from pan and degrease. (Pour into tall jar and let grease rise; then pour it off and discard.) Reheat sauce over medium-high heat and correct seasoning. Mound cooked wild rice between duck halves and liberally spoon sauce over both. Garnish with border of spiced red crab apples.

Preparation time: 45 minutes
Cooking time: 2–3 hours

Serves: 4

Barbara Brandt

WILD DUCK
Foil keeps meat moist and full of flavor

1 medium or large
  wild duck
Salt
1 apple, quartered, cored
1 T. butter
¼ cup honey
¼ cup orange juice
1 tsp. orange peel
¼ tsp. ginger
¼ tsp. basil leaves

Wash duck and dry with paper towel (can soak in salted water overnight). Salt body cavity and outside of duck; stuff duck with apple pieces. In small saucepan, heat next 6 ingredients until butter melts. Place duck in shallow roasting pan on piece of heavy-duty foil large enough to fold completely around duck. Pour ⅓ heated sauce in the cavity and ⅓ over duck. Seal all edges of foil so liquid does not drain out. Roast at 425° for 2 hours. To brown, open foil for last 15 minutes. To serve, discard apple and slice meat. Serve with remaining sauce.

Suggestion: Delicious with wild or brown rice and fruit salad (either Waldorf or tossed with citrus sections).

Wine suggestion: Côte de Nuits

Preparation time: 15 minutes
Roasting time: 2 hours

Easy

Serves: 2
Easily doubled

Sharon Garside

PHEASANT A LA VILLA BIANCA
Good for family or guests

3 (2½ lb.) pheasants,
  disjointed
3 T. olive oil
2½ tsps. salt
½ tsp. black pepper, freshly
  ground
1 cup dry sherry
1 onion, chopped
¼ lb. fresh mushrooms,
  sliced
1 can (10 oz.) Italian
  tomatoes
Wild or white rice (optional)

Brown pheasants in oil; add salt, pepper, and sherry. Cover and cook over low heat for 10 minutes. Stir in onion and mushrooms. Cook for 10 minutes. Add tomatoes; cover and cook over low heat for 30 minutes, or until tender.

Suggestion: Serve with wild or white rice.

Note: Guinea hen or chicken also good prepared in this manner.

Wine suggestion: Valpolicella or California "Claret"

Preparation time: 30 minutes
Cooking time: 30 minutes

Easy
Can make ahead

Serves: 8–10
Easily doubled

Gerry Steeby

CREVETTES AU VIN BLANC
Very attractive served in individual sea shells

2 small scallions or onions, minced
2 sprigs parsley, chopped
1 cup mushrooms, sliced
2 T. butter
1 cup white wine (can use vermouth)
1½ lbs. raw frozen shrimp, cleaned (equal amount of chunk crab meat may be substituted)
½ tsp. salt
Dash of white pepper
2 T. flour
2 T. butter
3 T. Crème Fraîche (see below)
1 egg yolk
2 T. Madeira
Parsley, chopped

The day before serving, make Crème Fraîche (see below). Sauté scallions, parsley, and mushrooms in butter for 2 minutes. Add wine and bring to boil. Reduce heat and simmer for 5 minutes. Add frozen shrimp. Gradually heat, breaking apart shrimp as they heat. When mixture boils, reduce heat and simmer for 2 minutes. Season with salt and pepper. Mash flour into butter and blend well. Add enough of this paste to thicken sauce. Combine Crème Fraîche and egg yolk, and stir a bit of hot sauce into it. Stir egg mixture into shrimp; heat but do not boil. Add Madeira. Sprinkle with parsley. Can serve in individual greased sea shells or over bed of hot rice.

Wine suggestion: Puligny Montrachet

Preparation time: 20 minutes

Easy
Can make ahead

Serves: 4–6

Ann Bennett

CRÈME FRAÎCHE

1 cup whipping cream, unwhipped
2 T. buttermilk

Stir together, put in a jar, and cover. Let stand at room temperature for 24 hours. Refrigerate.

Note: Crème fraîche is a combination of fresh whipping cream and buttermilk. The buttermilk acts to thicken the cream and change the taste. It is excellent for fish, vegetables, and fruit and can be kept in refrigerator for 4 to 6 weeks. Although it must be made in advance, it is very easy.

FILETS DE SOLE EN PAPILLOTES
Impress guests with this showy fare

4 (6 ozs. each) sole filets
Flour
2 T. butter
1 sheet (24 × 36 inches)
   parchment paper, cut into
   fourths
12 shrimp, boiled
12 scallops, boiled
4 sprigs parsley

Dust sole with flour; sauté in butter. Place on cut parchment paper.

CHICKEN SAUCE:
1 T. butter
1 T. flour
1 cup rich chicken stock
Salt and white pepper,
   freshly ground, to taste
2 T. white wine

To make chicken sauce: Melt butter in small pan. Blend in flour until smooth; cook on low heat for 2 minutes. Gradually whisk stock into flour mixture; cook until thickened (will not be very thick). Add salt, pepper, and wine. Set aside.

BÉARNAISE SAUCE:
3 T. white wine vinegar
3 T. white wine
3 shallots, finely chopped
½ tsp. tarragon
2 egg yolks
1 T. cold water
8 T. butter, melted
Salt and pepper to taste

To make béarnaise sauce: Combine vinegar, wine, shallots, and tarragon in small saucepan; simmer until reduced to 1 tablespoonful liquid. Lightly beat egg yolks in top of double boiler; stir in water and reduced liquid. Stir over hot water; very gradually add butter. Whisk until thick—DO NOT OVERCOOK. Add salt and pepper.

Combine chicken and béarnaise sauces. Place 3 shrimp and 3 scallops on each filet; pour equal amounts of sauce over each. Top with parsley. Fold paper; seal by stapling edges together. Bake at 350° for 10 to 15 minutes.

Wine suggestion: Muscadet or Sancerre

Preparation time: 40 minutes
Baking time: 15 minutes

Serves: 4

T. J. Butler
Chef, Gull Lake Country Club

FISH FILLETS POACHED IN WHITE WINE

2–2½ lbs. any fine white
   fish fillets (sole,
   flounder, etc.)
1 medium onion, sliced
2 shallots, minced
10 mushrooms, sliced
Dry white wine
1 tsp. lemon juice
1 sprig parsley
Salt to taste
White pepper, freshly
   ground
Pinch of nutmeg
Pinch of ground cloves
1 T. brandy
1 T. butter
1 T. flour
Pinch of cayenne pepper
2 T. parsley, minced
1 lemon, thinly sliced

Place fish in buttered oven-to-table baking dish. Sprinkle with onion, shallots, mushrooms, and wine—fish should not be covered with wine. Add lemon juice, parsley, salt, pepper, nutmeg, and cloves. Bake at 350° for 20 to 30 minutes, depending on thickness of fillets. Remove from oven and draw off all liquid with basting syringe. Place liquid in small saucepan. Keep fillets warm. Heat liquid until reduced to 1¼ cups. Warm brandy in ladle, light with match, and pour flaming brandy into sauce. Mix butter, flour, and cayenne pepper into smooth paste; carefully stir into sauce until slightly thickened. Pour over fish and sprinkle with parsley. Arrange lemon slices over top of fillets and serve at once.

Microwave: Place fish in buttered glass baking dish from which it can be served. Put onion, shallots, mushrooms, and butter in a 1-quart measuring cup; microwave on high for 2 to 3 minutes. Pour onions, shallots, mushrooms, wine (not quite covering fish), lemon juice, parsley, salt, white pepper, nutmeg, and cloves over fish. Cover with waxed paper; microwave on high for 9 to 10 minutes, or until fish flakes easily. Follow above directions beginning with "Remove from oven . . ."

Preparation time: 20 minutes   Serve immediately   Serves: 6
Baking time: 30 minutes
Microwave: 12 minutes

Ruth S. Anderson

Hint: To make court bouillon for poaching fish, combine 1 quart water, 1 tablespoonful salt, 1 teaspoonful pepper, a few sprigs parsley, 2 bay leaves, ½ tablespoonful dill seeds, 3 tablespoonfuls vinegar, ¼ teaspoonful marjoram, ¼ teaspoonful thyme, 1 chopped onion, and 1 stalk celery. Simmer for 30 minutes to blend flavors. Poach fish in this liquid. It can be strained and frozen for use at another time. Adds nice flavor to fish.

CHINESE-FRIED FISH ROLLS
Interesting addition to Chinese meal

½ lb. any fresh white fish
  fillets
1 T. ginger juice
1 T. soy sauce
Pinch of pepper
Pinch of Aćcent
1 T. wine
⅓ cup ham, shredded
¼ cup spinach, cooked,
  drained, chopped
⅔ cup cornstarch
⅓ cup flour
2 egg whites, beaten until
  frothy
2–4 T. water
2 tsps. sesame seeds
Oil (for deep frying)

Cut fish fillets into pieces 4 inches long × 2 inches wide. Dry on paper towel. Dredge fish with mixture of ginger juice, soy sauce, pepper, Aćcent, and wine. Using combined ham and spinach for filling, form fish into rolls and fasten with toothpicks. Can make ahead to this point and refrigerate. Mix together cornstarch, flour, egg whites, water, and sesame seeds. Coat fish rolls with this batter and fry in deep fryer for about 5 minutes. Serve hot. To increase recipe, double fish and filling but not batter.

Note: May be served as an hors d'oeuvre.

Wine suggestion: Domestic Riesling

Preparation time: 15 minutes
Cooking time: 5 minutes

Can make ahead

Serves: 2

Mrs. Young Hai Park

SALMON STEAKS WITH SPINACH MOUSSELINE
Mousseline sauce is heavenly!

1 small onion, sliced
1 cup celery with leaves,
  chopped
1 bay leaf
5 sprigs parsley
Juice of 1 lemon
Salt and white pepper,
  freshly ground, to taste
1 cup (approximately) water
1 cup chicken stock
4 salmon steaks

Put onion, celery, bay leaf, parsley, lemon juice, salt, and pepper in saucepan. Cover with water mixed with stock. Bring to a boil; simmer for 15 minutes. Carefully add salmon to pan (don't overlap). Cover; simmer for 10 minutes, or until fish flakes. Remove from heat but keep in pan until serving time.

(continued)

SALMON STEAKS (continued)

MOUSSELINE SAUCE:

2 cups fresh spinach,
  packed, or 1 pkg. (10 oz.)
  frozen spinach, chopped
¾ cup whipping cream,
  unwhipped
1 T. chives, snipped
Salt and white pepper,
  freshly ground, to taste
½ T. lemon juice

Pick apart spinach; use only leaves. Cook until tender. Drain. Process in food processor or blender until finely chopped. Bring cream to boil; remove from heat. Add spinach, chives, salt, and pepper. Cool. Add lemon juice; whisk until thick. Serve over steaks.

Note: Mousseline sauce can be made 1 or 2 hours ahead. Sorrel or watercress may be substituted for spinach.

Wine suggestion: White Rhône or Chardonnay

Preparation time: 20 minutes
Cooking time: 30 minutes

Can make ahead   Serves: 4

Sally Shipman Early

BAKED SHRIMP WITH FETA CHEESE
Uncommonly good!

1 cup onion, chopped
⅓ cup olive oil
2 large cloves garlic,
  crushed
2 cups fresh tomatoes,
  peeled, chopped
½ cup dry white wine
2 T. parsley, chopped
¾ tsp. oregano
½ tsp. sugar
Salt and pepper to taste
  (remember feta cheese is
  salty)
Dash of Tabasco sauce
1½ lbs. fresh or frozen
  shrimp
3 ozs. feta cheese

Sauté chopped onion in oil until transparent. Add garlic and cook for 1 minute. Add tomatoes, wine, parsley, oregano, sugar, salt, pepper, and Tabasco; simmer until thick—about 30 minutes. While sauce cooks, shell and devein shrimp, if necessary, and cook in simmering salted water for 5 minutes. Drain. Spoon half the tomato sauce into 4 individual ovenproof dishes. Place shrimp on top; spoon remaining sauce over shrimp. Crumble feta cheese over each. Bake at 375° for 15 to 20 minutes, until bubbly and cheese melts a little.

Wine suggestion: Red or White Domestica

Preparation time:
  30–45 minutes
Baking time: 15–20 minutes

Easy   Serves: 4
Can make ahead   Easily doubled

Dorothy Whallon

LOBSTER THERMIDOR
Looking for elegance? Your search is over!

4 (6 ozs. each) frozen
  lobster tails
2 T. butter
2 T. flour
1 cup half-and-half
Dash of Tabasco sauce
Salt and white pepper,
  freshly ground, to taste
¼ cup celery, chopped,
  sautéed
¼ cup mushrooms, sliced,
  sautéed
2 T. sherry
1 T. lemon juice
¼ tsp. dry mustard
3 T. Parmesan cheese,
  grated
3 T. corn flake crumbs
Paprika

Clean lobster tails; boil for 8 minutes. Cool. While tails cook and cool, make white sauce by melting butter in saucepan and blending in flour with whisk. Blend on very low heat for 2 minutes; gradually add half-and-half, Tabasco sauce, salt, and pepper. Cook, stirring constantly, for 2 minutes, until sauce is thick. Set aside and keep warm. Cut open tails lengthwise through outer shell. Remove meat from shells, saving shells, and cut meat into ½-inch cubes. Combine white sauce, celery, mushrooms, sherry, lemon juice, and dry mustard; fold in lobster. Put mixture in shells. Combine Parmesan cheese and crumbs; sprinkle over lobster tails. Sprinkle with paprika and brown at 375° for about 10 minutes.

Wine suggestion: Meursault or German Auslese

Preparation time: 30–40 minutes
Baking time: 10 minutes

Serves: 4

Amanda Clark Morrill

SHRIMP PELICAN
Make early in day; pop in oven before serving

32 slices bacon
32 jumbo shrimp in shell
Lemon wedges

CRAB MEAT STUFFING:
4 celery stalks, finely diced
1 small onion, finely diced
5 slices, bacon, diced
8 ozs. frozen or canned
  snow crab meat (reserve
  liquid)

Crab meat stuffing: Sauté celery, onion, and bacon until fairly soft. Cool. In mixing bowl, place remaining stuffing ingredients, including liquid from crab meat. Mix together. Add sautéed ingredients; mix well, adding water if needed for a good consistency. Let stand for 30 minutes.

Partially cook bacon. Peel and devein shrimp, leaving tails on. Split shrimp down backs but not through completely.

(continued)

SHRIMP PELICAN (continued)

7 ½ ozs. Salad Crispins, American style
⅛ tsp. salt
¼ tsp. pepper
⅛ tsp. celery salt
¼ tsp. poultry seasoning
2 chicken bouillon cubes dissolved in 1 T. warm water
2 eggs, slightly beaten

Place on board with back side up and flatten with hand. Put equal mounts of stuffing on shrimp; wrap each shrimp with 1 slice bacon. Place shrimp on baking sheet. Bake at 375° for 12 to 15 minutes. DO NOT OVERCOOK. Serve with lemon wedges.

Wine suggestion: Muscadet de Sèvre et Maine

Preparation time: 50 minutes
Baking time: 15 minutes

Easy
Can make ahead

Serves: 6–8

Wendell Meade
Chef, Kalamazoo Country Club

SHRIMP A BAHIANA
A Brazilian favorite

1 medium yellow onion, diced
2 T. oil or butter
1 can (6 oz.) tomato paste
¾ cup water
1 can (8 oz.) tomato sauce
1 tsp. celery salt
1 T. parsley, chopped
1½ lbs. shrimp, shelled, deveined
3 green onions, diced
Tabasco sauce to taste
1 cup unsweetened coconut milk*

Sauté onion in oil or butter until translucent. Add tomato paste, water, tomato sauce, celery salt, and parsley. Simmer for 20 minutes. Add shrimp, green onion, and Tabasco (carefully—taste as adding). Reserve a little green onion for garnish. Simmer for a few minutes until shrimp turn pink. Add coconut milk. Heat mixture but do not let boil. Serve over rice. Garnish with remaining green onion. This is nice served in individual casseroles.

Wine suggestion: White Rioja or Bardolino

*Available canned or frozen in specialty food stores, such as oriental stores. If unavailable, regular whole milk can be substituted, but it will lack unique flavor.

Preparation time: 30 minutes
Cooking time: 25 minutes

Easy
Can make ahead

Serves: 4
Easily doubled

Kristen Anderson-Quinn

TROUT MARJONE

Elegant—to the eye as well as the palate

6 T. butter or margarine
   (divided)
2 lbs. (3–4 small) trout,
   ready to bake
Salt and pepper to taste
Flour
6 small onions, thinly sliced
12 shrimp, cooked, minced
¼ lb. mushrooms, chopped
2 slices truffles or a few ripe
   olives, minced
Several sprigs parsley (for
   garnish)
Lemon slices (for garnish)

THIN HOLLANDAISE:
2 egg yolks
2 T. butter
⅓ cup boiling water
Juice of 1 large lemon or 4
   T. lemon juice
1 tsp. salt
½ tsp. paprika

Grease baking dish with 4 tablespoonfuls butter. Season trout with salt and pepper. Dust with flour and place in baking dish. Bake at 400° for 30 minutes, basting often. Cook onions in 2 tablespoonfuls butter until they turn yellow.

Thin hollandaise: Whisk egg yolks in top of double boiler. Place over hot water. Whisk small lumps of butter into egg yolks until butter is melted. Remove from heat. Very gradually add boiling water, lemon juice, salt, and paprika, beating constantly. Return to heat and stir until sauce is slightly thickened. Sauce will be thin. Fold onions, shrimp, mushrooms, and truffles into hollandaise. Pour over trout; garnish with parsley and lemon slices.

Wine suggestion: Chardonnay

Preparation time: 30 minutes
Cooking time: 30 minutes

Serves: 4–6

BAKED ATLANTIC FISH WITH CHEESE

6 fresh or frozen fish fillets
   (sole, haddock, cod, or
   halibut)
1 medium lemon or 3 T.
   lemon juice
Salt and pepper to taste
1½ cups Swiss or cheddar
   cheese, grated
Paprika
1 T. dry mustard

Thaw fish if frozen. Arrange fillets in single layer in buttered baking dish. Sprinkle both sides with lemon juice, salt, and pepper. Top with cheese and sprinkle with paprika. Mix together mustard and cream; pour over fillets. Sprinkle with crumbs. Bake at 350° for 35 minutes, or until fish flakes easily when tested with a fork.

(continued)

BAKED ATLANTIC FISH WITH CHEESE (continued)

½ pt. whipping cream,
unwhipped

½ cup fine dry bread
crumbs

Microwave: Arrange 1 pound of fish fillets in single layer in greased glass or pyroceramic baking dish. Sprinkle both sides of fillets with lemon juice, salt, pepper, and paprika. Combine mustard and cream; pour over fillets. Cover with wax paper. Microwave on high for 6 to 7 minutes, or until fish flakes easily with a fork. Sprinkle grated cheese and toasted bread crumbs on top; microwave on high for 1 to 2 minutes, or until cheese melts.

Wine suggestion: Hungarian White

Preparation time: 10 minutes   Easy   Serves: 4–6
Baking time: 35 minutes   Can make ahead   Easily doubled
Microwave: 7–9 minutes

Nancy Jacobs

SPANISH-STYLE BAKED FISH

1 cup onion, chopped
⅓ cup margarine
1 clove garlic, minced
½ cup celery, chopped
1 can (15 oz.) tomato sauce
  with onion, celery, and
  green pepper
⅛ tsp. ground cloves
1 bay leaf
1½ cups carrots, shredded
¾ cup chicken broth
Salt and pepper to taste
2 lbs. frozen fish fillets,
  thawed (flounder, perch,
  or turbot)
Fresh parsley, chopped

Sauté onion in margarine. Add garlic and celery; sauté until tender. Add tomato sauce, cloves, bay leaf, carrots, chicken broth, salt, and pepper. Cover and simmer for 30 minutes. Can make sauce ahead. Salt and pepper fish; roll up and secure with toothpicks. Place rolls in greased 2-quart baking dish. Top with sauce. Bake at 350° for 35 minutes. Sprinkle with parsley.

Microwave: Sauté onion, garlic, and celery in margarine in microwave on high for 1 to 2 minutes, or until lightly browned. Stir several times. Add tomato sauce, cloves, bay leaf, carrots, chicken broth, salt, and pepper. Cover: microwave on high for 4 to 5 minutes. Pepper fish (DO NOT SALT); roll up and secure with toothpicks. Place rolls in greased 2-quart glass baking dish. Top with sauce, cover with waxed paper, and microwave on high for 6 to 8 minutes, or until fish flakes easily. Sprinkle with parsley.

Preparation time: 15 minutes   Easy   Serves: 8
Baking time: 60 minutes
Microwave: 15 minutes

Gayle Kirkpatrick

ZARZUELA DE MARISCOS DE PADRE

1 lb. raw shrimp, shelled, deveined
1 qt. mussels in shell or 1 can (10½ oz.) minced clams
4 T. olive oil
1 lb. halibut or sole, cut into chunks
1 T. flour
½ tsp. salt
1 T. brandy
1 medium onion, chopped
1 pimiento, chopped
2 cloves garlic, crushed
3 T. almonds, crushed
2 fresh or 1 cup canned tomatoes, chopped
1 tsp. salt
White pepper, freshly ground, to taste
½ cup white wine
1 T. parsley, minced

Shell and devin shrimp. Scrub mussels and remove beards. Heat oil in large pan. Dust halibut with flour mixed with salt. Cook until browned lightly on both sides. Add shrimp; cook until pink. Warm brandy; add to pan and flame. Remove fish and shrimp when flame dies. To oil, add onion, pimiento, garlic, and almonds; sauté until tender, adding more oil if necessary. Add tomatoes and sprinkle with salt and pepper. Add wine and mussels or clams; bring to a boil. Cook over high heat until liquid is reduced and thickened and mussels open. If using clams, simmer gently to reduce liquid. Return fish and shrimp to sauce; cook for 2 minutes more. Place in a shallow casserole; sprinkle with parsley. Accompany with Saffron Rice (see page 160).

Wine suggestion: Mosel

Preparation time: 30 minutes
Cooking time: 20 minutes

Easy
Can make ahead

Serves: 4–6

Jean Kavanaugh

BAKED STUFFED CRAB LEGS
Makes a nice first course

4 lbs. frozen crab legs, split in half
1 large onion, finely chopped
1 clove garlic, minced
¼ cup butter
1½ cups bread crumbs
2 T. capers
½ tsp. thyme

Have crab legs split lengthwise at fish market. Plunge legs into boiling salted water to cover; simmer for 10 minutes. Remove. Cool. Pry meat from legs. Set meat aside and reserve shells. Sauté onion and garlic in butter until tender and golden. Remove from heat; mix with bread crumbs, capers, thyme, salt, and pepper. Moisten with sherry. Cut crab into bite-sized chunks; combine with bread-

(continued)

CRAB LEGS (continued)

Salt and pepper to taste
2 ozs. sherry
Sprig fresh thyme (for garnish)
Lemon wedges (for garnish)

crumb mixture. Fill split shells with crab mixture. Bake at 350° for 15 minutes, or until hot throughout. Garnish with thyme and lemon wedges.

Wine suggestion: Pouilly-Fumé

Preparation time: 30 minutes
Baking time: 15 minutes

Easy
Can make ahead

Serves: 6–8

Lina Nissim

NEW ORLEANS JAMBALAYA
Great for family or guests

1 lb. smoked sausage or ham, cut in ½-inch cubes
½ cup vegetable oil
2 medium onions, chopped
1 bunch scallions or green onions, chopped
1 large green pepper, chopped
½ cup celery, chopped
½ lb. fresh okra, chopped, or 1 pkg. (10 oz.) frozen okra
¼ typ. Thyme
2 bay leaves
2–6 cloves garlic, pressed
½ tsp. salt
Pinch of cayenne pepper
2 lbs. raw shrimp, peeled, deveined
2 cans (16 oz. each) tomatoes, undrained
1 can (6 oz.) tomato paste
½ lemon, quartered
3 cups cooked long grain rice

Cook sausage or ham in hot oil until light brown. Add onions, scallions, green pepper, celery, okra, thyme, bay leaves, garlic, salt, and cayenne pepper. Cook for 3 minutes longer. Add shrimp, tomatoes, tomato paste, and lemon. Simmer slowly, uncovered, tossing often with fork until shrimp are pink. Serve over hot rice.

Note: May substitute chicken livers or chicken for shrimp.

Wine suggestion: Grenache Rosé, Mâcon Blanc, or Beer

Preparation time: 1 hour
Cooking time: 30 minutes

Can make ahead

Serves: 6

Diane Basso

229

BAKED STUFFED SOLE WITH NANTUA SAUCE
Entertaining is simplified with this do-ahead dish

2 lbs. fresh or frozen sole
1½ cups unseasoned bread crumbs
½ cup butter, melted
1 T. parsley, flaked
¼ cup celery, chopped
1 can (7 oz.) crab meat, drained
Salt and pepper to taste

NANTUA SAUCE:
2 T. butter
2 T. flour
1 cup half-and-half or milk
½ tsp. salt
Dash of white pepper
½ cup Swiss cheese, grated
4 T. butter, melted
4 large shrimp, cooked, minced in blender
2 T. Madeira
Salt and pepper to taste

Thaw fish if frozen. Combine bread crumbs, butter, parsley, celery, and crab meat. Season with salt and pepper.

To make Nantua Sauce: Melt butter in pan. Blend in flour with whisk; cook on low heat for 2 minutes. Gradually blend in half-and-half; salt and pepper. Cook until thickened. Stir in Swiss cheese. Blend together butter and shrimp; add to cheese sauce. Add Madeira to sauce; season with salt and pepper. Arrange half the sole in buttered shallow oven-to-table dish. Cover with layer of crab meat stuffing, saving ⅓ for topping. Top with remaining fish. Pour Nantua Sauce over all, and sprinkle with remaining stuffing. Bake, uncovered, at 350° for about 45 minutes.

Wine suggestion: Dry Gewürztraminer

Preparation time: 30 minutes
Baking time: 45 minutes

Easy
Can make ahead

Serves: 6–8

Sally Ward Hume

BOILED CRAB LEGS

Chop 6 pounds frozen crab legs into 8-inch serving pieces. Set aside. Fill 2-gallon pot with water; add 2 whole juniper berries, 1 bay leaf, and a pinch of chervil. DO NOT ADD SALT! When water reaches a boil, add 1 to 1½ cups white wine (preferably a sweet German wine) that is room temperature. Place crab legs in water. Cover pot; cook for 15 minutes. Serve with melted unsalted butter. Serves 6.

Roger A. Gauntlett

SHRIMP WITH GRAPES

Delicate combination will have everyone asking for seconds

¼ cup butter or margarine
¾ cup celery, chopped
¼ cup green pepper, chopped
¼ cup onion, chopped
2 lbs. raw shrimp, shelled, deveined, rinsed, or 1½ lbs. frozen shrimp, ready to cook
1 tsp. salt
¼ tsp. pepper
1 T. bottled thick meat sauce (A.1.)
1 T. lemon juice
1½ cups seedless green grapes

In 10-inch skillet, melt butter or margarine. Sauté celery, green pepper, and onion in butter until tender—about 5 minutes—stirring occasionally. Add shrimp and sprinkle with salt and pepper; stir in meat sauce and lemon juice. Sauté until shrimp are pink. Add grapes and cook for 5 minutes longer. Good served with hot fluffy rice.

Wine suggestion: Vouvray

Preparation time: 45 minutes   Can make ahead   Serves: 6

Suzanne Sellers

SCALLOPS PROVENÇAL

Great as an hors d'oeuvre or entrée

2 lbs. scallops
Salt and pepper
Flour
½ cup butter
1½ tsps. garlic, finely minced
¼ cup fresh parsley, chopped

Rinse scallops (halve if large); pat dry. Sprinkle with salt and pepper. Dust with flour, shaking off excess. In a skillet, cook butter for 3 minutes, or until golden brown. Add scallops and sauté for 3 to 5 minutes, or until lightly browned and cooked through. Stir in garlic and parsley. Cook for 1 minute. Transfer to heated serving dish.

Wine suggestion: Muscadet

Preparation time: 10 minutes   Easy   Serves: 4
Cooking time: 5 minutes

Bettina Rollins

LEMON RICE-STUFFED WHITEFISH
Natural blend of lemon and fish makes this a hit

3–4 lbs. whitefish, freshly
dressed
1½ tsps. salt

STUFFING:
¼ cup butter
¾ cup celery, chopped
½ cup onion, chopped
1⅓ cups water
2 T. lemon rind, grated
1 tsp. salt
1 tsp. paprika
Dash of thyme
1½ cups instant rice,
uncooked
⅓ cup sour cream
¼ cup lemon, peeled, diced
2 T. butter, melted

WHITE SAUCE (optional):
2 T. butter
2 T. flour
1 cup milk
Salt and white pepper to
taste
⅓ cup Swiss cheese, grated
Juice of ½ lemon

Sprinkle fish inside and out with salt.

To prepare stuffing: In skillet, melt butter; add celery and onion. Sauté until tender. Add water, lemon rind, salt, paprika, and rhyme. Bring to a boil. Add rice and stir to moisten. Cover and remove from heat. Let stand for 5 to 10 minutes, or until liquid is absorbed. Add sour cream and lemon; mix lightly. Stuff cavity of fish loosely with dressing; tie securely with string. Place in buttered shallow baking dish; brush with butter. Bake at 350° for 40 to 60 minutes, or until fish flakes when tested with fork. Baste occasionally with butter. Serve extra dressing with fish. If desired, top with white sauce.

White sauce: Melt butter in small skillet; blend in flour over low heat. Cook for 1 to 2 minutes over low heat; gradually add milk, salt, and white pepper, stirring constantly. Cook over medium heat until sauce thickens. Add Swiss cheese and lemon juice; stir. Cook very slowly for a few more minutes.

Wine suggestion: Vinho Verde

Preparation time: 30 minutes
Baking time: 40–60 minutes

Can make ahead

Serves: 6

Reprinted with permission of
Jewel Companies, Inc.

BAKED OR BROILED CRAB LEGS

Cut split frozen crab legs into 4-inch sections and then butter them. Either bake at 375° for 12 to 15 minutes, or broil for 12 minutes, basting a second time.

Sharon Garside

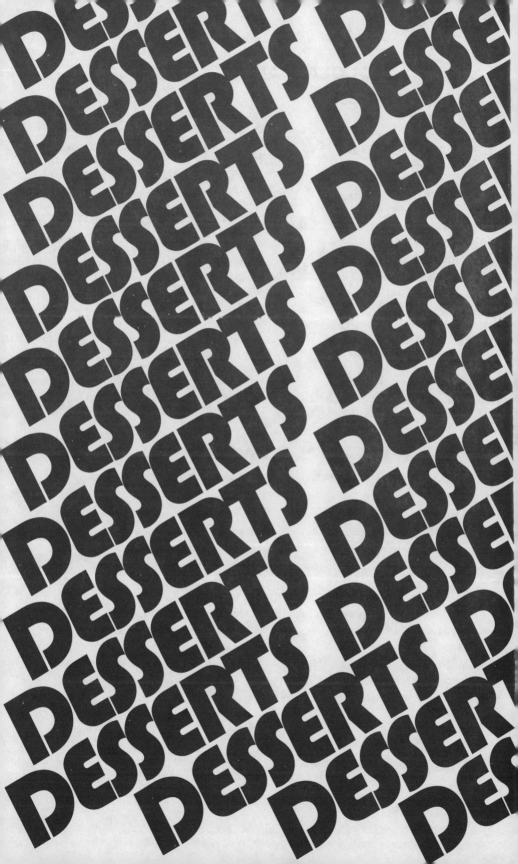

CHOCOLATE ANGEL STRATA PIE

9-inch pie shell, baked, cooled
2 eggs, separated
½ tsp. white vinegar
¼ tsp. salt
¼ tsp. cinnamon
¾ cup sugar (divided)
1 pkg. (6 oz.) semisweet chocolate chips
¼ cup water
1 cup whipping cream, whipped
Grated chocolate (for garnish)

Beat egg whites with vinegar, salt, and cinnamon. Gradually add ½ cup sugar and beat until meringue forms stiff peaks. Line pie shell with meringue and bake at 325° for 15 to 18 minutes. Cool. Melt together chocolate chips and water. Add egg yolks; mix well. Spread 3 tablespoonfuls chocolate mixture over meringue. Chill remaining chocolate. Add ¼ cup sugar and dash of cinnamon to whipped cream. Spread half of whipped cream over chocolate layer. Combine remaining whipped cream with chilled chocolate; spread over whipped-cream layer. Chill at least 4 hours. Garnish with grated chocolate.

Preparation time: 40 minutes
Baking time: 15–18 minutes

Must make ahead   Serves: 8

Marge Burns

ALASKAN PIE
Like a Baked Alaska in taste and elegance

CRUST:
1 cup chocolate wafer or Oreo cookie crumbs
⅓–¼ cup butter, melted

Combine cookie crumbs and butter. Press into 9 or 10-inch pie plate. Chill.

FILLING:
1–2 qts. peppermint stick or vanilla ice cream, softened

Spoon into chilled crust and freeze until firm (may be covered with baked meringue or served with chocolate sauce only).

MERINGUE:
3 egg whites
1 cup marshmallow crème
1 tsp. vanilla

Beat egg whites until stiff. Add marshmallow creme gradually and continue beating. Stir in vanilla. Spread meringue over ice cream, sealing to edge of crust. Bake at 450° for 2 to 3 minutes, or until lightly browned. Freeze immediately. Cut into pieces and serve with sauce.

(continued)

ALASKAN PIE (continued)

SAUCE:

2 ozs. unsweetened
   chocolate
1 T. butter
½ cup sugar
1 can (6 oz.) evaporated
   milk

Melt together chocolate and butter over low heat. Stir in sugar and milk; continue cooking until thick, stirring constantly. Either serve with the meringue or pour directly over the ice cream and freeze until serving.

Preparation time: 25 minutes
Baking time: 2–3 minutes

Must make ahead
Must be frozen

Serves: 8–10

Barbara Brandt
Mary Ellen Godfrey

RHUBARB CREAM PIE

CRUST:

1 cup flour
½ cup butter or margarine,
   softened
1 T. sugar

Mix together flour, butter, and sugar until crumbly. Press into 9-inch pie plate. Bake at 350° for 10 minutes, or until lightly browned. Cool.

FILLING:

2 T. butter, melted
2 cups rhubarb, chopped
1½ cups sugar (divided)
2 eggs, separated
¼ tsp. salt
2 T. cornstarch
¼ cup milk or cream

Add rhubarb and 1 cup sugar to melted butter and cook slowly until rhubarb is mushy. Mix egg yolks with ¼ cup sugar, salt, cornstarch, and milk. Add to rhubarb mixture and continue cooking until thick. Cool and pour into prepared shell. Beat egg whites until stiff; gradually add ¼ cup sugar. Top pie with meringue. Bake at 350° for 10 to 12 minutes.

Preparation time: 45 minutes
Baking time: 20 minutes

Best served the first day

Serves: 8

Nancy Jacobs

Hint: When using cornstarch in a recipe, sift or force it through a sieve to prevent lumping.

235

KENTUCKY CHOCOLATE CHIP PIE
This pie belongs in our "winner's circle"

1 cup sugar
½ cup flour
2 eggs, slightly beaten
½ cup butter, melted, cooled
1 cup English walnuts, chopped
1 cup semisweet chocolate chips
1 tsp. vanilla
9-inch pie shell, unbaked

Mix together sugar and flour; stir in eggs and beat. Add butter, nuts, chocolate chips, and vanilla; blend well. Pour into pie shell. Bake at 325° for 50 to 60 minutes. Cool.

Preparation time: 15 minutes
Baking time: 50–60 minutes

Easy
Can make ahead

Serves: 6–8

Evelyne Kilgore

FROZEN COFFEE PIE

CRUST:
1 T. butter, softened
1½ cups pecans, chopped
¼ cup sugar
Pinch of salt
1 egg white, stiffly beaten

Mix together butter, pecans, sugar, and salt. Fold in egg white. Spread into a *well-buttered* 9-inch pie plate. Bake at 375° for 12 minutes or microwave on high for 2 minutes. Remove from oven and cool.

FILLING:
1 T. instant coffee
½ cup milk
16 large marshmallows
1 egg yolk, slightly beaten
1 cup whipping cream, whipped
Shaved chocolate

In top of double boiler, over gently boiling water, or in microwave on high, heat coffee, milk, and marshmallows until melted, stirring frequently. Add a small amount of the hot mixture to the egg yolk and then blend egg yolk into remaining mixture. Mix until smooth and continue cooking, stirring constantly. Chill until thick. Fold in whipped cream and pour into crust. Freeze until firm. Garnish with shaved chocolate.

Preparation time: 30 minutes
Baking time: 12 minutes

Must make ahead
Must be frozen

Serves: 8

Shirley McCarty

FESTIVE EGGNOG PIE

Decorate this like a wreath to enhance your Christmas buffet

9-inch pie shell, baked, or
  9-inch coconut shell
1 env. unflavored gelatin
3 T. cold water
2 cups eggnog
1 cup whipping cream,
  whipped
¼ cup sugar
¼ tsp. salt
2 tsps. vanilla
½ tsp. almond extract
¼–½ tsp. nutmeg

Dissolve gelatin in water. Heat eggnog until warm and add to dissolved gelatin. Cool slightly. Fold in whipped cream, sugar, salt, vanilla, and almond extract. Pour into pie shell. Chill at least 2 hours. Sprinkle with nutmeg.

Holiday suggestion: Sprinkle edge with green colored coconut and cherries for a colorful Christmas wreath effect.

Preparation time: 20 minutes

Easy
Must be refrigerated
Must make ahead

Serves: 6–8

HUNGARIAN PINEAPPLE PIE

A unique offering from the old country

CRUST:
1 cup flour
1½ T. sugar
Pinch of salt
½ cup butter, softened

Blend flour, sugar, salt, and butter together in a bowl and mix with hands. Pat into a 9-inch pie plate. Bake at 350° for 5 to 10 minutes until lightly browned.

FILLING:
2 cups crushed pineapple,
  undrained
3 T. sugar
1 T. cornstarch
3 eggs, separated
1 cup whipping cream,
  whipped, sweetened

Place pineapple, sugar, cornstarch, and egg yolks in a saucepan. Cook over medium heat, stirring until mixture thickens; or microwave on high for 4 to 5 minutes, or until mixture thickens, stirring every 2 minutes. Remove from heat. Beat egg whites until stiff. Fold into hot mixture; blend well. Pour into prepared crust and bake for 5 minutes at 350°. Cool and chill. Cover with whipped cream and serve.

Preparation time: 20 minutes
Baking time: 10–15 minutes

Must make ahead
Must be refrigerated

Serves: 6–8

Geri Penniman

APPLESAUCE-SPICE PIE

1 lb. applesauce, sweetened
½ tsp. allspice
½ tsp. ground cloves
½ tsp. ground nutmeg
½ tsp. cinnamon
½ tsp. lemon rind, grated
½ cup butter, melted
3 egg yolks, slightly beaten
Pastry for 9-inch double-
   crust pie

Combine applesauce, spices, lemon rind, butter, and egg yolks; blend well. Pour into unbaked 9-inch pie shell. Cover with top crust, sealing well. Cut vents. Bake at 350° for 60 minutes. Remove from oven and cool.

GINGER MERINGUE:
3 egg whites
Pinch of salt
¼ tsp. cream of tartar
6 T. sugar
¼ tsp. ground ginger

Beat egg whites and salt until foamy. Add cream of tartar and continue to beat until egg whites stand in soft stiff peaks. Mix together sugar and ginger; gradually add to egg whites. Spread meringue over crust. Bake at 300° for 15 to 20 minutes, or until browned. Cool.

Preparation time: 40 minutes
Baking time: 75–80 minutes

Best served the first day   Serves: 8

Mary Maynard

SOUR CREAM-BLUEBERRY PIE

2 T. flour
⅛ tsp. salt
¾ cup sugar
1 egg, slightly beaten
1 cup sour cream
1 tsp. vanilla
1 tsp. lemon rind, grated
9-inch pie shell, unbaked
3 cups fresh blueberries

Combine flour, salt, and sugar. Add egg, sour cream, vanilla, and lemon rind; blend well. Pour into pie shell. Add blueberries. Bake at 400° for 15 minutes; reduce heat to 350° and continue baking 30 minutes longer. Remove from oven.

(continued)

BLUEBERRY PIE (continued)

TOPPING:

⅓ cup sugar
⅓ cup flour
3 T. butter or margarine, softened
1 tsp. cinnamon

Combine topping ingredients and mix until crumbly; sprinkle over top of pie. Bake at 400° for 10 to 15 minutes, or until lightly browned. Serve warm or cold.

Variation: Peaches can be substituted for blueberries; omit the lemon rind and add ¼ tsp. nutmeg.

Preparation time: 25 minutes
Baking time: 55–60 minutes

Best served the first day   Serves: 6–8

LEMONADE-ICE CREAM PIE
A tart afterdinner treat

BUTTER CRUNCH CRUST:

½ cup margarine, softened
¼ cup brown sugar, packed
1 cup flour
½ cup nuts, chopped
½ cup shredded coconut

Mix crust ingredients with hands. Spread in 9 × 13-inch pan and bake at 400° for 15 minutes, stirring occasionally. Remove from oven. Reserve ¾ cup mixture. Press remaining mixture into 9-inch pie plate while still hot. Cool.

FILLING:

1 qt. vanilla ice cream, softened
1 can (6 oz.) frozen lemonade, thawed

Mix together ice cream and lemonade. Fill prepared crust. Sprinkle with reserved crumbs. Freeze.

Preparation time:
    15–20 minutes
Baking time: 15 minutes

Easy
Must make ahead

Serves: 8
Must be frozen

Jan Wright

HOW TO MICROWAVE A PIECRUST

Place piecrust in a 9 or 10-inch glass deep-dish pie plate. Place another glass pie plate on top of crust. Microwave for 1 minute on high (to set the crust). Remove top pie plate. Microwave for 4 more minutes, or until crust appears dry, rotating once. Cool.

BEST-EVER CHEESECAKE

⅔ cup zwieback crumbs
3 pkgs. (8 oz. each) cream
   cheese, softened
4 egg whites
1 cup sugar
1 tsp. vanilla

Butter a 9-inch springform pan and dust with zwieback crumbs. Beat cream cheese until light and fluffy. Beat egg whites to soft peaks. Gradually add sugar and beat to stiff peaks. Fold egg whites into cream cheese. Add vanilla. Pour mixture into prepared pan. Bake at 350° for 25 minutes. Cool. May be topped with a glaze. Refrigerate overnight.

Preparation time: 25 minutes
Baking time: 25 minutes

Easy   Serves: 8–10
Must make ahead
Must be refrigerated

Jan Wright

LEMON GLAZE (MICROWAVE)

½ cup sugar
1 T. cornstarch
⅓ cup water
3 T. lemon juice, freshly
   squeezed
1 egg yolk, slightly beaten

Mix together sugar and cornstarch in a 1-quart glass measuring cup. Stir in water and lemon juice. Microwave on high, uncovered, for 2½ to 3 minutes, stirring every 60 seconds until mixture is thickened and bubbly. Stir some of the hot mixture into the egg yolk. Return yolk mixture to remaining hot mixture and stir until smooth. Microwave on high for 30 seconds. Spoon glaze over cheesecake; spread to the edge. Chill.

Preparation time: 10 minutes
Microwave: 3–3½ minutes

Easy

Deanna House
Instructor
Portage Community Education

Please note: Microwave directions in this book are for use with units having 600–700 watts (and above). If unit with lower wattage is used, baking times will need to be lengthened.

MELBA SAUCE OR RASPBERRY GLAZE

1 pkg. (10 oz.) frozen
  raspberries, thawed,
  crushed
1 T. cornstarch
½ cup currant jelly

Combine raspberries, cornstarch, and jelly in a saucepan. Cook and stir until thickened and bubbly. Remove from heat and strain. Cool. Spread over cheesecake.

Preparation time: 10 minutes   Easy

LIMELIGHT CHEESECAKE

CRUST:

1 cup coconut, shredded or
  flaked
2 T. flour
2 T. butter, melted

Combine coconut, flour, and butter. Press evenly into bottom of 9-inch springform pan. Bake at 350° for 12 to 15 minutes.

FILLING:

1 env. unflavored gelatin
3 eggs, separated
1 cup cold water (divided)
¾ cup sugar
2 pkgs. (8 oz. each) cream
  cheese, softened
¼ cup lime juice, freshly
  squeezed
1 tsp. lime rind, grated
Green food coloring
1 cup whipping cream,
  whipped
Lime slices, twisted
  (for garnish)

Soften gelatin in ¼ cup cold water (set aside). Combine egg yolks, ¾ cup water, and sugar in a saucepan. Bring to a boil over medium heat and simmer for 5 minutes, stirring constantly. Add gelatin; stir until dissolved. Remove from heat and cool slightly. Gradually add gelatin mixture to cream cheese; mix until blended. Stir in lime juice, rind, and food coloring. Fold in whipped cream and stiffly beaten egg whites. Pour over crust. Chill until firm. Garnish with twisted lime slices.

Preparation time:
  30–40 minutes
Baking time: 12–15 minutes

Must make ahead   Serves: 10–12
Must be refrigerated

Pat Nyblom

Hint: When grating the rind of limes, lemons, oranges, etc., use the smallest side of the grater. Take care not to include the white part of the rind in the gratings, because it will produce an undesirable bitter flavor.

"CHOCOHOLIC" CHEESECAKE
A chocolate lover's delight

CRUST:

1 cup chocolate wafer crumbs
¼ cup butter, melted
½ cup pecans or macadamia nuts, finely chopped

Combine wafer crumbs, butter, and nuts until well blended. Press evenly onto bottom and sides of a 10-inch springform pan. Cover outside of pan with foil to prevent leakage. Chill.

FILLING:

3 pkgs. (8 oz. each) cream cheese, softened
1 cup sugar
4 eggs
8 ozs. semisweet chocolate, melted, cooled
2 T. cocoa, sifted
2 tsps. vanilla
2 cups sour cream
½ cup butter, melted
Whipping cream, whipped (for garnish, optional)

Beat cream cheese until fluffy in a large mixing bowl. Gradually add sugar. Beat in eggs, 1 at a time, until well blended. Stir in chocolate, cocoa, and vanilla; mix well. Fold in sour cream and butter. Pour into prepared pan. Bake at 350° for 50 to 55 minutes, or until edges are set. Remove from oven and cool. Refrigerate overnight. May be garnished with whipped cream. Serve in small slices.

Preparation time: 45 minutes
Baking time: 45–50 minutes

Must make ahead   Serves: 16 or more
Must be refrigerated   Can be frozen

Mary Maynard

DELICATESSEN CHEESECAKE

CRUST:

4 ozs. zwieback crumbs
2 T. butter, melted
2 T. sugar
1 tsp. lemon rind, grated

Generously grease a 10-inch springform pan with butter. Cover the outside of pan with foil to prevent leakage. Combine zwieback crumbs, butter, sugar, and lemon rind until well blended. Press ¾ cup of mixture evenly onto bottom and up sides of pan. Chill. Reserve remaining crumbs.

(continued)

CHEESECAKE (continued)

FILLING:

3 pkgs. (8 oz. each) cream
  cheese, softened
1¼ cups sugar
6 eggs, separated
1 pt. sour cream
⅓ cup flour
2 tsps. vanilla
1–1½ T. lemon juice,
  freshly squeezed
Rind of 1 lemon, grated
Powdered sugar

Beat cream cheese until soft in a *large* mixing bowl. Gradually add sugar until mixture is light and fluffy. Beat in egg yolks, 1 at a time. Add sour cream, flour, vanilla, lemon juice, and rind; blend well. Beat egg whites until stiff, but not dry. Fold egg whites into cheese mixture until blended. Pour into prepared springform pan. Bake at 325° for 65 to 75 minutes or until center is firm. Turn off the heat and leave cake in the oven with the door closed 1 hour longer. Remove from oven and cool on wire rack. Sprinkle reserved crumbs on top. Chill overnight.

Remove from pan. Place bottom side up on serving plate. Dust top with powdered sugar just before serving.

Preparation time: 60 minutes
Baking time: 65–75 minutes
Standing time: 1 hour in oven

Must make ahead   Serves: 16 or more
Must be refrigerated

Mary Maynard

CHILLED ORANGE SOUFFLÉ
Perfect ending for that special luncheon

8 eggs
6 egg yolks
¾ cup sugar
3 envs. unflavored gelatin
4 tsps. lemon juice
6 T. cold water
2 T. orange rind, grated
4 cups whipping cream,
  whipped
1 cup currant jelly, melted,
  cooled slightly
3–4 oranges, sectioned

In a *large* bowl, beat eggs and egg yolks until thick; add sugar gradually. Dissolve gelatin in lemon juice and water over *low* heat. *Slowly* fold dissolved gelatin into egg mixture; add grated rind. Fold in whipped cream. Pour into ungreased 9-inch soufflé dish with collar. Refrigerate until set—at least 8 hours. Remove collar and carefully brush top with jelly. Arrange orange slices around outer edge of dish. Serve cold in dessert dishes.

Variation: Omit currant jelly and serve with Melba Sauce (see page 241).

Preparation time: 45 minutes

Must make ahead   Serves: 20
Can easily be halved

Virginia Bardeen

HAMPDEN-SYDNEY DESSERT
This heavenly mold is a showstopper

2 cups milk
6 eggs, separated
1½ cups sugar
2 envs. unflavored gelatin
½ cup cold water
½ tsp. almond extract
3 cups whipping cream,
  whipped
8-inch angel food cake
Flaked coconut (optional)
1 cup whipping cream,
  whipped (for icing, optional)

Scald milk in a double boiler. Stir a small amount of hot milk into egg yolks; add yolks to milk in double boiler. Add sugar gradually. Cook slowly, stirring constantly, until mixture thickens and coats a spoon (10 to 20 minutes). Remove from heat. Dissolve gelatin in cold water. Add dissolved gelatin to first mixture. Stir in almond extract. Cool about 20 minutes. Beat egg whites until stiff. Fold egg whites into cooled custard; fold in whipped cream.

Tear angel food cake into bite-sized pieces. Cover the bottom of a 10-inch tube pan with a thin layer of custard mixture. Arrange ⅓ cake pieces over custard. Pour ⅓ remaining custard over cake. Repeat layers, ending with custard. Chill until firm. Unmold on serving plate. Ice with whipped cream, if desired, and sprinkle with coconut.

Variations: Slice after unmolding. Top eah slice with whipped cream and fresh peaches or strawberries or serve sliced with Hot Fudge Sauce (see page 249).

Preparation time: 45 minutes

Must make ahead
Must be refrigerated

Serves: 12–18
Easily halved
in loaf pan

Mary Ann Hannah

CREPES WITH STRAWBERRIES

1½ cups flour (instant
  blending preferred)
¼ cup powdered sugar
Pinch of salt
1 cup milk
¼ cup butter, melted
2 T. orange liqueur
1 tsp. lemon rind, grated
5 eggs, well beaten

Combine flour, sugar, and salt. Stir in milk, butter, liqueur, and rind; blend well. Add eggs and beat until smooth. Cover and refrigerate for 30 minutes (allow a minimum of 2 hours if using all-purpose flour). Make crepes by placing 2 to 3 tablespoonfuls batter in a lightly buttered crepe pan (or small skillet, 5 to 6 inches in diameter). Tip pan so that batter covers the bottom. Fry until lightly browned; flip crepe and lightly brown other side. Stack between layers of paper towels. May be made ahead. Makes at least 24.

(continued)

CREPES (continued)

FILLING:

2 T. orange rind, grated
2 tsps. lemon rind, grated
2 pkgs. (8 oz. each) cream
cheese, softened
½ cup sour cream
¼ cup sugar

Combine filling ingredients; beat until smooth. May be refrigerated until serving. Spoon a heaping tablespoonful onto each crepe. Roll crepe. Tuck in ends.

SAUCE:

½–1 cup butter
1–2 qts. fresh strawberries,
sliced
2 ozs. Grand Marnier
4 ozs. brandy, hot
Powdered sugar

Melt butter in chafing dish. Arrange filled crepes around edge of chafing dish. Add sliced berries and juice; heat. Slowly pour Grand Marnier and warm brandy into center of dish and ignite. Remove to individual serving plates, and spoon sauce over crepes.

Preparation time:
1¼–1½ hours

Serve immediately

Serves: 12–16
Unfilled crepes
can be frozen

Greeta Douglass

COFFEE MOUSSE
Elegantly simple

1 cup water
4 T. instant coffee
35 large marshmallows
1 cup whipping cream,
whipped
Semisweet chocolate,
grated (for garnish)
12 cup crème de cacao

Place water, coffee, and marshmallows in top of double boiler. Cook and stir over gently boiling water until melted, or microwave for 3 minutes, or until melted. Remove from heat and cool. Fold in whipped cream. Pour into dessert dishes. Garnish with grated chocolate. Chill several hours before serving. Top each serving with 1 tablespoonful crème de cacao.

Preparation time: 20 minutes

Easy
Must make ahead
Must be refrigerated

Serves: 6–8

Scott Davison

BAKED PEARS WITH RASPBERRY SAUCE

6 fresh pears
12 ozs. ginger ale
3 T. lemon juice
1 cinnamon stick

Peel, halve, and core pears. Place, cut side up, in a 9 × 13-inch baking dish. Pour ginger ale and lemon juice over pears. Add the cinnamon stick. Cover with foil and bake at 375° for 30 minutes, or until tender. Cool. Drain pears on paper towel. Arrange pears on serving platter; cover and chill 2 to 3 hours or overnight.

RASPBERRY SAUCE:
2 pkgs. (10 oz. each) frozen
    raspberries, thawed,
    drained
1 tsp. lemon juice
2 tsps. kirsch

Puree raspberries by pushing through a sieve. Add lemon juice and kirsch to the puree; mix well. Pour over pears.

SOUR CREAM TOPPING:
1 cup whipping cream,
    whipped
2 T. powdered sugar
½ cup sour cream
1 tsp. vanilla

Add sugar to whipped cream. Fold in sour cream and vanilla. Chill. Serve over raspberry-covered pears.

Preparation time:
    30–40 minutes
Baking time: 30 minutes

Must make ahead
Must be refrigerated

Serves: 10–12

Shirley Weiss

SUPERB LIQUOR DESSERT

1 qt. fresh or frozen
    strawberries, hulled,
    whole
1 fresh pineapple, cut into
    bite-sized pieces
1 cup peaches, sliced
½ cup brandy
1 bottle champagne

Mix fruit together. Pour brandy over fruit and marinate for 24 hours. Pour champagne into goblets; fill with marinated fruit and juices. Serve.

Preparation time: 20 minutes

Must make ahead

Serves: 6–8

Isabel Stout

LEMON PUFF PUDDING

¼ cup butter, softened
½ cup sugar
1 tsp. lemon rind, grated
2 egg yolks
3 T. lemon juice
2 T. flour
¼ cup grape-nuts
1 cup milk
2 egg whites, stiffly beaten

Cream together butter, sugar, and lemon rind. Add egg yolks; beat until light and fluffy. Blend in lemon juice, flour, grape-nuts, and milk (will look curdled). Fold in egg whites and pour into greased 1-quart casserole. Place in pan of hot water. Bake at 325° for 1¼ hours or until top springs back. Serve warm or cold.

Preparation time: 20 minutes

Easy   Serves: 4–6
Should be refrigerated

Joann Data

FROZEN RASPBERRY SOUFFLE
A midsummer night's dream

4 pkgs. (10 oz. each) frozen
   raspberries, thawed,
   drained, or 3 pts. fresh
   raspberries
7 T. kirsch (divided)
6 ladyfingers, diced
1 cup sugar
¼ cup water
½ tsp. cream of tartar
5 egg whites
1 cup whipping cream,
   whipped
2 T. pistachio nuts, chopped

Puree raspberries in food processor or blender; strain to remove seeds. Mix ¼ cup kirsch into puree. Sprinkle ladyfingers with remaining kirsch; set aside. In a saucepan, mix together sugar, water, and cream of tartar. Bring to a boil over medium heat and continue cooking to soft ball stage (about 10 minutes). Beat egg whites to soft peak stage. Slowly pour hot sugar syrup into egg whites, beating continuously. Gradually fold raspberry puree into egg whites; fold in whipped cream. Pour half of mixture into collared 1-quart mold. Add ladyfingers; top with remaining mixture. Freeze for several hours. Remove from freezer 15 minutes before serving. Carefully remove collar and sprinkle with nuts.

Preparation time:
   45–60 minutes

Must make ahead   Serves: 10–12
Must be frozen

Sally Shipman Early

FROZEN PUMPKIN MOUSSE

1 pkg. (3 oz.) cream cheese, softened
1 cup superfine sugar
1 can (16 oz.) unseasoned pumpkin
2 T. brandy
1 tsp. cinnamon
½ tsp. ground ginger
¼ tsp. ground cloves
1 cup whole unblanched almonds, chopped
1 cup whipping cream, whipped
Almonds, sliced or slivered (for garnish)
Whipped cream (for garnish)

Beat cream cheese until fluffy. Gradually add sugar; blend well. Add pumpkin, brandy, spices, and almonds. Fold whipped cream into pumpkin mixture. Pour into an 8-inch springform pan. Freeze until firm. Remove from freezer 5 to 10 minutes before serving and remove rim of pan immediately. Place on serving plate and pipe whipped cream around base and top. Garnish with almonds. Slice and serve immediately.

Preparation time: 20 minutes   Easy   Serves: 8–12
                                Must make ahead   Must be frozen

STRAWBERRY SUSAN DESSERT

8 medium bananas, thinly sliced
2 qts. fresh strawberries, slightly crushed
2 T. currant jelly, melted
1 T. sugar
2 cups whipping cream, whipped
½ cup powdered sugar
Kirsch or Triple Sec to taste
10 small macaroons, crushed, lightly toasted

Arrange bananas in large deep bowl. (Can be sprinkled with lemon juice or Fruit-Fresh to prevent discoloration.) Mix strawberries, jelly, and sugar; spoon over bananas. Add powdered sugar and liqueur to whipped cream. Cover berries with whipped cream and sprinkle with macaroons. Chill at least 1 hour.

Preparation time: 30 minutes   Must be refrigerated   Serves: 16

Isabel Stout

HOT BRANDY SAUCE

1 cup butter
1 lb. dark brown sugar
6 T. lemon juice
2 tsps. lemon rind, grated
½ cup brandy
2 eggs

In the top of a double boiler, combine butter, sugar, lemon juice and rind, brandy, and eggs. Cook over boiling water until mixture thickens, stirring constantly. Serve hot over mincemeat pie, plum pudding, or fruitcake.

Preparation time: 15 minutes

Marion Putney

LIME DELIGHT
A great combination of lime and chocolate

1 pkg. (8½ oz.) chocolate
  wafers, crushed
¼ cup margarine, melted
1 pkg. (3 oz.) lime gelatin
1¾ cups hot water
1 cup sugar
⅓ cup lime juice
2 tsps. lemon juice
1 can (13 oz.) evaporated
  milk, chilled
Green food coloring

Mix together chocolate wafer crumbs and margarine. Press into 9 × 13-inch pan and freeze. Dissolve gelatin in hot water. Chill until it mounds (about 30 to 45 minutes). Whip gelatin; add sugar and juices. Whip evaporated milk until frothy; fold in whipped gelatin. Add a few drops of food coloring. Pour over crust and chill several hours, or until set.

FUDGE SAUCE:

4 ozs. unsweetened
  chocolate
4 T. margarine
1½ cups sugar
1½ cups evaporated milk
1 tsp. vanilla

Sauce: Melt together chocolate and margarine. Slowly add sugar and milk, stirring until sugar dissolves and mixture starts to thicken. Remove from heat and add vanilla. Sauce may need to be heated slightly before serving if stored in refrigerator.

Microwave: Melt together margarine and chocolate for 1½ minutes. Stir in sugar and evaporated milk. Return to microwave for 5 minutes, stirring every 2 minutes.

Preparation time: 30 minutes

Must make ahead
Must be refrigerated

Serves: 12–15

Joan deMink

FROZEN RAINBOW DESSERT
A light, cooling rainbow of flavors

6–8 macaroons, lightly
   toasted, crumbled
1 pt. whipping cream,
   whipped
3 T. sugar
1 tsp. vanilla
1 cup nuts, chopped
1 pt. orange sherbet,
   softened
1 pt. lemon sherbet,
   softened
1 pt. lime sherbet, softened
(3 pts. rainbow sherbet
   can be substituted for
   individual flavors)

Line a 9-inch springform pan with half the macaroons. Add sugar, vanilla, and nuts to whpped cream; spread half the whipped cream mixture over macaroons. Freeze until firm. Spread each sherbet layer evenly over whipped cream, freezing after each addition. Top with remaining whipped cream, then macaroons. Freeze for several hours. Remove rim of pan; serve.

Preparation time: 30 minutes   Must make ahead   Serves: 10–12
                                                                Must be frozen

Bonnie Boekeloo
Jan Shugars

APPLE-CHEESE BAKE

3 cups apples, peeled,
   chopped
⅛ tsp. cinnamon
¼ cup water
2 tsps. lemon juice
¾ cup sugar
½ cup flour
¼ tsp. salt
4 T. margarine, softened
¾ cup American cheese,
   shredded

Place apples in a greased 9-inch pie pan. Sprinkle with cinnamon. Combine water and lemon juice and pour over apples. Mix together sugar, flour, and salt; cut in margarine to form a crumbly mixture. Add cheese; mix lightly. Spread mixture over apples. Bake at 350° for 35 to 40 minutes, until apples are tender and topping is brown, or microwave for 10 minutes on high, rotating 2 times. Serve with ice cream.

Preparation time: 20 minutes   Easy   Serves: 6–8
Baking time: 35–40 minutes   Can be frozen
Microwave: 10 minutes   before baking

Patricia Ellwood

FRESH PEACHES BY JIMINY
A wonderful way to treat a peach

CRUST:
1¾ cups flour
2 T. sugar
½ tsp. salt
¼ tsp. baking powder
½ cup butter, softened

Mix together flour, sugar, salt, and baking powder. Cut in butter with a pastry blender until mixture is pebbly. Press evenly on the bottom and about 1 inch up the sides of an 8-inch square pan.

FILLING:
4–6 fresh peaches, peeled, halved
1 cup sugar
1 tsp. cinnamon
1 cup whipping cream
2 egg yolks

Arrange peach halves, cut side down, over crust. Mix together the sugar and cinnamon; sprinkle over the peaches. Bake at 400° for 15 minutes. Mix together whipping cream and egg yolks; pour over peaches. Continue baking for 30 to 35 minutes longer. Cool for at least 30 minutes before serving.

Preparation time: 20 minutes
Baking time: 45–50 minutes

Easy
Best served the first day

Serves: 6–8

Martha Hilboldt

Hint: The unused egg whites may be frozen in individual containers for later use.

FOAMY SAUCE

¼ cup butter, melted
1 cup powdered sugar, sifted
1 egg, slightly beaten
1 tsp. vanilla
1 cup whipping cream, whipped

Combine butter with sugar, egg, and vanilla; beat until smooth. Before serving, fold in whipped cream. Serve over steamed chocolate pudding, gingerbread, etc. Should be stored in refrigerator.

Preparation time: 5 minutes

Easy
Can make ahead
Should be refrigerated

Yield: 2 cups

Marilyn Walker

BLUEBERRY "THING"
Delicious morning or night

CRUST:
3 cups flour
1 T. sugar
1½ tsps. salt
1 cup vegetable oil
4½ T. milk

Mix together flour, sugar, salt, vegetable oil, and milk until well blended. Pat ⅔ mixture on the bottom and about 1 inch up the sides of an ungreased 9 × 13-inch pan.

FILLING:
5–6 cups blueberries
  (fresh or frozen)
1⅓ cups sugar
4 T. flour
1 T. tapioca
2 T. lemon juice
Dash of salt
4–5 T. butter

Toss blueberries with sugar and flour. Add tapioca, lemon juice, and salt. Spoon onto crust; dot with butter. Sprinkle remaining crust mixture over berries. Bake at 450° for 10 minutes; reduce heat to 350° and continue baking for 40 minutes. May be served warm or cold. Serve with ice cream or whipped cream.

Preparation time: 20 minutes
Baking time: 50 minutes

Best the first day

Serves: 12–15

Amanda Clark Morrill
Priscilla Washburn

LEMON SAUCE

3 egg yolks
⅓ cup sugar
⅓ cup butter, melted
1 tsp. lemon rind, grated
2 T. lemon juice
1 cup whipping cream,
  whipped

Beat egg yolks until thick and lemon colored. Add sugar and continue beating. Mix together butter, rind, and juice; add to egg mixture. Fold in whipped cream. May be served over apple crisp or other fruit dishes. Store in refrigerator.

Preparation time: 10 minutes

Easy
Can make ahead
Should be refrigerated

Yield: 2 cups

Carole Hawk

GRAPEFRUIT CAKE
As delicious as it is different

¾ cup butter, softened
1½ cups sugar
1 T. grapefruit rind, grated
½ tsp. lemon rind, grated
3 eggs
½ cup grapefruit juice
½ cup water
3 cups cake flour
¾ tsp. salt
3½ tsps. baking powder
¼ tsp. baking soda

Cream together butter and sugar until light and fluffy; add rinds. Beat in eggs, 1 at a time; blend well after each addition. Mix grapefruit juice and water together. Set aside. Sift together flour, salt, baking powder, and baking soda. Add sifted ingredients alternately with the juice-water combination to creamed mixture (use approximately ¼ of the dry ingredients and ⅓ of the liquid ingredients each time), beginning and ending with the dry ingredients. Pour batter into 2 greased 9-inch round pans. Bake at 375° for 30 minutes, or until browned and cake pulls away from the sides of the pan. Cool about 10 minutes; invert on wire racks. Cool. Put a thin layer of frosting between layers; use remaining frosting for top and sides. Alternate sections of oranges and grapefruit for garnish.

FROSTING:
3 pkgs. (3 oz. each) cream cheese, softened
1 T. butter, softened
4 tsps. grapefruit rind, grated
1 tsp. orange rind, grated
¼ tsp. vanilla
6 cups powdered sugar, sifted
1 T. lemon juice
1 T. orange juice
1 grapefruit, sectioned (for garnish)
2 oranges, sectioned (for garnish)

Cream together cream cheese, butter, rinds, and vanilla. Gradually add powdered sugar; beat until smooth. Add lemon and orange juices gradually; beat until frosting is of spreading consistency.

Preparation time: 1½ hours
Baking time: 30 minutes

Best the first day

Serves: 12–14

Pat LaMothe

APRICOT CASSEROLE FRUITCAKE
A uniquely delicious preparation of a holiday favorite

1 cup dried apricots
¾ cup shortening
1 cup sugar
4 eggs, separated
1 cup seedless white raisins
⅓ cup candied cherries, slivered
⅓ cup candied orange peel, sliced
⅓ cup citron, sliced
⅓ cup almonds, slivered
1 tsp. lemon peel, grated
2 cups flour
1 tsp. salt
½ tsp. baking soda

Place apricots in a small saucepan. Cover with cold water and bring to a boil; cook 1 minute. Drain. Slice coarsely. Set aside. Beat together shortening, sugar, and egg yolks until light and fluffy. Stir in apricots, raisins, other fruits, almonds, and lemon peel. Sift together flour, salt, and baking soda. Beat egg whites until stiff. Add dry ingredients to creamed mixture alternately with stiffly beaten egg whites. Pour into a well-greased 9 × 5 × 3-inch pan and bake at 275° for 2 hours, or until wooden pick inserted in center comes out clean. Cover with brown paper (during baking) after top is browned. Remove from oven and allow to stand 1 hour. Remove from pan and chill. Wrap tightly in foil and store in a cool place at least 1 week before serving.

Preparation time: 45 minutes
Baking time: 2 hours

Must make ahead

Serves: 10–12
Can be frozen

Barbara Brandt

APPLE PIE BROWNIES

¼ cup margarine, softened
1 cup sugar
1 egg
1 cup flour
1 tsp. cinnamon
½ tsp. nutmeg
½ tsp. salt
1 tsp. baking soda
2 T. hot water
2 cups apples, sliced
½ cup walnuts or pecans, chopped

Cream together margarine and sugar; add egg and mix well. Stir in flour, cinnamon, nutmeg, salt, and baking soda dissolved in water. Fold in apples and nuts. Pour into greased 9-inch pie plate. Bake at 350° for 40 to 45 minutes. Serve warm or cold with ice cream or whipped cream. May also be topped with caramel sauce.

(continued)

APPLE PIE BROWNIES (continued)

CARAMEL SAUCE:

¼ cup butter
¼ cup half-and-half
¼ cup sugar
¼ cup brown sugar, packed
½ tsp. vanilla

In a saucepan, combine butter, cream, and sugars. Bring to a boil and cook for 1 minute, stirring constantly. Remove from heat; add vanilla. May be served hot or cold.

Preparation time:
   20–30 minutes
Baking time: 40–45 minutes

Can make ahead   Serves: 8

Easily doubled in a 9 × 13-inch pan

Bonnie Eldridge
Mary Kelley

PUMPKIN ROLL

3 eggs
1 cup sugar
¾ cup canned unseasoned
   pumpkin
1 tsp. lemon juice
¾ cup flour
1 tsp. baking powder
½ tsp. salt
2 tsps. cinnamon
1 tsp. ginger
½ tsp. nutmeg
1 cup walnuts, chopped
Powdered sugar

Beat eggs with electric mixer on high speed for 5 minutes. Gradually beat in sugar; add pumpkin and lemon juice. Stir together flour, baking powder, salt, and spices; fold into pumpkin mixture. Spread into a greased 15 × 10 × 1-inch jelly roll pan lined with greased waxed paper. Sprinkle with walnuts. Bake at 375° for 15 minutes. Invert onto cloth sprinkled with powdered sugar. Carefully remove waxed paper; while hot, roll cake and towel from narrow end. Cool. Unroll and spread filling evenly over cake. Roll up and sprinkle with powdered sugar. Cover with plastic wrap. Refrigerate. Slice and serve.

FILLING:

1 cup powdered sugar
6 ozs. cream cheese,
   softened
4 T. margarine, softened
½ tsp. vanilla

Beat together powdered sugar, cream cheese, and margarine until smooth. Add vanilla.

Preparation time: 30 minutes
Baking time: 15 minutes

Can make ahead   Serves: 12

Kay Davison

CARROT CAKE

4 eggs, well beaten
2 cups sugar
2 jars (8½ oz. each) junior
 baby food carrots
1 can (8¼ oz.) crushed
 pineapple
1½ cups vegetable oil
2 cups flour
2 tsps. baking soda
1 tsp. cinnamon
1 tsp. salt
1 cup dates, chopped
1 cup pecans or walnuts,
 chopped
1 tsp. vanilla

In a large mixing bowl, combine eggs, sugar, carrots, pineapple, and oil. Sift together flour, baking soda, cinnamon, and salt. Add sifted ingredients to egg mixture. Stir in dates and nuts; add vanilla. Spread in ungreased 9×13-inch pan. Bake at 350° for 40 to 50 minutes. Cool. Frost with Cream Cheese Frosting (see page 259).

Preparation time: 45 minutes
Baking time: 40–50 minutes

Can make ahead
Should be refrigerated

Serves: 12–15

Joyce Hyde

HUNGARIAN DOBOS TORTE
An elegant dessert

CAKE:
6 eggs, separated
⅝ cup sugar (divided)
⅛ tsp. salt
1 cup flour

Beat egg yolks until thick and pale yellow. Gradually add ½ cup sugar; blend well. Beat egg whites until foamy; add salt and gradually add ⅓ cup sugar until stiff peaks form (*do not overbeat*). Gently fold egg yolks into egg whites; gradually fold in flour until blended (do not overwork). Spread into 3 greased 8-inch round pans (six 8-inch pans may also be used) lined with waxed paper. Bake at 350° for 12 to 15 minutes. It is best if all the cakes are baked simultaneously so that the egg whites do not sit too long. Cool 10 minutes and remove from pans. Cool. Slice each layer in half horizontally to make 6 layers.

APRICOT FILLING:
1 can (17 oz.) apricot
 halves, drained
½ cup apricot preserves
 (divided)
1 T. apricot brandy

Reserve 3 apricot halves for garnish. Chop remainder of apricots and mix with ¼ cup preserves and brandy. Set aside. Reserve remaining ¼ cup preserves for the top.

(continued)

HUNGARIAN TORTE (continued)

MOCHA CREAM FROSTING:
¾ cup sugar
3 eggs plus 2 egg yolks
2 ozs. semisweet chocolate, broken up
1 tsp. instant coffee powder, sifted
1 tsp. vanilla
1 cup unsalted butter, softened
½ cup almonds, toasted, chopped (for garnish)
Chocolate curls (for garnish)

In top of a double boiler, beat together sugar, eggs, and yolks. Add chocolate, coffee powder, and vanilla. Cook over simmering water for 10 to 15 minutes, or until thickened, stirring constantly. Remove from heat and cool completely. Beat butter until fluffy. Gradually beat butter into chocolate mixture.

Assembly:
1. Place first layer on serving plate; spread with ¼ cup mocha frosting.
2. Stack second layer on top; spread with half the apricot filling.
3. Repeat layers, ending with cake.
4. Spread remaining ¼ cup preserves on top of cake.
5. Frost sides of cake; reserve ½ cup for piping around border at the top.
6. Press nuts on the sides.
7. Garnish top with sliced apricots and chocolate curls; pipe border with reserved frosting. Chill 3 hours before serving.

Preparation time:
  1 hour 20 minutes
Baking time: 12–15 minutes

Must make ahead
Must be refrigerated

Serves: 16

Thomas Berglund

ARKANSAS CAKE

3 cups sugar
1 cup shortening
4 eggs
3 cups flour, sifted
¼ tsp. salt
¼ tsp. baking soda
1 cup buttermilk
1 T. plus ½ tsp. vanilla

Cream together sugar and shortening. Beat in eggs, 1 at a time. Sift flour with salt and baking soda. Add flour mixture alternately with buttermilk to creamed mixture, beginning and ending with the flour. Stir in vanilla. Pour into a well-greased 10-inch tube pan. Bake at 300° to 325° for 80 minutes. Cool 10 minutes. Remove from pan. Continue cooling on rack. May be served with fresh fruit.

Preparation time: 20 minutes
Baking time: 80 minutes

Easy
Can make ahead

Serves: 12–14

Nancy Jacobs

Hint: Vanilla extract is always preferred over vanilla flavoring.

GINGERBREAD-SPICE CAKE

½ cup shortening
½ cup sugar
1 egg, slightly beaten
2½ cups flour, sifted
1½ tsps. baking soda
½ tsp. salt
1¼ tsps. ground ginger
1 tsp. cinnamon
½ tsp. ground cloves
½ tsp. allspice
1 cup molasses
1 cup Concord grape juice,
    boiling
1 tsp. lemon rind, grated
½ cup golden raisins
½ cup walnuts or pecans,
    chopped
Powdered sugar

Cream together shortening and sugar. Beat in egg. Sift together flour, baking soda, salt, and spices. Set aside. Combine molasses and grape juice. Add sifted ingredients alternately with molasses-grape juice mixture to creamed mixture (beginning and ending with dry ingredients); beat well after each addition. Fold in lemon rind, raisins, and nuts. Pour batter into greased 7½ × 11¾-inch pan. Bake at 350° for 45 to 50 minutes, or until cake pulls away from sides of pan. Cool. May sprinkle with powdered sugar or serve with applesauce, Foamy Sauce (see page 251), or Lemon Sauce (see page 252).

Microwave: Prepare cake following above directions. Pour batter into greased and sugared microwave bundt pan. Microwave on high for 6 to 7 minutes, rotating once, or until cake pulls away from sides of pan. Cake will appear moist on top and will dry during cooling.

Preparation time: 40 minutes
Baking time: 45–50 minutes
Microwave: 6–7 minutes

Best served the first day   Serves: 8–10

APPLESAUCE CAKE

3 eggs
2 cups sugar
1¼ cups vegetable oil
2 cups flour
1 tsp. salt
2 tsps. baking soda
2 tsps. cinnamon
1 jar (8½ oz.) junior baby
    food carrots
1 jar (8½ oz.) junior
    baby food apricots -
    applesauce

Combine eggs, sugar, and oil; blend well. Sift together flour, salt, baking soda, and cinnamon; add sifted ingredients to egg mixture. Blend in baby food. Pour into an ungreased 9 × 13-inch pan. Bake at 350° for 30 minutes. Cool. Frost with cream cheese frosting.

(continued)

APPLESAUCE CAKE (continued)

CREAM CHEESE FROSTING:
½ cup butter, melted
1 tsp. vanilla
1 pkg. (8 oz.) cream cheese, softened
1 lb. powdered sugar, sifted

Combine melted butter with vanilla and cream cheese. Beat in powdered sugar until smooth.

Preparation time: 20 minutes
Baking time: 30 minutes

Easy
Can make ahead
Should be refrigerated

Serves: 12–15

Ann Kneas

CHOCOLATE FUDGE CAKE

CAKE:
½ cup butter or margarine, softened
1 cup sugar
4 eggs
1 cup flour
½ tsp. salt
1 tsp. baking powder
1 can (16 oz.) chocolate syrup (Hershey's preferred)
1 tsp. vanilla

Cream butter and sugar. Add eggs, 1 at a time; beat well after each addition. Sift together flour, salt, and baking powder; mix in alternately with chocolate syrup, beginning and ending with flour mixture. Stir in vanilla. Pour into greased and floured 9 × 13-inch pan. Bake at 350° for 35 minutes. Cool 10 minutes and frost.

FROSTING:
½ cup margarine
1 can (5.33 oz.) evaporated milk
2 cups sugar
1 pkg. (6 oz.) semisweet chocolate chips
½ cup nuts, chopped

In a saucepan, bring to a boil margarine, milk, and sugar. Boil for 2 minutes; remove from heat. Stir in chocolate chips and beat until smooth. Add nuts. Pour over warm cake—spread quickly.

Preparation time: 20 minutes
Baking time: 35 minutes

Easy
Can make ahead

Serves: 12–15

Jan Cornell

GÂTEAU CHOCOLAT
Typically French; typically gourmet

CRÈME FRAÎCHE:

1 cup whipping cream
2½ tsps. buttermilk

Combine whipping cream and buttermilk in a jar. Shake at least 1 minute; allow cream to stand at room temperature for at least 8 hours (may be stored in refrigerator 4 to 6 weeks).

4 eggs
¾ cup sugar
1 cup flour, sifted
4 ozs. semisweet chocolate, grated
⅔ cup Crème Fraîche

Beat together eggs and sugar for 5 minutes, or until mixture is thick and light in color. Fold in flour, chocolate, and Crème Fraîche (batter will have a speckled appearance). Pour batter into a well-buttered and floured 9-inch round cake pan. Bake at 325° for 40 minutes, or until set. Cool completely on a rack. Remove from pan and place on a serving dish; spread icing on top. Serve in very small pieces.

ICING:

4 ozs. semisweet chocolate, broken up
2½ T. butter, melted
2 T. strong coffee
½ tsp. vegetable oil

In top of double boiler, over hot water, melt chocolate and butter with coffee. Remove from heat and beat in vegetable oil (frosting should have a shiny appearance).

Preparation time: 45 minutes
Baking time: 40 minutes

Can make ahead

Serves: 12–14

Betty Maxwell

WHISKEY (OR BOURBON) SAUCE

½ cup butter, softened
1¾ cups powdered sugar, sifted
¼ cup plus 1 T. blended whiskey or bourbon

Blend together butter and powdered sugar. Add whiskey; blend well. Serve with bread pudding.

Preparation time: 5 minutes

Easy
Can make ahead

Yield: 2 cups

Susan Bowers

CASSATA
An easy, yet festive, dessert

9 × 5-inch pound cake

Day before serving: Chill pound cake 1 hour. Slice cake horizontally in 6 slices (approximately ½ inch thick). Place bottom slice on serving plate.

FILLING:
2 cups ricotta cheese
4 ozs. semisweet chocolate, finely chopped or grated
1 oz. orange liqueur
1½ cups raspberry jam

Force ricotta through a sieve. Beat until smooth. Set aside. Mix chocolate with liqueur and jam. Spread ⅕ of ricotta over bottom layer of cake, spread ⅕ of chocolate mixture over ricotta. Repeat layers of cake, ricotta, and chocolate mixture, ending with cake. Press the filled cake gently; use a spatula to even up sides. Cover with plastic wrap and refrigerate 24 hours.

FROSTING:
2 cups chocolate frosting or whipped cream, sweetened
Whole unblanched almonds, toasted (for garnish)

Frost cake with chocolate frosting or whipped cream before serving. Garnish with almonds.

Preparation time: 30 minutes   Must make day ahead   Serves: 8–10

Barb Long

MIAMI BEACH BIRTHDAY CAKE

½ cup graham cracker
  crumbs
⅓ cup butter, melted
½ cup walnuts, chopped
⅔ cup semisweet chocolate
  chips
½ cup butter, softened
1½ cups sugar
2 eggs
⅓ cup semisweet chocolate
  chips, melted, cooled
1 tsp. vanilla
2 cups flour, sifted
1 tsp. baking soda
1 tsp. salt
1¼ cups buttermilk
1 cup whipping cream,
  whipped, sweetened

Combine graham cracker crumbs and melted butter; cool. Stir in nuts and ⅔ cup chocolate chips; set aside. Cream together ½ cup butter and sugar. Add eggs; beat well. Blend in melted chocolate chips and vanilla. Sift together flour, baking soda, and salt. Add sifted ingredients alternately with buttermilk to creamed mixture. Spread in 2 greased and floured 9-inch round pans. Sprinkle top with graham cracker crumb-chocolate chip mixture. Bake at 375° for 30 to 40 minutes. Cool 10 minutes and remove from pan. Continue cooling on racks. Frost cake with whipped cream. Refrigerate.

Preparation time: 45 minutes
Baking time: 30–40 minutes

Can make ahead
Best served the first day

Serves: 10–12

Ginny Costenbader

MERINGUE CREAM TORTE

MERINGUE:
4 egg whites
¼ tsp. cream of tartar
Pinch of salt
1 cup sugar

Beat egg whites with cream of tartar and salt until frothy. Gradually add sugar; beat to stiff peaks. Arrange three 8-inch circles cut from waxed paper on baking sheets. Spread meringue ¼ inch thick within each circle. Bake at 250° for 50 minutes, or until lightly browned. Remove from oven. Cool. Carefully remove waxed paper.

1½ tsps. unflavored gelatin
3 T. kirsch or orange-
  flavored liqueur
2 cups whipping cream
⅓ cup sugar

Dissolve gelatin in liqueur. Beat whipping cream; gradually add sugar and then gelatin. Chill.

(continued)

MERINGUE TORTE (CONTINUED)

1 pkg. (6 oz.) semisweet chocolate chips
3 T. water
2 T. butter

Melt chocolate with water and butter. Cool slightly.

1 pt. strawberries, hulled, sliced

Assembly: Place a meringue round on serving plate. Spread with a thin layer of chocolate; cover with ½-inch layer of whipped cream. Arrange half of strawberries on top. Repeat layers once more. Top with remaining meringue. Garnish with a chocolate-drizzled design and strawberries. Sides of torte may be frosted with whipped cream. Chill 6 hours.

Preparation time: 1½ hours
Baking time: 50 minutes

Must make ahead
Must be refrigerated

Serves: 10

Judy Brown

APRICOT BRANDY POUND CAKE

1 cup butter or margarine, softened
3 cups sugar
6 eggs
¼ tsp. almond extract (optional)
1 tsp. orange extract
½ tsp. lemon extract
1 tsp. vanilla
1 cup sour cream
½ cup apricot brandy
3 cups flour
½ tsp. baking soda
½ tsp. salt

Cream together butter and sugar until light and fluffy. Add eggs, 1 at a time; beat well after each addition. Stir in extracts. Mix together sour cream and brandy. Set aside. Sift together flour, baking soda, and salt. Add dry ingredients alternately with sour cream and brandy to creamed mixture, beginning and ending with the dry ingredients. Pour into a greased and floured 10-inch tube pan. Bake at 325° for 75 to 85 minutes. Cool in pan on rack; remove from pan and store. Best after 24 hours. Serve with fresh fruit or plain.

Preparation time: 20 minutes
Baking time: 75–85 minutes

Can make ahead

Serves: 12–14

Mary Jo Garling

APRICOT BARS

1 cup dried apricots,
  chopped
¾ cup water
1 cup flour
6 T. margarine, softened
1½ cups brown sugar,
  packed (divided)
1 T. cornstarch
¼ tsp. salt
2 tsp. orange rind, grated
2 T. orange juice,
2 eggs, beaten
1½ cups flaked coconut
  (divided)

Combine apricots and water in a sauce-pan. Bring to a boil. Cover and simmer for 20 minutes. Mix flour, margarine, and ½ cup brown sugar; press mixture into greased 7 ½ × 11¾-inch pan. Bake at 350° for 20 minutes.

Mix 1 cup brown sugar, cornstarch, and salt; add to undrained apricots and cook until thickened, stirring constantly. Remove from heat; stir in orange rind, orange juice, eggs, and 1¼ cups coco-nut. Spread apricot mixture over baked crust. Sprinkle top with remaining coco-nut. Bake at 350° for 25 minutes. Cool. Cut into bars.

Preparation time: 30 minutes
Baking time: 45 minutes

Should be refrigerated

Joann Data

MELTING MOMENTS
So good they melt in your mouth

⅔ cup cornstarch
1 cup flour
⅓ cup powdered sugar
1 cup butter, softened

Combine cornstarch and flour. Cream together powdered sugar and butter until light and fluffy. Gradually add flour mixture to butter mixture. Drop by tea-spoonfuls onto ungreased baking sheet. Bake at 325° for 15 to 18 minutes. Cool. (Cookies are very fragile while hot.)

FROSTING:
¾ cup butter or margarine,
  softened
3 T. fresh lemon juice
Approximately 3 cups
  powdered sugar, sifted

Cream together butter and lemon juice. Gradually add powdered sugar, beating until smooth. Frost cooled cookies.

Preparation time: 30 minutes
Baking time: 15–18 minutes

Yield: 4–5 dozen
Can be frozen

Marge Burns
Jean Rainsford

WALNUT PATTIES

½ cup shortening
1 cup light brown sugar,
    packed
1 egg, slightly beaten
1 tsp. vanilla
1½ cups flour, sifted
½ tsp. baking soda
½ tsp. salt
1 cup walnuts, chopped

Cream together shortening and brown sugar until fluffy. Beat in egg and vanilla. Sift together flour, baking soda, and salt and add to shortening-egg mixture. Fold in walnuts. Drop on greased baking sheet by rounded teaspoonfuls. Bake at 375° for 12 to 15 minutes. Cool.

FROSTING:
½ cup light brown sugar,
    packed
4 T. butter
4 T. half-and-half
¾ to 1 cup powdered sugar,
    sifted

In a saucepan, cook brown sugar and butter over low heat until melted and bubbling. Remove from heat and slowly add cream, beating until smooth. Add powdered sugar gradually, mixing until frosting is barely thick enough to spread.

Preparation time: 45 minutes
Baking time: 12–15 minutes

Yield: 4 dozen
Can be frozen

Betty Maxwell

MAUREEN'S REFRIGERATOR COOKIES
Slice and bake when the children get home

1 cup butter, softened
1 cup powdered sugar
2 tsps. vanilla
1½ cups flour
1 cup quick-cooking oats
Chocolate shot (sprinkles)

Beat together butter, powdered sugar, and vanilla until fluffy. Add flour, mixing well. Stir in oats. Wrap in waxed paper to shape into logs approximately 1 to 1½ inches in diameter. Roll in chocolate shot. Chill overnight. Slice and bake at 325° for 15 minutes on ungreased baking sheet.

Preparation time: 10 minutes
Baking time: 15 minutes

Easy

Yield: 5–6 dozen
Can be frozen before
    or after baking

Dorrie Kelly

ALMOND RASPBERRY BARS
A testing favorite

¾ cup butter or margarine,
  softened
¾ cup powdered sugar
1½ cups flour
¾ cup raspberry jam
3 egg whites
¾ cup sugar
½ cup shredded coconut
1 cup blanched almonds,
  slivered

Cream butter and sugar. Add flour, mixing well, and press into a greased 9 × 13-inch pan. Bake at 350° for 12 to 15 minutes, or until lightly browned. Spread jam over hot layer. Beat egg whites until foamy. Gradually add sugar, beating until stiff. Fold in coconut. Spread over jam. Sprinkle with almonds, and bake for 20 minutes. Cool and cut into squares.

Preparation time: 30 minutes
Baking time: 32–35 minutes

Can be made ahead
but not frozen

Louise Godfrey

YUMMY CARAMEL CRUNCH

32 caramel candies or 1 cup
  caramel syrup
⅓ cup evaporated milk or
  half-and-half
½ cup flour
½ tsp. baking soda
¼ tsp. salt
⅓–½ cup dark brown sugar,
  packed
½ cup old-fashioned oats,
  uncooked
4 T. butter or margarine,
  softened
1 pkg. (6 oz.) semisweet
  chocolate chips
½ cup pecans, chopped

In the top of a double boiler, combine caramels and milk. Heat over simmering water until melted, stirring occasionally. Remove from heat and set aside. Sift together flour, baking soda, and salt. Stir in brown sugar and oats. Cut in butter with a pastry blender until mixture looks like coarse crumbs. Press half of mixture evenly into greased 7 ½ × 11¾-inch pan. Sprinkle chocolate chips and nuts on top. Pour caramel mixture over chocolate chips and nuts. Sprinkle with remaining crumbs. Bake at 350° for 20 minutes, or until lightly browned. Cool. Refrigerate until set. Cut into squares.

Preparation time: 45 minutes
Baking time: 20 minutes

Must make ahead

SUNFLOWER SEED COOKIES
As tasty as they are healthful

1 cup butter, softened
1¼ cups brown sugar, packed
2 eggs, slightly beaten
2 tsps. vanilla
1⅓ cups unbleached flour
1 tsp. salt
1 tsp. baking soda
3 cups old-fashioned oats, uncooked
¾ cup sunflower seed kernels
½ cup wheat germ

Cream together butter and sugar. Beat in eggs and vanilla. Sift together flour, salt, and baking soda; add to creamed mixture. Fold in oats, sunflower seed kernels, and wheat germ. Drop by teaspoonfuls onto ungreased baking sheet. Bake at 375° for 10 to 12 minutes. Cool. Store in tightly covered container.

Preparation time: 25 minutes
Baking time: 10–12 minutes

Easy

Yield: 4½ dozen

Brenda Murphy

CREAMY FUDGE

1 pt. marshmallow creme
1 pkg. (12 oz.) semisweet chocolate chips
3 bars (4 oz. each) German sweet chocolate, broken up
1 can (13 oz.) evaporated milk
2 T. butter
4½ cups sugar
Dash of salt
2 cups pecans, chopped

Place marshmallow creme and chocolate in a large bowl. Set aside. In a heavy saucepan, combine milk, butter, sugar, and salt. Bring to a vigorous boil; stir often. Reduce heat and simmer 6 minutes. Remove from heat and gradually pour syrup over chocolate-marshmallow mixture; beat until chocolate is melted. Stir in nuts. Pour into 2 buttered 9 × 13-inch pans. Cool. Cut into squares.

Preparation time: 20 minutes

Easy
Can make ahead
Should be refrigerated

Joan deMink

267

BOHEMIAN COOKIES

½ cup shortening
½ cup butter, softened
1¼ cups powdered sugar
1¼ cups flour
1½ tsps. vanilla
¼ tsp. salt
6 ozs. semisweet chocolate
  chips, ground
1 cup walnuts, ground

Cream together shortening, butter, and powdered sugar. Add flour, vanilla, and salt. Stir in ground chocolate chips and walnuts. Shape into small balls and place on greased baking sheet. Flatten balls with the bottom of a glass. Bake at 250° for 40 minutes. Cool. May frost with chocolate frosting if desired.

Preparation time: 20 minutes
Baking time: 40 minutes

Easy

Yield: 3 dozen

Marianne Struckmeyer

SPICED NUTS
Great Christmas gift for that special teacher

2 cups walnut or pecan
  halves
1 cup sugar
5 T. water
½ tsp. cinnamon
¼ tsp. salt
1¼ tsps. vanilla

Toast nuts at 350° for 8 minutes. In a saucepan, mix together sugar, water, cinnamon, salt, and vanilla. Heat about 5 or 6 minutes, stirring constantly, to soft ball stage (240°). Remove from heat; stir in nuts and place on waxed paper to cool. Store in tightly covered container.

Preparation time: 10 minutes

Easy
Can make ahead

Yield: 2 cups

Patricia Ellwood

BANANA-NUT BROWNIES
Super lunch box treat

⅓ cup margarine
1 pkg. (6 oz.) semisweet
  chocolate chips
2 eggs
¾ cup sugar
1 tsp. vanilla
½ cup bananas, mashed
  (about 1 large)

Melt together margarine and chocolate chips. Cool slightly. Beat eggs until thick and lemon colored. Gradually add sugar, then vanilla. Add melted chocolate to egg mixture, and beat until blended. Stir in bananas. Sift together flour, baking powder, and salt; add to batter, mixing well. Stir in nuts. Spread into greased 9-inch

(continued)

BANANA-NUT BROWNIES (continued)

1 cup flour, sifted
½ tsp. baking powder
½ tsp. salt
½ cup pecans or walnuts,
   chopped

square pan. Bake at 350° for 25 to 30 minutes, or until top springs back when lightly touched. Cool.

Preparation time: 20 minutes
Baking time: 25–30 minutes

Can be frozen

Ann Paulson

FRESH SPICE BARS

1 cup apples, unpeeled,
   chopped
1 cup dates, chopped
1 cup sugar
½ cup butter
1¾ cups flour
1 tsp. baking soda
1 tsp. cinnamon
½ tsp. ground cloves
¼ tsp. salt

In a saucepan, combine apples, dates, sugar, and butter. Bring to a boil over medium heat. Reduce heat and simmer for 5 minutes, stirring occasionally. Cool. Sift together flour, baking soda, cinnamon, cloves, and salt. Add to cooled mixture, blending well. Spread into a greased and floured 7 ½ × 11¾-inch pan. Bake at 350° for 25 to 30 minutes. When cool, frost with either Cream Cheese Frosting (see page 273) or a powdered sugar frosting.

Preparation time: 20 minutes
Baking time: 25–30 minutes

Should be refrigerated

Emma Born

PEANUT CLUSTERS
An easy, yet professional-looking, candy

1 pkg. (12 oz.) semisweet
   chocolate chips
1 pkg. (12 oz.) butterscotch-
   flavored chips
1 cup peanut butter
1 lb. salted Spanish peanuts

In top of double boiler, melt together chips and peanut butter over hot water. Remove from heat; stir in nuts. Drop by tablespoonfuls onto waxed paper. Refrigerate.

Variation: Chinese noodles or raisins may be substituted for peanuts.

Preparation time:
   15–20 minutes

Easy
Should be refrigerated

Yield: 7 dozen
Can be frozen

Mary Louise Avery

OATMEAL-CHOCOLATE CHIP CRISPS

1 cup margarine
1 cup brown sugar, packed
1 cup sugar
1 egg
1 tsp. vanilla
1 cup vegetable oil
3½ cups flour
1 tsp. baking soda
1 tsp. salt
1 cup Rice Krispies
1 cup quick-cooking oats
12 ozs. semisweet
  chocolate chips

Cream together margarine and sugars. Add egg, vanilla, and oil. Sift together flour, baking soda, and salt. Add sifted ingredients to sugar mixture, blending well. Stir in Rice Krispies, oats, and chocolate chips. Drop by rounded teaspoonfuls onto greased baking sheet. Bake at 375° for 10 to 12 minutes. Cool. Store in tightly covered container.

Preparation time: 20 minutes
Baking time: 10–12 minutes

Easy

Yield: 4–6 dozen
Can be frozen

Judy Brown

MINCEMEAT BARS
Perfect for a holiday open house

1 T. butter, softened
1½ cups brown sugar,
  packed
2 eggs
2 T. molasses
1 tsp. vanilla
2 cups flour, sifted
½ tsp. salt
½ tsp. baking soda
1 tsp. cinnamon
1 tsp. ground cloves
3 T. hot water
¼ cup almonds, chopped
¼ cup seedless raisins
9 ozs. mincemeat
  (packaged), broken up

Mix together butter, brown sugar, eggs, molasses, and vanilla. Sift together flour, salt, baking soda, cinnamon, and cloves. Add sifted ingredients to creamed mixture. Stir in water, almonds, raisins, and mincemeat, mixing well. Spread into greased 9 × 13-inch or 10 ½ × 15 ½-inch pan. Bake at 400° for 12 to 15 minutes. (May require longer baking time in 9 × 13-inch pan.) Cool.

(continued)

MINCEMEAT BARS (continued)

GLAZE:

1½ cups powdered sugar, sifted
3 T. hot milk
½ tsp. vanilla
½ tsp. almond extract

Mix together powdered sugar, milk, vanilla, and almond extract; beat until smooth. Spread frosting on cooled bars.

Preparation time: 30 minutes
Baking time: 12–15 minutes

Ruth Kasdorf

PEANUT BUTTER BARS
Not for kids only

1 cup crunchy peanut butter
⅔ cup butter or margarine, softened
1 tsp. vanilla
2 cups brown sugar, packed
3 eggs
1 cup flour, sifted
½ tsp. salt

Cream together peanut butter, butter, and vanilla. Beat in sugar, then add eggs one at a time. Blend in flour and salt. Spread in greased 9 × 13-inch or 10 × 14-inch pan. Bake at 350° for 30 to 35 minutes. Cool.

FROSTING:

4 T. butter, melted
2 cups powdered sugar, sifted
2–3 T. half-and-half
¼ tsp. salt
1 tsp. vanilla

Stir melted butter into powdered sugar alternately with the cream. Beat until smooth. Add salt and vanilla. Frost cooled bars. Allow to set.

GLAZE:

1 oz. unsweetened chocolate
1 T. butter
½ tsp. vanilla

Melt chocolate and butter together. Remove from heat and add vanilla. Drizzle over frosting.

Preparation time: 30 minutes
Baking time: 30–35 minutes

Marion Ludlow

ALMOND BUTTER TOFFEE

1 cup roasted unblanched
  almonds, chopped
1 cup butter or margarine
1 cup sugar
⅓ cup brown sugar, packed
2 T. water
½ tsp. baking soda
3 ozs. semisweet chocolate,
  grated or shaved

Sprinkle half of the almonds in the bottom of a buttered 9 × 13-inch pan. In a heavy saucepan, melt butter; add sugars and mix well. Bring to a boil, stirring constantly, and continue cooking to hard crack stage (300°) or until candy becomes brittle when dropped in cold water. Remove from heat. Stir in baking soda which has been dissolved in 2 tablespoonfuls water. Pour mixture carefully over almonds in pan. Sprinkle chocolate over hot toffee and allow to stand 1 or 2 minutes, or until melted; spread melted chocolate evenly. Sprinkle remaining almonds over chocolate and press lightly. Cool completely. Break into pieces.

Microwave: Microwave butter and sugars on high in a 3-quart glass container for 9 to 11 minutes, stirring every 3 to 4 minutes, or until candy reaches the hard crack stage (300°). To complete, follow above directions.

Preparation time:
  30–45 minutes

Must make ahead

Yield: 1½ lbs.

Jan Cornell

HARVEST SQUARES

½ cup butter or margarine,
  softened
1 cup sugar
2 eggs
¾ cup canned unseasoned
  pumpkin
1¾ cups flour
1 tsp. baking soda
1 tsp. cinnamon
½ tsp. nutmeg
¼ tsp. ground ginger
¼ tsp. ground cloves
½ tsp. salt
1 cup semisweet chocolate
  chips or raisins

Cream together butter and sugar. Add eggs and pumpkin, mixing well. Sift together flour, baking soda, spices, and salt. Add to pumpkin mixture. Stir in chocolate chips. Pour into greased and floured 9 × 13-inch pan. Bake at 350° for 20 to 25 minutes, or until toothpick comes out clean. Cool and frost with cream cheese frosting. Cut into squares.

(continued)

HARVEST SQUARES (continued)

CREAM CHEESE FROSTING:

**4 ozs. cream cheese,
  softened**
¼ cup margarine, softened
**2 cups powdered sugar,
  sifted**
1 tsp. vanilla

Cream together cream cheese and margarine. Gradually add powdered sugar, beating until smooth. Stir in vanilla.

Preparation time: 20 minutes
Baking time: 20–25 minutes

Easy
Should be refrigerated

Can be frozen

Mary Maynard

ORANGE-NUT BARS

CRUST:
1 cup flour
½ cup butter, melted
2 T. sugar
Dash of salt

Combine flour, butter, sugar, and salt. Pat into a 9-inch square pan. Bake at 350° for 10 minutes.

FILLING:
1 cup brown sugar, packed
2 T. flour
1 tsp. baking powder
2 eggs
1 tsp. vanilla
**½ cup pecans or walnuts,
  chopped**

Combine brown sugar, flour, baking powder, eggs, vanilla, and nuts. Spread over crust. Bake for 25 minutes more at 350°. Cool.

FROSTING:
½ cup butter, melted
2 T. orange juice
1 tsp. orange rind, grated
**2 eggs yolks, slightly
  beaten**
**2–2¼ cups powdered sugar,
  sifted**

Combine butter, orange juice, rind, and egg yolks. Add powdered sugar, beating well. Spread on cooled bars.

Preparation time: 30 minutes
Baking time: 35 minutes

Should be
refrigerated

Can be frozen
before frosting

Ruth Herendeen

TURTLES

1 lb. light brown sugar
1 can (14 oz.) sweetened
  condensed milk
½ cup light corn syrup
1 cup margarine
4 cups pecan halves
12–18 ozs. milk chocolate
  chips
½ bar paraffin

In a heavy saucepan, mix together sugar, milk, corn syrup, and margarine. Bring to a boil and cook to the soft ball stage (230°), stirring often. Remove from heat and stir in pecan halves. Drop by teaspoonfuls onto a buttered baking sheet; allow to stand until firm. Melt together chocolate and paraffin. Dip candy into chocolate and place on waxed paper; chill until firm.

Microwave: Combine brown sugar, milk, corn syrup, and margarine in a glass container. Microwave on high for 8 to 10 minutes, or to the soft ball stage (230°), stirring every 4 minutes. Continue with the above directions.

Preparation time: 60 minutes   Must make ahead   Yield: 6–7 dozen
                                 Should be refrigerated

Patricia Ellwood

PEANUT BUTTER FUDGE

1 cup margarine
1 cup peanut butter
1 tsp. vanilla (optional)
1 lb. (3½ cups) powdered
  sugar, sifted
8 oz. chocolate bar
  (Hershey's preferred)
  (optional)

Place margarine, peanut butter, and vanilla in saucepan and heat until melted. Remove from heat. Add powdered sugar; blend well. Spread into a 9-inch square pan; refrigerate until firm. Melt chocolate and spread evenly over peanut butter layer. Chill. Cut into squares.

Preparation time: 10 minutes   Easy
                                 Should be refrigerated   Can be frozen

Linda Brown
Nancy Jacobs

ADELAIDES

1 cup shortening
1 cup sugar
1 cup light brown sugar, packed
2 eggs, slightly beaten
3 cups flour
1½ tsps. baking soda
1 tsp. salt
2 tsps. vanilla
1 cup dates, chopped
1 cup walnuts, chopped
Sugar

Cream together shortening and sugars. Beat in eggs. Sift together flour, baking soda, and salt. Add sifted ingredients to sugar mixture, blending well. Add vanilla. Stir in dates and walnuts. Form into balls. Place on greased baking sheet about 3 inches apart. Flatten each ball with the bottom of a glass. Bake at 375° for 12 to 15 minutes. Remove from oven; sprinkle with sugar while hot.

Preparation time: 25 minutes
Baking time: 12–15 minutes

Yield: 7 dozen
Can be frozen

Betty Maxwell

MARTHA WASHINGTON CANDY
Tastes like miniature Mounds candy bars

1 can (14 oz.) sweetened condensed milk
2 cans (3½ oz. each) angel flake coconut
5 cups powdered sugar, sifted
½ cup margarine, melted
1 tsp. vanilla
2 cups pecans, chopped
½ bar paraffin
12–18 ozs. semisweet chocolate chips

Combine milk, coconut, sugar, margarine, and vanilla; blend well. Stir in nuts. Cover and chill for several hours. Roll candy into small balls and chill. Melt together paraffin and chocolate. Dip balls in chocolate and place on waxed paper. Refrigerate until firm.

Preparation time: 60 minutes

Should be refrigerated

Yield: 6–8 dozen

Nancy Jacobs

ALMOND MACAROONS
Delightfully easy and delicious

½ lb. almond paste
2 egg whites, unbeaten
1 cup sugar

Have almond paste and egg whites at room temperature. Mix almond paste, egg whites, and sugar together with a pastry blender or slotted spoon until lumps are removed. Drop by rounded teaspoonfuls 1½ inches apart onto baking sheets lined with foil. Bake at 325° for 25 minutes. Cool; peel foil from cookies. Stores cookies in plastic bag; store in airtight container. Best the first 2 days.

Preparation time: 10 minutes   Easy   Yield: 2½ dozen
Baking time: 25 minutes

Leola Stocker

Hint: Egg whites should be brought to room temperature before beating to increase the volume. If they're still cold, place them in a bowl and set the bowl in warm water for a few minutes.

CHOCOLATE MINT STICKS
Beware! These are irresistible!

CRUST:
½ cup butter
2 ozs. unsweetened
  chocolate
2 eggs
1 cup sugar
½ tsp. peppermint extract
½ cup flour
½ cup blanched almonds,
  chopped (optional)

Melt butter and chocolate together and cool. Beat eggs and sugar until frothy. Add chocolate mixture, blending well. Stir in peppermint extract, flour, and almonds. Spread into greased 9-inch square pan. Bake at 350° for 25 to 30 minutes. Cool.

FILLING:
3 T. butter, softened
1½ cups powdered sugar,
  sifted
1–2 T. milk or half-and-half
½ tsp. peppermint extract
3–4 drops green food
  coloring

Cream butter and powdered sugar. Add milk and peppermint extract, beating to a smooth frosting consistency. Add food coloring. Spread over cooled chocolate crust. Allow to set.

(continued)

MINT STICKS (continued)

GLAZE:
2 ozs. semisweet chocolate
2 T. butter

Melt chocolate with butter. Cool slightly, and spread or drizzle over top of filling. Refrigerate until set. Cut into bars.

Preparation time: 45 minutes
Baking time: 25–30 minutes

Should be refrigerated

Easily doubled using 9 × 13-inch pan

Jean Stringfellow
Jane Todd

PINEAPPLE CAKE

2 cups sugar
2 cups flour
2 tsps. baking soda
2 eggs, slightly beaten
1 can (20 oz.) crushed pineapple, undrained
½ cup pecans or walnuts, chopped

Mix together sugar, flour, and baking soda. Add eggs and pineapple; stir in nuts. Pour into greased and floured 9 × 13-inch pan. Bake at 325° for 40 minutes. Frost with cream cheese frosting while cake is warm.

FROSTING:
1 pkg. (8 oz.) cream cheese, softened
½ cup butter or margarine, softened
1½ cups powdered sugar, sifted
1 tsp. vanilla
½ cup walnuts or pecans, chopped

Cream together cream cheese and margarine. Gradually add powdered sugar; beat until smooth. Stir in vanilla and nuts.

Preparation time: 20 minutes
Baking time: 40 minutes

Easy
Should be refrigerated

Serves: 12–15

Ann Block

KNOBBY APPLE CAKE

¼ cup butter or margarine,
  softened
1 cup sugar
1 egg
1 cup flour
1 tsp. baking soda
½ tsp. cinnamon
¼ tsp. nutmeg
¼ tsp. salt
3 cups apples, pared,
  chopped
½ cup walnuts or pecans,
  chopped
½ cup raisins

Cream together butter and sugar; add egg. Sift together flour, baking soda, cinnamon, nutmeg, and salt. Mix sifted ingredients into creamed mixture. Fold in apples, nuts, and raisins. Spread in a 9-inch square pan. Bake at 350° for 40 minutes. Cool. Frost with ½ recipe Cream Cheese Frosting (see page 259), to which ¾ cup chopped nuts has been added.

Preparation time: 30 minutes
Baking time: 40 minutes

Easy

Serves: 8–10

Sally Smyrnios

ORANGE CAKE

Juice of 2 oranges
1¾ cups sugar (divided)
½ cup butter, softened
⅔ cup buttermilk
2 eggs, beaten
2 cups flour
1 tsp. baking powder
Pulp and rind of 1 orange
1 cup raisins, ground
Whipping cream, whipped,
  sweetened (for garnish)
Nuts (for garnish)
Orange slices (for garnish)

Squeeze oranges; reserve pulp and rind of 1 orange. Mix together orange juice and ¾ cup sugar. Set aside. Cream together butter and 1 cup sugar until fluffy. Add buttermilk and eggs. Sift together flour and baking powder; add to creamed mixture. Stir in pulp and rind of 1 orange and raisins. Spread into a greased 10-inch tube pan. Bake at 350° for 45 minutes, or until firm to touch. Remove from oven and pour orange juice-sugar mixture over the top. Cool. Remove from pan. Garnish with whipped cream, nuts, and orange slices.

Preparation time: 20 minutes
Baking time: 45 minutes

Can make ahead

Serves: 12–15

Norma Stancati

PUMPKIN COOKIES

1 cup shortening
1 cup sugar
1 cup canned unseasoned
  pumpkin
1 egg
2 cups flour
1 tsp. baking soda
1 tsp. cinnamon
½ tsp. salt
1 cup raisins

Cream together shortening, sugar, and pumpkin. Add egg and mix well. Sift together flour, baking soda, cinnamon, and salt. Add sifted ingredients to pumpkin mixture. Stir in raisins. Drop by rounded teaspoonfuls onto greased baking sheet. Bake at 375° for 10 to 12 minutes.

FROSTING:
3 T. butter
2 T. milk
½ cup brown sugar, packed
1 cup powdered sugar,
  sifted
¾ tsp. vanilla

In a saucepan, cook butter, milk, and brown sugar until dissolved. Cool. Add powdered sugar and vanilla and beat until smooth. Spread on warm cookies.

Preparation time: 45 minutes
Baking time: 10–12 minutes

Yield: 4–5 dozen
Can be frozen

Betsy McOmber

EASY TOFFEE

1 cup walnuts, chopped
¾ cup brown sugar, packed
½ cup butter
¼ cup semisweet chocolate
  chips

Butter the bottom and sides of an 8-inch square pan. Sprinkle nuts evenly over the bottom. In a heavy saucepan, combine brown sugar and butter; cook over medium heat to the soft crack stage (260°), stirring constantly. Remove from heat and spread over nuts. Sprinkle chocolate chips over top and allow to stand 1 or 2 minutes, or until melted. Spread melted chips evenly over toffee. Cool. Break into pieces.

Preparation time: 15 minutes

Easy
Can make ahead

Bernadine Simpson

GLORIOUS STRAWBERRY PIE

3 egg whites
¼ tsp. cream of tartar
Dash of salt
1 cup sugar
1 tsp. vanilla
10 (2-inch square) soda
  crackers, finely crushed
½ cup pecans, chopped
1 qt. fresh strawberries,
  sliced, sweetened to taste
1 cup whipping cream,
  whipped, sweetened

Beat egg whites until foamy. Add cream of tartar and salt and continue beating until stiff. Gradually add sugar, then vanilla. Fold in crackers and nuts. Spread meringue into a *well-greased* 10-inch pie plate. Scoop out the center of meringue slightly. Bake at 275° for 60 minutes. Turn off heat and allow meringue to remain in oven with the door closed for 1 hour. Remove from oven and cool completely. Fill crust with strawberries and top with whipped cream. Garnish with additional strawberries.

Preparation time: 25 minutes
Baking time: 60 minutes

Must be refrigerated

Serves: 8

Barbara Campbell

SWEDISH CHOCOLATE-ALMOND TORTE
Outstanding! A five-star rating!

½ cup almond paste
3 eggs, separated
½ cup butter or margarine,
  softened
¼ cup sugar
1 pkg. (6 oz.) semisweet
  chocolate chips, melted,
  cooled
⅓ cup flour
1 tsp. baking powder
1 can (8¾ oz.) apricot
  halves, sliced
1 cup whipping cream,
  whipped
1 T. powdered sugar

Cream together almond paste and egg yolks. Add butter and sugar; beat until light. Stir in chocolate. Sift together flour and baking powder; add to almond mixture until well blended. Beat egg whites until stiff and fold into above. Spread into 2 greased 9-inch round cake pans. Bake at 350° for 15 minutes. Cool 5 minutes. Remove from pan and continue cooling on racks.

Drain apricots; reserve ¼ cup syrup. Add syrup and sugar to whipped cream. Spread between layers and on top. Garnish with apricot slices. Chill

Preparation time: 45 minutes
Baking time: 15 minutes

Must make ahead
Must be refrigerated

Serves: 8–10

Suzanne Sellers

280

ORANGE-COCONUT LAYER CAKE

8 eggs, separated
1⅔ cups sugar
3 T. lemon juice (divided)
1 cup flour
⅓ cup cornstarch
½ tsp. salt

Beat egg yolks until thick and lemon colored. Gradually add sugar; blend well. Stir in 2 tablespoonfuls lemon juice. Mix together flour, cornstarch, and salt; add to egg mixture. Add 1 tablespoonful lemon juice and beat slowly until smooth. Beat egg whites until stiff, but not dry. Fold in egg whites; blend. Spread in 2 greased 15 × 10 × 1-inch jelly roll pans lined with waxed paper. Bake at 375° for 15 minutes, or until lightly browned. Remove from oven and immediately invert cakes onto waxed paper. Carefully peel paper from bottom. Cool.

FILLING:
½ cup cake flour, sifted
1 cup sugar
¼ tsp. salt
¼ cup water
1¼ cups orange juice
¼ cup lemon juice
Rind of 1 lemon, grated
Rind of 1 orange, grated
4 egg yolks, slightly beaten

In a heavy saucepan, mix flour, sugar, and salt. Add water; mix until smooth. Add juices and rinds. Cook over low heat, stirring constantly, until mixture thickens and becomes translucent. Add small amount of hot mixture to egg yolks and stir. Return eggs to remaining hot mixture and cook slowly a few minutes longer. Cool.

FROSTING:
1 cup sugar
¼ tsp. cream of tartar
⅛ tsp. salt
⅓ cup hot water
3 egg whites, stiffly beaten

In a saucepan, combine sugar, cream of tartar, salt, and water. Cook over medium heat, without stirring, until mixture reaches the soft ball stage (240°). Meanwhile, beat egg whites until stiff, but not dry. Add hot syrup to egg whites (pour in a continuous stream); beat constantly until frosting holds shape.

Grated rind of 1 orange
3½ ozs. shredded coconut

Mix rind and coconut together.

Assembly: Slice each cake into thirds. Stack cake layers on serving plate, using 1/5 of filling between each layer. Frost entire cake with frosting. Sprinkle with coconut.

Preparation time: 1½–2 hours
Baking time: 15 minutes

Serves: 12–14
Best served the first day

Kay Davison

LEMON CHESS PIE
An old Southern favorite

2 cups sugar
1 T. flour
1 T. cornmeal
¼ tsp. salt
¼ cup butter, melted
¼ cup lemon juice, freshly
  squeezed
2 tsp. lemon rind, grated
4 eggs, slightly beaten
¼ cup milk
9-inch pie shell, unbaked

Mix together sugar, flour, cornmeal, and salt. Stir in butter, lemon juice, lemon rind, eggs, and milk. Pour into pie shell and bake at 350° for 50 minutes.

Microwave: Microwave on high for 8 minutes, or until pie is set around the edges, rotating twice. Transfer to preheated 350° conventional oven and continue baking for 10 minutes, or until lightly browned.

Preparation time: 25 minutes
Baking time: 50 minutes
Microwave time: 8 minutes
  plus 10 minutes in
  conventional oven

Easy
Best served the first day
Should be refrigerated

Serves: 8

Fran Cruise Garvey

APPLE-CREAM CHEESE TORTE

CRUST:
½ cup margarine
⅓ cup sugar
¼ tsp. vanilla
1 cup flour

Cream together margarine, sugar, and vanilla. Blend in flour; mix well. Pat dough onto the bottom and about 1 inch up the sides of a 10-inch springform pan. Crust will be very thin.

FILLING:
1 pkg. (8 oz.) cream
  cheese, softened
¼ cup sugar
1 egg
½ tsp. vanilla
⅓ cup sugar
¾ tsp. cinnamon
6 cups tart apples,
  peeled, sliced
¼ cup almonds, sliced

Cream together cream cheese and sugar. Add egg and vanilla; beat until smooth. Pour into prepared pan. Combine sugar and cinnamon; toss apples in mixture. Spoon or arrange apples over cream cheese layer; sprinkle with nuts. Bake at 450° for 10 minutes. Reduce heat to 400° and continue baking for 35 minutes, or until apples are tender. Cool before removing rim of pan. Serve soon or refrigerate.

Preparation time: 45 minutes
Baking time: 45 minutes

Best the first day

Serves: 8–10

Barbara Brandt

PRALINE CAKE

½ cup butter
1 cup buttermilk
2 cups brown sugar, packed
2 eggs
2 cups flour
1 tsp. baking soda
3 T. cocoa
1 tsp. salt
1 T. vanilla

Melt butter in a saucepan; add buttermilk and heat until warm. Place buttermilk mixture in a large mixing bowl. Add brown sugar and eggs; beat well. Sift together flour, baking soda, cocoa, and salt; stir into above. Add vanilla. Pour into greased and floured 12 × 14-inch pan. Bake at 350° for 30 to 35 minutes. Remove from oven; pour topping over hot cake. Return to oven about 1 minute, or until topping bubbles. Serve warm with ice cream or whipped cream.

TOPPING:
½ cup butter
1 cup brown sugar, packed
⅓ cup half-and-half or
   evaporated milk
1 cup pecans, chopped

Melt butter and brown sugar in a saucepan over low heat. Gradually add cream; cook and stir until warm. Add pecans.

Preparation time: 30 minutes
Baking time: 30–35 minutes

Serves: 20
Easily halved in 7½ × 11¾-inch pan

Mary Ann Hannah

FRENCH CHOCOLATE CANDY

1 pkg. (12 oz.) semisweet
   chocolate chips
1 cup walnuts, chopped
¾ cup sweetened
   condensed milk
1 tsp. vanilla
⅛ tsp. salt
1 cup chocolate sprinkles
   (optional)

In top of double boiler, melt chocolate chips over hot water. Stir in walnuts, milk, vanilla, and salt. Chill. Shape into 1-inch balls and roll in chocolate sprinkles. Refrigerate until firm.

Preparation time: 10 minutes

Easy
Can make ahead
Should be refrigerated

Yield: 36

Peggy Fouts

METRIC

Approximate equivalents of U.S. and metric kitchen weights and measures.

LIQUID MEASURE

1 teaspoon		= 5 milliliters
2 tablespoons	= 1 fluid ounce	= 30 milliliters
1 cup	= 8 fluid ounces	= 0.24 liters (240 ml.)
2 cups	= 1 pint	= 0.47 liters
4 cups	= 1 quart	= 0.95 liters
4 quarts	= 1 gallon	= 3.8 liters

DRY OR LIQUID MEASURE

3 teaspoons	= 1 tablespoon	= 15 milliliters
16 tablespoons	= 1 cup	= 0.24 liters

WEIGHT

1 ounce	= 28 grams
3½ ounces	= 100 grams
16 ounces	= 454 grams
1 pound	= 454 grams
1 pound	= 0.45 kilograms

MENU SELECTIONS

HOLIDAY BRUNCH FOR A CROWD
CHAMPAGNE PUNCH
HAM AND CHEESE STRATA
CURRIED EGGS WITH SHRIMP SAUCE
CRANBERRY COFFEE CAKE   GLAZED LEMON NUT BREAD
WAIT-A-DAY SALAD

BRUNCH FOR HOUSE GUESTS
RAMOS GIN FIZZ
SWISS CHEESE PUFF WITH LOBSTER SAUCE
GRAPEFRUIT HALF   OR   ASSORTED FRUIT BOWL
TWISTED MAPLE-BUTTER RING

LADIES LUNCHEON
SAUSAGE-FILLED CREPES   OR   CHICKEN-AVOCADO CREPES
COBB SALAD
FROZEN RASPBERRY SOUFFLÉ
Chenin Blanc

PIQUE-NIQUE
THERMOS OF GAZPACHO
GREEK-STYLE SANDWICHES IN ARABIC BREAD
DESSERT FRUITS AND CHEESES
CHOCOLATE MINT STICKS
Domestica Red

SOUPLINE PARTY
MY LENTIL SOUP   CANADIAN CHEESE SOUP
NEW ENGLAND CLAM CHOWDER
CAESAR SALAD   MEL'S CRISP HERB TOAST
HARVEST SQUARES
California Chablis

DINNER À DEUX
ESCARGOTS WITH FRENCH BREAD
LOBSTER-STUFFED BEEF TENDERLOIN
TOSSED GREENS WITH ROQUEFORT DRESSING
SPINACH-STUFFED TOMATOES   OR   FRESH GREEN BEANS
COFFEE MOUSSE
Light Burgundy

CANDLELIGHT DINNER FOR EIGHT
FLAMING CHEESE HORS D'OEUVRE
CREAM OF BROCCOLI SOUP
VEAL WITH ARTICHOKES
EGGPLANT TOWERS   GREEN NOODLES SUPREME
FRESH SPINACH SALAD WITH GEINSING DRESSING
GÂTEAU CHOCOLAT
Classified Bordeaux

SUMMER'S NIGHT SUPPER
CHILLED CUCUMBER SOUP
SALMON STEAKS IN SPINACH MOUSSELINE
WILD RICE
TOSSED GREENS WITH RUSSIAN DRESSING
STRAWBERRY SUSAN DESSERT
Grey Riesling or Muscadet de Sèvre et Maine

AUTUMN DINNER
CROWN ROAST OF PORK
WITH
SAUSAGE OR CRANBERRY STUFFING
FESTIVE SPINACH RING WITH SHERRIED ONIONS
CRANBERRY RING   BUTTERFLAKE ROLLS
PUMPKIN ROLL
Beaujolais

PATIO BARBEQUE
CHILLED ARTICHOKE HORS D'OEUVRE
GRILLED BUTTERFLIED LEG OF LAMB IN MINT SAUCE
HASH BROWNS AU GRATIN   EUROPEAN-STYLE CARROTS
FRUIT-FILLED WHITE WINE-APRICOT MOLD
LIME DELIGHT
Cabernet Sauvignon

SOUTH OF THE BORDER BUFFET
SANGRIA
GUACAMOLE AND TORTILLA CHIPS
KING RANCH CHICKEN   ENCHILADAS
TACOS   GREEN CHILIES AND RICE
FRESH FRUIT FANTASIA
FROZEN COFFEE PIE

A GREEK CLASSIC
FILO CHEESE TRIANGLES
COSSACK LAMB KABOBS
RICE PILAF   GREEN SALAD
BAKLAVA   HOT SPICED TEA
Red Bordeaux

AFTER THE THEATER
CHILLED CREAM OF TOMATO SOUP
SALMON PIE WITH CUCUMBER SAUCE
GARDEN MARINADE
DINNER ROLL
CHEESECAKE
Vouvray or Fumé Blanc

SUPERBOWL PARTY
BEER PARTY PUNCH
POTATO SOUP
BAKED HAM IN RYE CRUST
WITH
SWEET-AND-SOUR MUSTARD SAUCE
ITALIAN BEEF SANDWICHES
SWEDISH RYE BREAD   COLONIAL BREAD
ORANGE-NUT BARS

HOLIDAY OPEN HOUSE
EGGNOG   TEA-BASED PUNCH
ASPARAGUS ROLL-UPS   CHEESE-ONION SOUFFLÉ
SHRIMP MOUSSE   BEER-CHEESE PUFFS
CRUDITÉS AND CURRIED DIP   CHICKEN LIVER PÂTÉ

INDEX

298

ORDERING INFORMATION

I'VE GOT A COOK IN KALAMAZOO is $25.00 per copy plus $5.00 postage and handling (Michigan residents add $1.50 sales tax per book). Cookbooks may be purchased online at www.jlkalamazoo.org.

JUNIOR LEAGUE OF KALAMAZOO
2121 HUDSON STREET, SUITE 101 • KALAMAZOO, MICHIGAN 49008

Please send _____ copies of I'VE GOT A COOK IN KALAMAZOO. Enclosed please find a check for $_____. Make checks payable to Junior League of Kalamazoo.

NAME _____

STREET _____

CITY _____

STATE _____ ZIP _____

PHONE _____ EMAIL _____

JUNIOR LEAGUE OF KALAMAZOO
2121 HUDSON STREET, SUITE 101 • KALAMAZOO, MICHIGAN 49008

Please send _____ copies of I'VE GOT A COOK IN KALAMAZOO. Enclosed please find a check for $_____. Make checks payable to Junior League of Kalamazoo.

NAME _____

STREET _____

CITY _____

STATE _____ ZIP _____

PHONE _____ EMAIL _____

JUNIOR LEAGUE OF KALAMAZOO
2121 HUDSON STREET, SUITE 101 • KALAMAZOO, MICHIGAN 49008

Please send _____ copies of I'VE GOT A COOK IN KALAMAZOO. Enclosed please find a check for $_____. Make checks payable to Junior League of Kalamazoo.

NAME _____

STREET _____

CITY _____

STATE _____ ZIP _____

PHONE _____ EMAIL _____

ORDERING INFORMATION

I'VE GOT A COOK IN KALAMAZOO is $25.00 per copy plus $5.00 postage and handling (Michigan residents add $1.50 sales tax per book). Cookbooks may be purchased online at www.jlkalamazoo.org.

JUNIOR LEAGUE OF KALAMAZOO
2121 HUDSON STREET, SUITE 101 • KALAMAZOO, MICHIGAN 49008

Please send _____ copies of I'VE GOT A COOK IN KALAMAZOO. Enclosed please find a check for $_____. Make checks payable to Junior League of Kalamazoo.

NAME _____

STREET _____

CITY _____

STATE _____ ZIP _____

PHONE _____ EMAIL _____

JUNIOR LEAGUE OF KALAMAZOO
2121 HUDSON STREET, SUITE 101 • KALAMAZOO, MICHIGAN 49008

Please send _____ copies of I'VE GOT A COOK IN KALAMAZOO. Enclosed please find a check for $_____. Make checks payable to Junior League of Kalamazoo.

NAME _____

STREET _____

CITY _____

STATE _____ ZIP _____

PHONE _____ EMAIL _____

JUNIOR LEAGUE OF KALAMAZOO
2121 HUDSON STREET, SUITE 101 • KALAMAZOO, MICHIGAN 49008

Please send _____ copies of I'VE GOT A COOK IN KALAMAZOO. Enclosed please find a check for $_____. Make checks payable to Junior League of Kalamazoo.

NAME _____

STREET _____

CITY _____

STATE _____ ZIP _____

PHONE _____ EMAIL _____
